Difference in translation

Difference in
Translation

Edited with an Introduction by

JOSEPH F. GRAHAM

CORNELL UNIVERSITY PRESS

Ithaca and London

Contents

6   Contents

Preface

As a rule, we understand new ideas by following their lead and exploring their consequences, wherein we discover their real substance or significance and their specific differences or defining traits. We also judge new ideas by their consequences, usually in relation to some familiar theory or practice. Ideas about language and meaning are no exception to that rule, especially since much of modern thought has taken a linguistic turn which looks to language for progress in understanding of all sorts. Its general strategy is to start with language as the basis for inquiry and then to proceed as usual by extrapolation. The essays in this collection do just that, but their idea of language is very different from the most familiar. It is an idea about the constitutive, and therefore positive, function of differences in language, as they characterize not only the basic fact of language but also every linguistic act, whether expressive or interpretive. This volume illustrates that idea with specific reference to translation, and the essays elaborate its consequences in pointed contrast to those of the dominant tradition, which construes the task of the translator in such a way that difference means defeat. The combined effect of these essays is to reverse that judgment by showing how the operation of language already includes translation, just as it requires difference. In the process the use and value of deconstruction are also demonstrated.

Difference in Translation is the work of a new generation that has emerged with a new sense of the difficulty and complexity of dealing with language. That same outlook on language brings a growing sense of responsibility in communication and shows the need for greater solidarity across the established barriers and facile oppositions of language, discipline, and tradition. These essays already embrace French and English, literature and philosophy—and philosophy both analytic and continental. But their appeal extends even further, in that they invite and encourage participation from other disciplines and points of view and thereby promote an open discussion of difference in translation for the common benefit of understanding.

This book began with a conference sponsored by the Research Foundation of the State University of New York and held at Binghamton in October 1980. Papers read at the conference have been revised for publication here. I thank all who contributed to the conference and to the volume for their diligence as well as for their patience.

In translating "Des Tours de Babel," I have received considerable help from my friends. Gina Collins and Walter Verschueren prepared a rough draft for the conference. I began with their version and subsequent suggestions from James Hulbert. Later I went through my first draft with Richard Henning and the members of a graduate seminar. A careful reading by Jacques Derrida brought further improvement. Catherine Porter then read the manuscript and her comments prompted many of the final revisions. My thanks to all.

For aid of various kinds during my stay at the University of Oregon, I am grateful to my department chairman, Jack Powers, to my dean, Robert Berdahl, to my programmer, Lorie Wigle, and especially to my students Jane Todd, Janet Sutherland, Titus Suck, Marion Martin, Catherine Villemin, and Anne Leblans. I received similar assistance in Binghamton from Julio Rodriguez-Luis, Sheldon Grebstein, Carol Doherty, and Stefano Rosso. Finally, I thank Loretta G. Keller for help with the proofs and index, and for so much more.

JOSEPH F. GRAHAM

Santa Cruz, California

Difference in Translation

Introduction

JOSEPH F. GRAHAM

Translation is a topic of general interest for various reasons, but inasmuch as those reasons are diverse, there may be less to be said about translation in general than about it as a critical exercise for particular ideas of language, meaning, and interpretation. In this book several prominent notions of the sort are put to the test of translation. The results have immediate significance within certain specific contexts—literary or philosophical, linguistic or psychoanalytic—and to that extent they are not only specific but also strategic. The scope of the work done in each case also defines its own limits; yet questions are bound to arise about these essays in relation to some wider context and also about their ultimate significance.

Questions of significance and relevance are bound to arise in connection with translation or interpretation all the more readily since these particular matters seem to involve operations of language determined by some general notion that answers to those very questions. So it is that both translation and interpretation are commonly thought to have an essential concern with meaning or significance and with relevance or context. There is real concern for the respective identity and difference of meaning

and context inasmuch as both operations are supposed to preserve meaning through or despite a change in context. The essays in this volume exhibit that concern, even when they challenge established ideas of what in fact the significance or
relevance at issue may be. They are doubly relevant as a result,
because they are reflexive in already suggesting answers to the
sort of questions that might be asked about their own significance and relevance. Yet those answers are best understood in
response to specific questions about meaning and context, especially where such questions are so framed as to call for answers
of greater simplicity and generality. There is a common resistance to the assumption that either significance or relevance
could be any one thing.

Philip E. Lewis gives an example in his contribution to this
volume. He begins with the predicament of actually translating
his own work and then considers various consequences of transposing into English thoughts already expressed in French. To
the extent that the two languages are different, they impose
differences in translation, either as necessary compensation or as
inevitable distortion. Drawing on recent work in comparative
linguistics, Lewis shows in particular how the discursive mode of
English tends to resist the French, and so attenuate, even oblite-
rate, some of its characteristic effects by requiring concrete,
direct, and cohesive specifications for all kinds of objects and
relations. Lewis takes the translation of an essay on metaphor by
Jacques Derrida as his prime example and compares its effects
with those of the original. He also chooses a specific effect because there is no point in taking just any one at random and no
way of comparing all effects possible.

The crucial effect in question results from what Lewis calls a
"disruptive or deconstructive" force of writing in Derrida. It is
the force of this effect that usually gets reduced in translation,
especially where the effect operates by means that are not only
"interrogatory, descriptive, or explanatory" but also "demonstrative or even performative" in their discursive mode. The
effect is lost, in other words, when the original relation between

"telling and showing, thesis and expression, program and performance," is allowed to lapse in translation. Such differences in rhetoric are surely important for any text that works by example as well as by analysis. And what is significant for Derrida in the use of language includes not only what he says about rhetoric but also what he does with rhetoric.

A weak translation of a work that was originally and perhaps intentionally disruptive, would obviously affect the work's reception in that other language, if only by reducing its force of example. But that is not all. Quite easily though less obviously, such loss in translation could even affect the same work in the original. As Lewis suggests, once a weak translation enters the context of discourse pertaining to the work, it has the effect of drawing or directing commentary to its own disparity or inadequacy. The task of interpretation can then become all too reactive and protective. Now, this reverse effect of translation on the original may not seem important, for it may not seem to affect or in any way change the essential significance or meaning of the original. Yet it does have consequence in determining what is relevant and important to say about the original, if only to correct false impressions derived from the translation itself. That kind of difference in and through translation, however, would still imply some notion of similarity and identity of meaning, and its correction or compensation requires some distinction between the significance of a text as such and the recognition or appreciation of that significance in our interpretation of that text.

We might want first to distinguish the process or act of interpretation from its object and then compare interpretation to perception or cognition, processes in which the result of any given act is some judgment or statement that designates some independent object. We could then think of interpretation as a type or mode of description, subject, like any other, to criteria of adequacy in getting things right yet prone to failure and error in getting them wrong. We already assume something of the sort: we ask that interpretation be valid or correct, and we expect interpretive statements to be true rather than false, as if there were an object to interpret and a fact of the matter. But for any given text, as for any given object, all kinds of descriptions and all kinds of true statements are possible. Interpretive statements are presumably the kind that specify what a text means as against what it merely is or does; they are statements about its meaning or significance in some specific sense and not just any kind of statement, however relevant or important when true. If we could only sort out that simple difference in kind, we would solve a major problem for interpretation and translation. We would then know, at least in principle, just what interpretation was supposed to describe and just what translation was supposed to preserve.

Ordinary language is characteristically vague on the matter of meaning or significance, for we really have no definitive or even very definite criteria to distinguish meaning in some relatively narrow sense from significance in the widest sense. We talk about the meaning of a text, and ask what it means, without fully knowing what we mean by the words so readily used for that purpose. We say that a text is somehow significant, but we also say that it signifies something, without being very sure of the exact difference between the two. The essays in this collection are concerned to a large extent with some distinction of the sort and, ultimately, with the possibility or impossibility of drawing such a general distinction once and for all. In terms I have already borrowed from Lewis, it would be a matter of distinguishing the thesis of a text from its force and its effect, where the thesis would simply be what was said or asserted and the effect would be a consequence of how it was read or received. The difference so construed would comport with the notion that for any given text, something like meaning, in the narrow sense of thesis, was intrinsic (linguistic or semantic, and therefore invariable), whereas something like significance, in the widest sense of effect, was extrinsic (rhetorical, and determined by context).

Now, it may seem quite plausible to distinguish meaning from significance in this way, as if meaning were a property of texts and significance a relation between texts and contexts, or as if the one were objective, like a primary quality, and the other subjective, like a secondary quality. It may even seem necessary to maintain such a distinction in order to explain the practice of translation. But the matter of language is neither that clear nor that easy.

To get a sense of the difficulty, consider the claim that some discourse has a disruptive or deconstructive effect. Both disruption and deconstruction are presumably relations; something disrupts or deconstructs something else. Disruptive effects, then, would vary with context, even for one and the same text, which might well cause disruption here but not there. And such would surely be the case with deconstruction, were not its effect promised to be so rigorous as to reach the widest possible context. If deconstruction were indeed a strategic effect of some discourse touching the very possibility of all discourse, there could be no—other, wider, or broader—context for discourse that would be exempt from its effect. It would be absolute, as far as we could know, affecting language prior to utterance and irrespective of context—always already, in each and every language. But we can hardly grant such a claim without question, especially when it concerns the very nature of theoretical claims and their practical effects.

We might set translation as a test for claims about deconstruction or any other disruptive effects of discourse. The same test would apply in sorting out the differences between meaning and significance or those between a thesis, its force, and its effect, to the very extent that they are limited by language. If deconstruction does in fact deal with basic modes of expression, and not just specific means of expression, then its effects should cross language barriers, at least within its declared domain and context of relevance. To be truly and fully effective on its own terms, deconstruction has to operate throughout the sphere of influence exercised by Western metaphysics. If it were limited to lan-

guages like French and German, it would, as critics have observed, look more like word play and, as a result, little more than
a set of bad puns or rhymes without reasons.

Though we may readily admit that translation constitutes a
test of sorts for various claims about language, surely we should
consider the exact nature of that test before we interpret or
evaluate any results that would settle those claims. After all, a
given test could be significant in various ways, depending upon
just what was revealed and just what was tested. Because translation is supposed to preserve meaning without alteration from
language to language, it is generally supposed to present criteria
for the identity of meaning. Hence translation is often proposed
as a test for meaning, a test for telling the difference, in particular, between one meaning and another. Yet such a test remains
equivocal: meaning is not always equivalent to what can be translated from one language to another, so that even the results of a
good translation may require interpretation. There might well
be inevitable differences and serious loss in translation simply
because one language lacked the expressive power of another: its
vocabulary might be insufficient or its grammar inadequate by
comparison. Negative results would reflect contingent facts
about a specific language rather than anything essential about
meaning. Meaning is not just what can be translated in practice
but rather what can be translated in principle, which is also what
can be expressed in principle. We might say that meaning is the
aspect of language that is indifferent to form, since it could be
expressed just as well in any other form and so translated from
one form to another quite indifferently or arbitrarily.

When construed as such, translation is more an idea or an
ideal, because it no longer depends upon the actual relations of
form and meaning in any one language but requires only the
possibility of expression in some form or other. At that level of
generality, translation coincides with expression, there construed as the translation of meaning into some form of language.
What then matters is not just the fact that any practice of transla-

tion could define meaning but especially the fact that some claim about the difference between form and meaning would determine that practice. Yet translation itself has to be defined—and it is regularly defined by recourse to some notion of meaning or significance. It is not as if the practice of translation were given as such, independent of any claim about language, or as if that practice could somehow serve to evaluate other claims in a crucial yet perfectly neutral test. Translation constitutes a test that is only as good as the idea governing its application. The idea in question has to be good for the results to be right. We thus face this reversal: if we insist that deconstruction pass the test of translation, we can hardly avoid the converse injunction. Both operations involve theory as much as practice. Their theoretical claims and their practical effects may well be very different yet nonetheless comparable. The comparison could, then, favor either one over the other and would be decisive as to their relative force of explanation.

As a radical element in discourse, deconstruction constitutes a decisive test for thought about discourse in general and for all the usual talk about translation as the transfer of meaning from one language to another. The consistent effort of deconstruction has been to analyze the thought that underlies such talk and then to criticize certain basic distinctions that once seemed invulnerable or inevitable. As a result of that challenge, it has become as difficult to define as to defend the difference between words and concepts, sounds and meanings, or any other version of the difference between a transcendental signified and a material signifier, including that between real thought and mere talk. Yet those are the very rhyme and reason that translation is supposed to distinguish by discarding the one and preserving the other in transit from language to language. Hence the effect of deconstruction has already been to question the very notions that have long defined translation. In particular, deconstruction has always defied, though not simply denied, the system of categories that divides language into form, meaning, and effect, the very system that still presides over the standard theory and ordinary practice of translation as if nothing had ever happened to call it into question.

The contributors to this volume are convinced that something has indeed happened to change our thinking about language radically, and they are determined to elaborate some of the specific and strategic consequences for translation. They begin with an established idea of what translation involves, revoke any privileged status or special exemption that it may have enjoyed, and then raise serious doubts about its legitimacy or validity. A common strategy in such criticism is to reverse the direction of inquiry for a given problem by considering the solution proposed as yet another problem—and, most likely, yet another instance of the very same problem. No solution that is part of or prey to the problem it aimed to solve is really a solution. Hence translation can hardly solve the problem of meaning if any question remains about the meaning of terms that define translation itself.

Several of these essays render translation in the ordinary sense problematic by finding problems precisely with that ordinary sense. When the focus shifts to the meaning of words, the question becomes more obviously semantic, though neither trivial nor pendantic as a result. There is surely some connection between the meaning of words and the nature of things such that knowing what "translation" means is significantly or substantially related to knowing what translation is. Unless we know what we mean, we can hardly know what we are talking about. These essays probe the limits of our knowledge in the whole matter of translation by stretching some point about the word or stressing some aspects of the thing. They also change the configuration of that knowledge by suggesting that translation may be quite different from what we think.

In the contributions of Cynthia Chase and Richard Rand, something like translation is shown to operate in a single language and even in a single text. Cynthia Chase describes as a form of translation the specific relation between a revery by Rousseau and an essay by Baudelaire. Baudelaire translates

Rousseau, but in reverse, by transforming Rousseau's moral pleasure into physical disgust. On such an interpretation, Baudelaire's meaning is not anything he takes from Rousseau but something he does to Rousseau. What is truly significant is not how much Baudelaire preserves but how readily he perverts the substance of the original. [The real meaning for both then becomes that difference in translation, the difference that transforms one text into another and thereby changes textual meaning as a property of texts into contextual significance as a relation between texts.] Richard Rand finds translation in an ode by Keats. Autumn is seen translating in the action of the poem, as she transforms certain elements into others and as her poem transforms other elements from the poetry of Keats. Here translation is something that informs one and the same poem, poetry, and even poet, for Keats also translates Autumn. Because it is internal to a language, a text, and an author, this example of translation changes the very notion of what is original or integral to every language, text, and author. With such translation, difference is already there in the original.

Barbara Johnson and Alan Bass also describe translation in terms rather different from the ordinary. Johnson brings love and marriage, along with fidelity and adultery, into the discussion; she even talks about reproduction and dissemination, impotence and castration, family and incest with reference to translation. Bass traces the effects of a mistranslation through Freud and others in the psychoanalytic movement to the point where the unconscious becomes a mode of transportation that actually carries psychoanalysis, both the theory and the practice. Whether translation is considered social or psychological, mechanical or biological in essence, its ordinary sense appears a special or limited case in those wider contexts, and any attempt either to restrict or to reduce translation as such to some type or specific instance would then be taken as very suspicious.

Given that much diversity of usage about translation, we may well wonder about its real unity. If and when it is possible to say so many different things about translation, how can we ever know that we are all talking about one and the same thing? We may well ask whether the differences correspond to different aspects of the same operation or rather to some aspect shared by different operations. Surely objects can be similar without being the same, just as they can be diverse in aspect without being distinct. Or we may simply ask what advantage we might derive from changing the way we talk and think about translation. If our use of language is to serve some purpose, we should know what purpose is served by any given usage as against some other. Presumably it is no better to expand than to contract the meaning of a word in principle, but only better or worse in practice for some specific reason. If so, there can be no general answer to such questions. Each case for revision has to be urged on its own grounds and judged on its own merits. We can hardly know just what translation is or even know what to say and think on the matter without considering the evidence in detail.

There remains at least one related question that has general significance as well as practical consequence: it concerns the possibility or feasibility of arguing with reason, and adjudicating on principle, such cases of dispute about the reference or use of basic terms like those for language, meaning, and translation. The differences often seem so great as to defy mediation. Here is another case in point. Recent debate about Derrida and deconstruction in America has been characterized by acute if not complete disagreement on fundamental issues, resulting in more confrontation than real discussion, satisfaction, or resolution. At times it has almost seemed as if there were no common language or no means of translation from one language to another—and therefore no way of knowing whether the parties to the dispute really understood each other because there was no way of knowing whether they were in fact talking about the same things even when they used the same words. In that confusion of tongues, we need a theory of language to explain the possibility of serious discussion beyond such differences and so to encourage its pursuit. Robert J. Matthews offers something of the sort in his essay by suggesting the conditions that are necessary to sustain and so to continue the discussion of translation.

Among these conditions are the following. At least some agreement about the use of basic terms in question must be reached. Words like "meaning" and "translation" are to be used in ways that will permit rather than prevent further revision of our ideas about the objects and actions they designate. No immediate or even ultimate agreement about the real nature of such referents is required; what is needed is simply a willingness to consider various proposals as possibly true and perhaps more plausible than others advanced in the past. Those basic terms ought to be used indexically, almost like proper names, without bearing any meaning that would determine as necessary or a priori the truth of statements expressing a particular theory or individual belief on the matter under discussion. Conventional notions of meaning and translation tend to be self-defeating in that they imply their own infallilibity and so deny or somehow preclude the collective search for agreement, despite differences, that characterizes the inevitably historical pursuit of an essentially empirical subject.

But even if we can agree that some guarded use of language allows us to continue talking and thinking about translation with reasonable expectations, we still do not know just where that leaves us in practice. We have no definitive theory of language or meaning and no definitive criteria for translation either. What we know is tentative at best, neither full nor final but fragmentary and temporary. We have common examples of translation, and we can designate others as appropriately similar. But we have no real definition, no description with enough empirical substance or logical force to say just what it is about translations that makes them what they are.

Now, it could well be, as in the case of language and of meaning, that translation does not constitute a natural kind and that the term itself is not constant in meaning but varies with context. We are hardly prepared, however, to reach any conclusion, either positive or negative, on that point since we have just begun to figure out the differences between grammar and rhetoric, syntax and semantics, designation and description, as they determine meaning relative to language. So much ignorance seems to leave translation in limbo, still relying on pragmatic or heuristic devices, awaiting a systematic theory of meaning in language. Yet we can always use translation as we know it to develop the very theory that we need in order to define translation itself. Such is the way to solve a problem with several factors. No reasonable inquiry can proceed without holding certain questions in abeyance while pursuing others. Along that line we can follow the lead of Jacques Derrida reading Walter Benjamin.

In describing what he calls "the task of the translator" ("die Aufgabe des Übersetzers"), Walter Benjamin suggests how translation could—and urges it should—contribute significantly to something like a theory of meaning for language. Of course, he does not say just that. Benjamin first considers bad translations and bad translators. Their success is a failure in itself, he points out, the failure of a mistake in purpose. They assume the wrong task and then do the wrong thing. The essential purpose of translation and the worthy task of the translator do not consist merely in getting the sense right by saying the same thing in the words of some other language. The real achievement is not the restitution of sense ("die Wiedergabe des Sinnes") or even the preservation of sense ("die Erhaltung des Sinnes"). Rather it concerns the claim or the demand of literality and what Benjamin calls "the pure language" ("die reine Sprache"). Here the obvious crux is the notion of sense. Benjamin explains what he means by sense with recourse to the scholastic idiom of *intentio* and that "fundamental law in the philosophy of language" which distinguishes the mode, or manner, of meaning ("die Art des Meinens") from the thing meant ("das Gemeinten"). But this is surely the difference between meaning as the content of intention and reference as the object of intention. Bad translators get the reference right and the meaning wrong by neglecting the letter of the text and the form of the language. A true or real translation is transparent to the extent that it exhibits the literal difference of language in translation. Such differences are divergences of meaning, divergent ways of meaning from language to language. And so it is an error to oppose form and meaning, eventually sacrificing the one for the other, since the very aim of translation is to resonate in one language the meaning that adheres to the form in another.

It is the idea of a pure language that gives real purpose to the task of the translator. Yet the exact nature of that language and its relation to translation remains enigmatic even for Benjamin. His use of metaphor and his own comments on the problem draw attention to the inherent difficulty of describing just what it is that he is talking about. Indeed, as he explains it, we have no direct access to that pure language but only intimations or indications conveyed particularly, though not exclusively, through differences in translation. What is striking in this context is that Benjamin should present a positive or constructive view of such differences.

Translation is directed in principle to the expression of the innermost relation among languages, and the consequent relation of a translation to an original is complementary in nature. Each text complements the other much like the fragments of some larger whole and just like different meanings with a common reference. The same complementarity ("Ergänzung") applies to individual languages as well. The pure language is finally the object of reference for translation, and even the end of all linguistic reference, in that it is the ultimate referent for each and every language as a language. In order to express that convergence of languages, translation cannot simply reproduce either the reference or the meaning of the original; it cannot be simply equivalent in content and arbitrarily different in form like any ordinary version. Translation has somehow to signify and not just satisfy that very relation of difference in meaning between languages if it is ever to contribute more than evidence for a theory of language.

When commenting on his own relation to Benjamin in "Des

Tours de Babel," Jacques Derrida emphasizes the fact of translation. He says that in some way, his own way, he is translating,
and translating not only someone who was a translator but also
something on translation that served as a preface to a translation.
He even says that he is translating a translation and so translating
a text already in translation. Yet it is hardly obvious in what way
or in what sense Derrida can truly be said to translate Benjamin.
Certainly not in any simple or literal sense, and not in the sense
that Maurice de Gandillac first translated Benjamin from German into French.[1] Perhaps it is rather in the special sense that
Benjamin assigns to translation as right or proper for it. If it were
then a matter of complementation, Derrida would be translating
Benjamin by complementing his text with regard to some larger
whole, some wider context, some purer language.

Indeed, Derrida complements Benjamin in many ways—even
in the very choice of text for discussion. Derrida chooses the text
on the task of the translator rather than another, which actually
mentions Babel with reference to proper names, and he thereby
extends the context of discussion. Whereas Benjamin presents
the task of the translator in relation to the common end and final
reconciliation of languages, Derrida begins with Babel, the origin and dispersion of languages. Benjamin stresses not only the
teleological but also the theological aspects of translation, whereas Derrida brings out the archaeological, the political, and the
legal. The same complementarity also shapes Derrida's actual
commentary on Benjamin. Not only is what was missing supplied, but what was implicit in the one becomes explicit in the
other. The minor becomes major and the peripheral becomes
central, in an elaborate counterpoint of terms and themes.

Such a complement may rightly be taken as a compliment, and
Derrida clearly acknowledges a debt to Benjamin in the very act
of elaborating the notion of debt that he finds in Benjamin. The

[1]Derrida works from the text found in a collection of essays translated by
Maurice de Gandillac: Walter Benjamin, *Oeuvres I, Mythe et violence* (Paris:
Denoël, 1971).

task of the translator involves a debt in that the translator is beholden to the author of the original. Yet a complement can also take the form of criticism, and Derrida insists upon the initial debt of any author to an eventual translator. If the relation of the translation to the original is that of complement, the reverse is also true, and the relation is by nature symmetric. But if the essential relation is symmetric, there is no provision to mark any essential difference between an original and a translation. The two need each other in the same way, and they complement each other in the same way. To that extent they are equivalent.

Derrida insists that the debt of translation is not only mutual or reciprocal but also "insolvent" by nature. The author is no less beholden to the translator than the translator is to the author, and yet neither can possibly repay the other. Their texts are complementary and thereby equivalent in structure, as in reference, but not in substance or meaning. They lack a common coin, as it were. Here Derrida complements Benjamin first by emphasizing the paradox of that debt, with its structure of complementarity short of identity, and further by exhibiting the very same structure in what he calls "the Babelian performance," or simply "Babel," and in what looks like an essential, hence irreducible, complementarity of reference and meaning in language. He begins with the proper name and asks if we really know what it is that we are talking about. He asks if we know what we name when we say "Babel." The biblical account and a philosophical-*cum*-philological commentary are then invoked to suggest that Babel represents not only the multiplicity of languages but also the impossibility of a certain construction or completion due to something like a formal limit—a limit to form or formalization. The story of Babel figures both the necessity and the ultimate or absolute difficulty of translation in a sequence of events. Moreover, the very word bears that same significance as an event, as a specific utterance in a specific language. The reference, if not the meaning, of the word for Babel is precisely the confusion of meaning and reference. At its original occurrence in the language of Babel, the proper name for Babel was confused with the common noun for confusion.

What is peculiar about this confounding is the very way in which the grammatical and rhetorical values of the word "Babel" get crossed by the context. That particular utterance involves a difference in syntax between nouns and names, a difference in semantics between some meaning and none, as well as a difference in pragmatics between description and designation. But it would not help to force the issue of what "Babel" really meant in and of itself, as if the sound alone could have meaning independent of that provided by some grammar or other system of interpretation. Whether phonetic, syntactic, semantic, or pragmatic in kind, the phenomena of language are intensional. They are descriptions according to rule, so that the real or right form and meaning for a word depend on the grammar. And just as language is relative to grammar, so grammar is relative to context, in that the real or right grammar for an utterance depends on the context. The problem of interpretation thus shifts to the context and its consistency. The question is finally whether the context is relative to anything else or even whether that other thing could possibly be anything but relative.

Now, it is true that the argument against objectivity for meaning can also be mounted against syntax to the effect that there is no objective, rather than relative, fact of the matter that warrants assigning either semantic categories like synonym and antonym or syntactic categories like noun and name to utterances of any word. It makes no sense to ask about the form or the meaning of such a word as "Babel" prior to some choice of grammar and thus prior to some decision about the right context. If you grant as much, the skeptical claim is that no such choice or decision can be anything but arbitrary. Neither the grammar nor the context is given or even justified by the available evidence. The example of the confusion at the utterance of "Babel" shows an obvious limit of form as evidence for meaning. Yet that is just the point about intensionality: the syntactic and semantic properties of language do not have acoustic counterparts, hence you cannot possibly know what they are if all you know is the sound. You have to know the grammar that assigns those descriptions. But you can know the grammar only if you can somehow learn it, and you can learn it only if you can have sufficient evidence for it.

Evidence is also a matter of context, a matter of what counts as evident in context. Moreover, there is the further and deeper question of relevance, since not all evidence is relevant any more than all relevance is evident. What really counts as context for language use is, finally, whatever counts as relevant to the utterance in question, which may be the grammar alone or may be even less or a lot more, whether evident or not. But what is relevant will depend upon the specific interest or purpose of inquiry. Where the object is simply truth as an empirical fact, there is no abstract or absolute standard of evidence or any comparable standard of relevance. There can be no a priori definition or delimitation of context for language or its use as a result.

Here is a further and perhaps final limit on form: it is impossible to calculate or even estimate the full extent of relevant context for any form of language, either grammatical or rhetorical. You can never know in advance what might prove significant only in the end. Still, this conclusion does not warrant skepticism about language or its significance unless you have to know everything in order to know anything. That the context of relevance for an empirical inquiry is neither given nor evident does not mean that it cannot be discovered or inferred. The most relevant context is the one that offers the best explanation, whether it be the meaning of a sentence or the grammar of an utterance. Such a context is both right and real, for it is indeed the very causal mechanism that determines the phenomena in question. With respect to the truth of a statement about meaning, grammar, or anything of the sort, that context is no less than whatever makes it true as well as whatever it makes true. If you then include complements along with antecedents and consequents, as suggested by Derrida and Benjamin, you have your hands full of relevance.

Complements are relevant to the extent that they fill in or flesh out the context of a claim. They complement the meaning of a common reference by providing different descriptions for the same designation; they also complement the reference of a common meaning by providing different designations for the same description. Not all claims are complementary, however; some are contrary and some even contradictory, while others are so independent or distant as to be virtually irrelevant. The task of comprehending and eventually concluding is then a matter of elaborating the relevant complement in a manner of translation or interpretation.

Consider this collection of essays as a case in point. The collection itself provides a context with some presumption of relevance that concerns difference in translation as designated by its title. Some of the essays actually describe a complementarity of interests and relations. Yet there remain all kinds of effects to be tried by comparing these texts with each other and with others. The results may well be disparate, if not dissonant. But such is surely the way of understanding and perhaps the very task of reading. It is, in any event, the task finally left to the reader.

1

The Measure
of Translation Effects

PHILIP E. LEWIS

Difference in Translation

Can we or should we be indifferent to the fact that this essay about the difference that translation makes is itself a kind of "free" translation? Does it matter that, under a quite different title,[1] the first version of these remarks was composed, presented, eventually revised, and published in French?[2] In what respect might it be significant that a piece for this book, *Difference in Translation*, enacts the process of translation, is a performance of translation?

We shall never really leave the terrain on which these somewhat embarrassed questions lie. For the moment, however, let us not pretend that we can tackle them head-on, or indeed that we can ever address them decisively. Let us be content with developing, in order to introduce the problem of translation with

[1]"Vers la traduction abusive," paper presented in the seminar "La Traduction" at the summer 1980 colloquium "Les Fins de l'Homme" at Cerisy-la-Salle, France.
[2]"Vers la traduction abusive," in *Les fins de l'homme* (Paris: Galilée, 1981), pp. 253–61.

which we are trying to reckon, a single comment concerning the change in title. The original essay bore a resolutely tentative title, "Vers la traduction abusive," and had a somewhat programmatic cast; it sought to set forth in more or less theoretical terms a strategy that a translator of Derrida might well consider adopting. By contrast, the title "The Measure of Translation Effects" displaces the emphasis so as to take into account and reappropriate the ambivalence of the portentous heading "Difference in Translation." In the first place, "measure" refers to the means or process by which we can perceive the action of difference—the workings of a principle of fragmentation—in translation. In the second place, "effects" shifts the stress away from the program for strong translation toward a consideration of the results or consequences of translation. Putting these two references together, the preposition "of" discreetly allows an alternative sense of measure—as a state of moderation, restraint, regulation—to come into play, just as the preposition "in," in "Difference in Translation," allows difference to signify either the active principle in translation or the product of translation. "Of" and "in" are charges of discursive dynamite. In titles, where they are parts of nominal phrases that initially appear underdetermined (since the titular function is precisely to inaugurate the elaboration of a context as yet unset), these stealthy little prepositors are versatile and indecisive; they readily enable a vacillation between two modes, active and passive, transitive and intransitive, on either side of the relation they splice. "Of" and "in" are interpositional yokes allowing the nominal forms— "difference," "translation," "measure," and even "effect"—to designate *indifferently* here a state or accomplished fact, there an activity or operative principle. So the new title backs away from the lean into theoretical prescription of the French "Vers la traduction abusive" (by contrast with "of" or "in," the preposition *vers* is unequivocally directional); it shifts the accent away from the tentative program for translating Derrida and toward reflection on what translation actually is and does, on how we might measure—understand and evaluate—its effects. But in what sense does this shift entail translation? Is "The Measure of Translation Effects" indeed a translation?

The literal rendering "Toward Abusive Translation" would doubtless be a possible title in English. Yet that title fails to ring true. In part the reason is that the English word "abusive" (meaning wrongful, injurious, insulting, and so forth) does not immediately pick up another connotation of the French cognate: false, deceptive, misleading, and so forth. Yet this is by no means the only consideration underlying the recourse to a different title and with it an immediately altered slant. The shift in question here has to do with the English language and concomitantly with the Anglo-American intellectual environment that is circumscribed by the language. In translating the French text, I want to achieve more than a stilted transfer of meanings, to make it "work" in English, to endow it with the texture of a piece written in English for an English-speaking audience. Now, my intuitive sense as a native speaker of English who teaches in an American university is that a discussion emphasizing the practical processes and concrete results of translation will work better, fit in better, go down and over better, than a somewhat more theoretical excursus on shall we say, "translativity"—on the conditions that make possible and govern the work of translation.

This initially subjective hunch about what will sit well with an Anglophonic audience—and how, therefore, the French original of this paper might best be carried over (translate: from the Latin ✓ trans + latus, "carried across") into an English version—is strongly reinforced by empirical research in contrastive linguistics. An excellent case in point is a powerful book by the French linguist Jacqueline Guillemin-Flescher, *Syntaxe comparée du français et de l'anglais: Problèmes de traduction*.[3] In this work of applied discourse analysis, a comparative study of several translations of Flaubert's *Madame Bovary* serves as the

---

[3]*Syntaxe comparée du français et de l'anglais: Problèmes de traduction* (Paris: Editions Ophrys, 1981).

principal basis for identifying a number of important differences between French and English. Following the lead of Antoine Culioli, Guillemin-Flescher sets her comparison of French and English within a complex system of linguistic communication that includes the utterance, the enunciation or act of utterance, the interlocutionary relations of an enunciator and a coenunciator, and the dimension of reference. This allows for a number of levels of comparison and leads to remarks on syntax (for example, English tends to prefer fully formed, assertive clauses, whereas French is content with participial phrases or relatively elliptical expressions) and on aspect (English requires more, and more precise, aspectual markers) that analytically confirm tendencies long recognized by grammarians.

The big step forward in Guillemin-Flescher's work depends on the generalized scope of her analysis. Her achievement of a broadly inclusive comparison of the two languages is all the more impressive, since she carries it out while nonetheless pursuing exceedingly meticulous analysis of minute details. This interplay of microscopic analysis and large-scale comparison is one advantage that appears to derive directly from the purview of discourse analysis: the specific, often quite delicate operations it studies happen to be the ones that are responsible for cementing together large segments of discourse; when viewed collectively, those questions appear to constitute the structural orders or articulatory frames that allow extended textual constructs to develop cohesively. As Guillemin-Flescher's study proceeds, two such structural orders acquire over-arching importance: (1) "modes of enunciation," that is, besides the traditional grammatical modes, observation as distinct from commentary, direct discourse as distinct from indirect discourse, and also, in the last analysis, narrative as distinct from discourse; and (2) means or forms of *repérage*, that is, the frames of reference or processes of contextual binding internal to discourse, or, to put it a bit less abstrusely, the diverse relations—often made perceptible by deictics, sequence of tenses, iteratives, personal pronouns, positional adverbs, and so on—whereby terms refer to one another so as to mark the linkage between the enunciative situation and predication, between the subject and complement linked by predication, and between separate propositions or sentences. It is, of course, necessary to take stock of the detail and ordering of Guillemin-Flescher's analyses in order to appreciate their power and sophistication adequately. For our purposes here, however, we can derive the gain we need to make simply from weighing a handful of major points that her wide-sweeping comparison establishes demonstratively.

Here, then, are some of the characteristics of English that serve to contrast it with French:

1. A strong tendency to favor *actualization* (this word means roughly "concrete occurrence in a context"; actualization is thus defined in opposition to "abstract notion," so that, for example, the abstract term "heart" is actualized in the utterance "Frances' heart stopped beating at 10:47 this morning"; because it depends on the entire set of enunciative relations, actualization is a matter of degree, and its role is to be understood in relation to various forms of "disactualization," such as use of a term in conditional or hypothetical propositions, in statements that position it as having already occurred, and so forth).

2. A tendency to prefer direct or constative relations to the referent over commentary (this latter term is used in a technical sense to designate the operation whereby the discourse refers back to an element or set of elements or to a statement previously introduced in some manner; in other words, the constative/commentary distinction bears a certain resemblance to the familiar opposition of narrative to description: the latter comments on elements posited by the former).

3. A strong tendency to tighten the network of internal linkages that bind the elements of discourse together and thereby to prefer a strict, precise, homogeneous set of relations to the looser, less forcefully determined relations that prevail in French.

4. As a corollary of point 3, a tendency to require consistency and compatibility of terms that are related in representations of reality (notable manifestations of this tendency surface in state-

ments involving perception: (a) the tendency to orient the prevailing viewpoint around the category "alive/*human*"; and (b)
the requirement of clear differentiation between observed and
imagined reality).

What do contrastive observations such as these, arising from
the comparison of original texts to translated texts, tell us about
the problem of translating French into English? Clearly enough,
there is a motif common to the four points summarized above. In
both of the key domains—enunciative relations and referential
operations—that Guillemin-Flescher highlights, English calls
for more explicit, precise, concrete determinations, for fuller,
more cohesive delineations than does French.

This difference, Guillemin-Flescher demonstrates massively,
makes for innumerable problems in translation. The point is no
longer merely the hackneyed though doubtless sensible claim
that translation is "impossible" because the lexical correspon-
dences between languages are imprecise (for example, because
la porte in French does not have exactly the same meaning as
"door" in English); nor, indeed, is the point the much more
decisive one that translation is doomed to be inadequate because
attempts to construct contrastive grammars powerful enough to
support machine translation have revealed that a strong theory of
translation, capable of prescribing correct choices, is not within
reach. The point now is also that translation, when it occurs, has
to move whatever meanings it captures from the original into a
framework that tends to impose a different set of discursive relations and a different construction of reality. When English rearticulates a French utterance, it puts an interpretation on that
utterance that is built into English; it simply cannot let the
original say what it says in French, since it can neither allow the
translated utterance to relate to previous utterances in the same
chunk of discourse in the way the French statement does nor
allow the English substitute to relate to the world it positions or
describes in the way the French original does.

What comes into English from French will therefore be something different. This difference that depends on the dissimilarity of the languages is the difference always already in translation. As the very ground of translation—its raison d'être and its principle—it cannot be overcome. The difference that blocked or deferred communication in the mythical Babelian situation may be glossed over, but it never completely disappears; translation never suppresses it totally. The problem for the English-speaking interpreter of the French text might then be, initially, to specify in English what lost or modified enunciative and discursive relations are functioning in the French and what construction of reality is enacted by the French. For the translator, however, the problem is not the same; it is rather to reinscribe the French message so as to make it comply with the discursive and referential structures of English, to put on the French text the particular interpretation inherent to English.

Or is it? For in fact the conventional view of translation puts the translator under pressure not simply to produce a version of the original that reads well or sounds right in the target language but also to understand and interpret the original masterfully so as to reproduce its messages faithfully. The very translation that imposes the interpretation attendant to its language should also offer an accurate interpretation, a re-presentation of the original. This contradictory exigency constitutes the classical translator's predicament: a good translation should be a double interpretation, faithful both to the language/message of the original and to the message-orienting cast of its own language. To say that translation is always already interpretation is therefore not enough: an adequate translation would be always already two interpretations, a double interpretation requiring, so to speak, a double writing; and it is the insurmountable fact that these two interpretations are mutually exclusive that consigns every translation to inadequacy.

The thrust of this comment on our question concerning the practice of translation being undertaken here, in this essay, should by now be fairly evident. Thanks to the opportunity to translate freely and expansively, a translator who is also the author of the original can undertake to do precisely what is not possible for the translator who works on the text of another author: in the present case, the author-translator can both interpret according to English and according to French, can shift at will between conventional translation that has to violate the original and commentary that attempts to compensate for the inadequacy of the translation. Such, it would seem, is the ready option of a translator determined not to allow the incidence of the translating language to assume a subtle priority, to do in the intricacies of the translated language. Even this option, we shall see, has insurmountable drawbacks. But by opening it up, perhaps we can appreciate better the lot of the translator who cannot have recourse to it, who is obliged, for example, simply to reproduce, for better or for worse, an English version of Derrida's ultra-refined French. The question for the translator deprived of the commentarial option is whether, and to what extent, anything can be done in translation to preserve the tenor or texture or tangents of the French that English would override. In the first instance, as I begin actually translating portions of the French version of this essay, I shall put the question to Derrida: what indicators might his writing offer us concerning the conduct of translation? Subsequently, I shall reapply the question, along with the answer, to the English translation of one of Derrida's most influential essays, "La mythologie blanche."

Abuse in Translation

Translation could well, of course, be treated as a leitmotif in Derrida's work. Indeed, for initiates it is surely all too obvious that translation, as a concept and as a practice, falls within the larger framework of representation and mimesis, of analogy and metaphoricity, that Derrida has ushered through deconstructive analysis in his pursuit of a wide-ranging critical/historical account of metaphysics. Those same initiates will already have noticed a certain allusion to that analysis in my free introduction to this free translation: I have positioned translation as a form of representation that necessarily entails interpretation; and furthermore, I have observed that this re-presentation must seek futilely to mine two contradictory veins of interpretation. Such probing into representation and its derivatives could hardly fail to reflect, in its outlines, the project of deconstructive analysis that Derrida's early work persistently brought to bear on representation and that his recent work has often pursued specifically with respect to translation.

But I am not pretending to perform or reproduce Derridean deconstruction here in any serious or sustained way. For to attempt to repeat or resume or somehow reconstruct that analysis as it applies to translation would surely lead to precisely the form of failure—incompletion, distortion, infidelity—that is the inescapable lot of the translator. (We may reckon, then, that if the opportunity to disclaim makes the commentator's lot relatively more comfortable than the translator's, commentary is by no means an adequate solution: the only fidelity is exact repetition—of the original, in the original; and even that, it can well be argued, is finally a superficial fidelity.) As I have suggested, under normal circumstances the translator, confronted with the impossibility of importing signifiers and their associative chains from one language into another, and with the impossibility of transferring the original's structures of reference and enunciation, must try and fail to do the impossible, to elude infidelity. So granting this deplorable impasse occasioned by difference in translation, how, I am now asking, would Derrida deal with the risk and necessity of infidelity?

In "Le retrait de la métaphore," an essay translated into English under the daringly transliteral title of "The Retrait of Metaphor,"[4] Derrida has occasion to assert parenthetically, concerning the word *retrait*, with the adjective "good" in quotation marks, "une 'bonne' traduction doit toujours abuser"—"a 'good' translation must always commit abuses." Or perhaps "a good

---

[4]"The Retrait of Metaphors," *Enclitic* 2 (Fall 1978), 5–33.

translation must always play tricks." Now, the point here is by no
means to revalidate a superficial opposition of good to bad translation (to do so would be to fall prey to the kind of critical blows
that are struck on the opposition of good and bad metaphor in
"La mythologie blanche"); the point is rather to make clear the
sense of a translation effect—the rendering, in Derrida's commentary, of the German *Entsiehung* by the French term *retrait*—that, in relation to the text of Heidegger that Derrida is
discussing, does not result from a simple concern for fidelity or
adequacy but that, additionally, plays a strategic role in unveiling the possibility conditions that underlie Heidegger's statements on metaphor and doubtless underlie as well Derrida's
extremely scrupulous criticism of Heidegger. In any case, the
retrait functions not so much as a form of equivalence but as a
factor in an *economy* of translation in a process of gain as well as
loss that has to be conceived quantitatively rather than
qualitatively, energetically rather than topically. The *retrait* will
occasion a kind of controlled textual disruption: insofar as it is
abusive, it exerts an unpacking and disseminating effect, and
precisely that effect of the *retrait* as a textual operator makes it a
"good" translation, justifies the translator's work on the original.
The possibility that interests us here has to do with the use of
abuse that is epitomized by this example: can we take it as a
model? Can we reasonably extrapolate from it a kind of abuse
principle? Can we proceed legitimately to use such a principle to
measure effects wrought by the translation of Derrida's work?

Behind examples of capable translations such as the retrait or
Derrida's celebrated rendering of Hegel's *Aufhebung* by a term,
la relève, that can actually be incorporated into direct translations of Hegel's work, an inchoate axiology of translation can
perhaps be glimpsed. On the one hand, the impossibility of a
fully faithful translation points to a risk to be overcome, that of
weak, servile translation, of a tendency to privilege what Derrida
calls, in "La mythologie blanche," the *us*-system, that is, the
chain of values linking the *us*ual, the *us*eful, and common linguistic *us*age. To accredit the use-values is inevitably to opt for

what domesticates or familiarizes a message at the expense of whatever might upset or force or abuse language and thought, might seek after the unthought or unthinkable in the unsaid or unsayable. On the other hand, [the real possibility of translation—the translatability that emerges in the movement of difference as a fundamental property of languages—points to a risk to be assumed: that of the strong, forceful translation that values experimentation, tampers with usage, seeks to match the poly-valencies or plurivocities or expressive stresses of the original by producing its own. But, it will quickly be asked, suppose we concede that the strength of translation lies in its abuses—in the productive difference consisting in that twist or skewing signaled by the prefix *ab* that is attached to the dominant c(h)ord of use: how far can the abuse be carried? does an abuse principle not risk sacrificing rigor to facility? sacrificing the faithful transmission of messages to playful tinkering with style and connotation?]

No. The basic scruples of conventional translation—fidelity and intelligibility—remain intact and are indeed, in a sense, reinforced. Here is why. If the play of signifiers and the manipulation of enunciative and referential relations seem to make translation an activity of constant, inevitable compromise, this is not solely because the impossibility of transferring the linguistic substance of the original, as graphic or phonic elements on which both the higher-level relations and the effects of reception depend, makes for an inescapable difference in the translation. The translator's compromises also result from a tendency, specific to the translation of expository writing, to privilege the capture of signifieds, to give primacy to message, content, or concept over language texture. Now this means that the translating text works principally and principially by substitution and gives priority to re-presentational processes—to the identification of substitute signifiers, to metaphoricity—whereas it tends to subordinate or lose sight of the order of syntax or metonymy, in which the signifiers of the original are linked to one another and in which that more or less poetic activity that we might term "textual work" is carried on.

Now, on the horizon traced by Derrida, where the metaphoric concept of translation is thrown into question and where the clear-cut separability of signifier and signified, of force and meaning, is dismantled, what we face is never—never possibly—an utter collapse of distinctions or a withdrawal from the intelligible work of expression and translation; it is rather a new axiomatics of fidelity, one that requires attention to the chain of signifiers, to syntactic processes, to discursive structures, to the incidence of language mechanisms on thought and reality formation, and so forth. No less than in the translation of poetic texts, the demand is for fidelity to much more than semantic substance, fidelity also to the modalities of expression and to rhetorical strategies. A practice of abuse belongs, part and parcel, to this toughened exigency precisely because that abusiveness, in its multiple forms and functions, constitutes a modality in which this fidelity—we might call it an ab-imitative fidelity—to an analytic practice that is bound to a necessarily stratified, double-edged writing practice can be pursued. For the translator, the problem here can no longer be how to avoid the failures—the reductive and redirective interpretations—that disparity among natural languages assures; the problem is rather how to compensate for losses and to justify (in a graphological sense) the differences—how to renew the energy and signifying behavior that a translation is likely to diffuse. In terms more germane to Derrida's move to displace the translation problem away from a logic of identity or equivalence, the question is how to supply for the inevitable lack.

So what is crucially at stake here is what the translation itself contributes, is that abuse, committed by the translator, whereby the translation goes beyond—fills in for—the original. But again, can this be just any abuse? The absurd question points up the salient features of the example we have used, the word *retrait*. In the first place, the abusive move in the translation cannot be directed at just any object, at just any element of the original; rather, it will bear upon a key operator or a decisive textual knot that will be recognized by dint of its own abusive features, by its resistance to the preponderant values of the "usual" and the "useful" that are placed under interrogation in "La mythologie blanche" and "Le retrait de la métaphore." Thus the abusive work of the translation will be oriented by specific nubs in the original, by points or passages that are in some sense forced, that stand out as clusters of textual energy—whether they are constituted by words, turns of phrase, or more elaborate formulations. In the second place, the abuse itself will take form in the translation in an ambivalent relation both with the text that it translates and with the language of the translation (the latter incorporates its own system of use-values to be resisted from within). No doubt the project we are envisaging here is ultimately impossible: the translator's aim is to rearticulate analogically the abuse that occurs in the original text, thus to take on the force, the resistance, the densification, that this abuse occasions in its own habitat, yet, at the same time, also to displace, remobilize, and extend this abuse in another milieu where, once again, it will have a dual function—on the one hand, that of forcing the linguistic and conceptual system of which it is a dependent, and on the other hand, of directing a critical thrust back toward the text that it translates and in relation to which it becomes a kind of unsettling aftermath (it is as if the translation sought to occupy the original's already unsettled home, and thereby, far from "domesticating" it, to turn it into a place still more foreign to itself).

Here again, given this strained relation between original and translation, an objection is sure to arise: does not the demand for reproduction of the original abuse, on the one hand, and for adaptive and reactive transformation of the abuse, on the other, simply constitute an untenable contradiction? Is this not just a radical version of, or reversion to, the irresolvable tension between French and English that we have already uncovered? Is not the practice of abuse doomed to give in to the preclusionary dominion of use in and under which it operates? If you can abuse only by respecting and thereby upholding the very usages that are contested, if the aggressive translator merely falls into a

classic form of complicity, whereby, for example, deviation
serves to ground and sustain the norm, then why all the fuss
about abuse? Maybe this is just the same old trap, well known to
the most conventional theories of translation, that Benjamin de-
rides in "The Task of the Translator."

Precisely in this impasse, up against an apparent contradiction, one rediscovers the necessity of a double articulation, of
that pluralized, dislocutory, paralogical writing practice that
Derrida has so often cultivated and explained. In relation to the
tensions within translation-as-representation that we have dis-
cerned, we might well situate Derrida's experiments with a double-edged writing as, precisely, a response to the pressure for
two interpretations—the one in compliance with the target language, the other in realignment with the original text—that I
have been underscoring. The response would consist in assuming the contradiction and attempting to make something of it. If
such a response proves necessary in commentary on the prob-
lematics of representation, then a fortiori it would be necessary
in the translation of that commentary. In terms of method, the
question would, predictably, focus on a paradoxic imperative:
how to say two things at once, how to enact two interpretations
simultaneously? Or in the framework of our inquiry here, how to
translate in acquiescence to English while nonetheless resurrect-
ing a certain fidelity to the original French.

In principle, there would be a great deal to say here about the
encounter with, or recourse to, or use and abuse of, operators of
undecidability. Suffice it to refer to the interview entitled "Positions,"[5] and to add just one remark: the strategy, analytic as well
as discursive, is grounded in the capacity of discourse to say and
do many things at once and to make some of the relations among
those things said and done indeterminate; recourse to such a
strategy obviously makes certain texts of Derrida exceptionally
resistant to translation. To deny that language has this capacity is
demonstrably foolish, and to claim that philosophy or linguistic
theory should not, or need not, reckon with the incidence of

---

[5]*Positions*, trans. Alan Bass (Chicago: University of Chicago Press, 1979).

untranslatability seems hopelessly defensive. Far from arguing this point, however, let me stick with my quite limited project of delineating the elements of a translation practice that devolves from a disruptive or deconstructive writing practice, so as to suggest that, in translation, the difficulty of an already complex performance of language is aggravated, and with that heightened difficulty the very abusiveness that is made more difficult becomes that much more necessary.

Given two terms, original and translation, in a relation of thoroughgoing coimplication; and two registers, use and abuse, in simultaneous relations of contrariness and complementarity; and a translating operation that works in three zones, the language of the original, the language of the translation, and the space between the two; and two complicated aims, first to reproduce the use and abuse of the original in the translation and second to supply for what cannot in fact be reproduced with a remobilization of use and abuse that further qualifies the original as used and thus disabused. Now, after codification of these givens, we could construct logical and mathematical schemes to account for the modest number of combinations that come into play here; yet it is evident that, in the translator's experience, these combinations are elusive, that it is logistically impracticable to conduct the translational operations in a systematized or programmed fashion, and thus that, in the work of translation, the integration that is achieved escapes, in a vital way, from reflection and emerges in a experimental order, an order of discovery, where success is a function not only of the immense paraphrastic and paronomastic capacities of language but also of trial and error, of chance. The translation will be essayistic, in the strong sense of the word.

Use in Translation

We now have in place, via some abusive use of snatches of Derrida, a modest scheme for measuring the effects of translating Derrida. In a nutshell, the proposal is (1) to concentrate evaluative attention on moments of density and intensity where the play of concepts and expression is affected by the disruptive, disseminatory power of language; (2) to insist on the transformations that the translation carries out, not just on the semantic, but also on syntactic and discursive levels; (3) to ask whether the translation articulates on its own textual effects that are consequentially and tellingly abusive with respect to the original. In order to see whether and how guidelines such as these might illuminate translation practice, it is of course necessary to examine a translation through the lenses they provide. The remarks that follow are based on a reading of a translation of "La mythologie blanche," selected for this purpose because it appears to have had, for circumstantial reasons, a considerable influence on the reception of Derrida's work in this country. The translation, "White Mythology," appeared in *New Literary History* in 1974.[6] The analytic work, which is extremely tedious, was concentrated on one portion of the essay, the final pages of its second section, "The Ellipsis of the Sun," where Derrida undertakes a commentary on Aristotle's discourse on metaphor. The very simple ad hoc procedure adopted was to compare the translation to the original, line by line and word by word, and to note diverse manifestions of difference. I shall now list some of the kinds of difference that are visible to a strictly amateur analyst.

1. *Punctuation and markers.*   Derrida happens to be exceedingly and quite transparently careful about textual geography. It is therefore surprising to observe that the translation allows the italics that set off certain terms to be dropped; puts quotation marks around very important terms such as *métaphorologie* that do not have them in the French text; and goes so far as to insert in parentheses translator's notes that are not clearly identified as such. The effect of these alterations is subtractive: the translated version flattens or softens the original.

[6]"White Mythology," *New Literary History* 6:1 (1974), 5–74. I refer to "La Mythologie blanche," in *Marges de la Philosophie* (Paris: Minuit, 1972), 247–324.

2. *Translation of translation.*   "La mythologie blanche" has its own translation strategy, indicated not only in its elaborate explanations about terms in Aristotle and its explicit allusions to the difficulties of translation but also by its use of the well-established practice whereby a given Greek or German word that is being translated is given in brackets after the French term. At times, moreover, Derrida elects to refer only to the foreign word, set in italics. The text of "White Mythology" sometimes drops the words in brackets, making do with just the English word. One effect of this kind of omission is to reduce the attention to translation that is sustained in the original.

3. *Suffixes.*   At the level of "semes," that is, elemental units of signification, we encounter—over and beyond a predictable "Anglo-Saxon" resistance on the part of the translator to forms ending in *-ist* and *-ism* (as in continuist, continuism, and so forth)—a curious hesitation with respect to the suffix *-ique* (*-ic* in English). Thus, for example, the widely used French term *la métaphorique,* for which the English equivalent would be "metaphorics," sometimes becomes in "White Mythology" simply "metaphor." Or again, the coined term *l'anthropophysique,* carefully backgrounded by Derrida in analyses of *physis* and its antitheses before it is adopted, is simply rejected in favor of a paraphrase that refers to "l'homme physique" without suggesting that an abstract conceptualization that takes systemic outlines is at the nub of the argument. A still more disquieting and very frequent case is the suppression of the suffix *-ème,* as in the word *mimême* and especially in *philosophème.* The special conceptual value of this term, as a basic unit in a structured system, is trivilized in the translation, which resets it in common parlance as an "element of philosophy."

4. *Words.*   There are innumerable examples in this category. Let us therefore note only a few terms that relate to important Derridean motifs, to begin with, the reflexive verb *se suppléer.* In the now-familiar logic of supplementarity so brilliantly analyzed and remobilized by Derrida, this verb is convenient for articulating the dual relations of "lack" and "supplement" pre-

cisely because it can convey a two-sided articulation, here meaning "to add to, to supplement," there meaning "to substitute for,
to replace." The first time the term appears with this double
function, the translation chooses the second of these meanings
(rather than, for example, choosing to adopt the somewhat archaic English verb "supply," which can serve as a carrier of the two
meanings). Among other important examples, let us note: (1) the
crucial term "effect," although a key part of its connotational
force clearly depends on the etiological context from which it is
taken, is often translated by the word "phenomenon" (which is
reserved for guarded use in Derrida's vocabulary); (2) the crucial
term *valeur*, despite a very insistent discussion of the meaning it
acquires in Saussurean linguistic theory, is often translated by
"notion"; (3) the equally vital term *articulation*, even though it is
pointedly coupled with the term *article* in a statement that al-
ludes to the syntactic function of articles, is nonetheless translated by the word "joint." In the case that I mention here, where
a relatively literal alternative is available in English, the selec-
tion of semantic neighbors does not necessarily modify the
meaning of a statement in a radical way, but it does occasion an
unnecessary loss of precision.

5. *Phrases.*   In this zone of constructions still smaller than
full sentences, there can of course be very difficult translation
problems. The question is again, in the case of vitally important
expressions, how far to deviate from a "literalist" rendering. Let
us note two examples. First, the phrase "la métaphoricité par
analogie," the process that is constitutive of the orders of similarity and proportionality, becomes "analogy producing metaphor." This conversion does not simply entail a slight displacement of meaning; it sets aside a key term designating the general
status and operation of metaphor, both a state and an energetics;
later on the general term will prove indispensable enough for the
translation to deploy the word "metaphoricality" (a less satisfactory choice, since by analogy with words like "musicality" it
would seem to designate a quality, than the more literal alternative, "metaphoricity"). Second, the somewhat tricky phrase

"*la condition d'impossibilité* d'un tel projet" becomes "*the conditions which make it in principle impossible* to carry out such a project" (the project of constructing a future metaphorics). So Derrida is not looking for a set of conditions (it would be interesting to know why the plural was adopted in the translation) that are constitutive of the operative principle; on the contrary, he is in fact proposing to search out the principle underlying a single impossibility condition that disables the project from the outset. Ultimately at stake in the slippage that this passage allows is the transmission, in translation, of Derrida's discourse on possibility conditions, which happens to be the veritable armature of a deconstructive analytic practice in general.

6. *Discourse.* This is of course the broad category on which we focused a good deal of attention in the first section of this essay thanks to the decisive investigations of Guillemin-Flescher. The range of phenomena encountered in this vast domain is so wide as to preclude a systematic accounting. Examples could be as discrete as the introduction of a single adverbial marker or as far-reaching as a series of syntactic adjustments extending over a full page or more. But here again, a handful of cases will suffice to give us a sense of the stakes.

(*a*) French original: "C'est depuis l'au-delà de la différence entre le propre et le non-propre qu'il faudrait rendre compte des effets de propriété et de non-propriété" (p. 273). English version: "Account has to be given of the effects of that which is proper and that which is not by going beyond that difference itself" (p. 28). Here we can, of course, identify many changes: syntactic inversion, shift from the conditional verb (*il faudrait*) to the assertive "has to be" (an instance of English favoring actualization), deletion of the parallels between *propre/propriété* and *non-propre/non-propriété,* together with dilution of the conceptual specificity of these terms, and so forth. The shift at the start, however, involving the opening prepositional phrase of the French, "depuis l'au-delà de la différence," is perhaps most telling. The English adopts the present participial form (no doubt some purists would wish to protest that the participle, awkwardly appended to a passive construction and lacking a specified subject, dangles), which has two effects: it implies the presence of an agent who is absent in the French version, and it substitutes for the spatial positioning of "depuis l'au-delà" (indicating a locus from which the explanation would originate) a movement, an action of the agent or subject. We might then say that the resetting of Derrida's theoretical comment in the translation gives it a more immediate, practical tenor.

(*b*) Consonant with the tendencies Guillemin-Flescher ascribes to English, the translator takes the liberty of adding conjunctions, concessives, and adversatives that tie sentences together much more tightly than does the French, which often leaves them crisply separated. There are also instances where the translation adds substantial phrases so as to transform elliptical utterances into well-formed sentences with subject and verbal complement. (This characteristic is more surprising than it might be in other French-to-English conversions because "La mythologie blanche," in its third major section "L'ellipse du soleil: l'énigme, l'incompréhensible, l'imprenable," contains forceful commentary on the effects of ellipsis. There can hardly be any doubt, therefore, that Derrida is making a deliberate, pointed use of ellipsis in his text.) Overall, the syntactic and programmatic adjustments that the translator allows himself to multiply rather freely do seem to conform to a bias openly stated in the translator's note, where we are told that natural, intelligible English renderings have been preferred except in a few cases where the argument required retention of more strained, literal forms. By and large, the tendency was then to respect the *use*-values of English.

(*c*) In his studied writing practice, Derrida plays masterfully on the associative, poetic resources of French, generating articulatory structures that a reader of the French can hardly miss. He thus creates, to be sure, many a problem for the translator. To put it approximately, we might say that the global problem is to determine what to do about anaphoric structures (association of terms via parallel placement in sentences, paragraphs, and so forth) and anasemic formations (association of semes or terms in serial relations, often via word play), whether to stress retaining them or to let them lapse as English imposes its discursive order. A couple of examples follow.

1. In this passage, Derrida is weaving a commentary on the relation of *physis* and *mimesis* in Aristotle to which we have referred once before: "Le *mimesis* est le propre de l'homme. Seul l'homme imite proprement. Seul il prend plaisir à imiter, seul il apprend à imiter, seul il apprend par imitation. Le pouvoir de vérité, comme dévoilement de la nature (*physis*) par la *mimesis*, appartient congénitalement à la physique de l'homme, à l'anthropophysique" (p. 283). Now, the translation. "*Mimesis* is the property of man. Only man properly speaking imitates. He alone takes pleasure in imitating, learns to imitate, and learns by imitation. The power of truth, as an unveiling of nature (*physis*) by *mimesis*, is a congenital property of man as a physical being" (pp. 37–38). Attention to the anaphoric dimension here leads us at once to two remarks.

First, at the level of the passage's internal dynamics, a salient feature is the repetition, in the two middle sentences, of *seul* and of *imiter/imitation*. The English keeps the latter but drops the former, thereby diminishing the rhetorical effect of the series, which is by no means just a matter of elegance or sonority. Repeating the limitative adverbs "Seul . . . seul . . . seul" serves to set off the three members of the compound sentence as parallel propositions and thereby to confer on them a certain equivalence, to mark the three propositions of the second sentence as refinements that further specify the sense of the first sentence. The rhetoric is crucial to the placement of the two sentences in an interlocking definitional mode, and some of the vigor with which the two sentences and their four propositions are thus imbricated is drained off in the translation.

Second, at the level of the passage's connection with the motifs of the essay at large, a particularly decisive marker is the term *propre* and all its derivatives. With good cause the translator's note calls attention to *propre* and *propriété*, observing that in some cases the use of "proper" instead of "distinctive" or other equivalents seems strained, but that this literal rendering is nonetheless justified "so that the strategic role of 'the proper' in the argument may remain manifest" (p. 6). When the passage in question was translated, this sound remark was doubtless remembered. But how far is its application carried? In the context, it is clear that mimesis is the defining quality that distinguishes man from animals, and the shift in the translation from the adjectival noun *le propre* to the standard English noun "property" seems acceptable from this standpoint (an alternative, "mimesis is what is proper to man," would, however, be closer to the adjectival/definitional form and would cut back on the ambiguity of the assertion "mimesis is the property of man," which can also be read as meaning "mimesis is the possession of man"). The difficulty comes with the next proposition, "Seul l'homme imite proprement," and with its sense in relation to the preceding one and to the discourse on the *proper* in the essay at large. For the adverb *proprement,* the translation gives us "properly speaking," placed before the verb rather than after it, as in the French, so as to suggest that in the proper sense of the word "imitate," only man does it. The trouble is that the sentence with *proprement,* set up by *le propre* of the previous sentence, says poignantly "only man imitates *properly.*" The sense of the adverb at this point depends on its function as a modifier of the verb "imitate": it specifies the manner of imitation. This certainly implies the meaning given by the proposition "only man properly speaking imitates," but it also says more in that it posits the actualization of the property, which the form "properly speaking" leaves in its notional guise, and it does something with the term *propre* that the English does not do, rearticulating it as an action-qualifying adverb (man's imitation is appropriative and self-defining). This capacity to signify literally and actively in the discourse on the proper could also be conferred upon the English "properly."

In all events, what is crucially at stake here is the sense, the meaning-capacity, the inferential resonance that the terms of an elaborate discourse can take on and draw upon as they are rearticulated.

2. The passage considered hereafter concerns the metaphor external to philosophy that presides over the system of metaphors within it, that is, in sum, the metaphor of metaphor.

> Cette métaphore en plus, restant hors du champ qu'elle permet de circonscrire, s'extrait ou s'abstrait encore ce champ, s'y soustrait donc comme métaphore en moins. En raison de ce que nous pourrions intituler, par économie, la supplementarité tropique, le tour de plus devenant le tour de moins, la taxinomie ou l'histoire des métaphores philosophiques n'y retrouverait jamais son compte. A l'interminable *déhiscence* du supplément (s'il est permis de jardiner encore un peu cette métaphore botanique) sera toujours refusé l'état ou le statut du complément. Le champ n'est jamais saturé. [P. 261]

> This extra metaphor, remaining outside the field which it enables us to circumscribe, also extracts or abstracts this field for itself, and therefore removes itself from that field as one metaphor the less. Because of what we might for convenience call metaphorical supplementation (the extra metaphor being at the same time a metaphor the less), no classification or account of philosophical metaphor can ever prosper. The supplement is always unfolding, but it can never attain the status of a complement. The field is never saturated.

Here we have a clear, straightforward instance of the logic of supplementarity, that of tropical supplementarity, which the translation actualizes as "metaphorical supplementation." For the moment, let us not quibble over this debatable choice of terms, over the omissions of Derrida's parenthesis pointing to the botanical metaphor in his own discourse, over the loose rendering of "la taxinomie ou l'histoire des métaphores n'y retrouverait jamais son compte." Let us now consider only the anasemic play whereby tropical supplementarity is defined: "le tour de plus devenant le tour de moins," which the English moves into parentheses and renders "the extra metaphor being at the same time a metaphor the less."

The English transmits the main point about the operation of supplementarity well enough: from the standpoint of philosophy, the surplus trope on the outside is also a missing trope, it functions here as a plus but there as a minus, on this hand as a supplement but on the other one as a lack; whether added to the metaphorics of philosophy or subtracted from it, the unmanageable external metaphor assures its incompletion. Thus the set of philosophy's metaphors can never be the whole set. Now, since this point is made, why be concerned with a few little changes in the translation? Does it matter, for example, that *le tour* is translated as "metaphor," that *devenant* ("becoming") is translated as "being at the same time"?

It does matter if the anasemic play on the word *tour* matters. That it does indeed matter is easy enough to determine, since Derrida elects to re-mark the term by italicizing it and by distinguishing it from metaphor in the overture of the next section of the essay: "Chaque fois qu'une rhétorique définit la métaphore, elle implique non seulement *une* philosophie mais un réseau conceptuel dans lequel *la* philosophie s'est constituée. Chaque fil, dans ce réseau, forme de surcroît un *tour*, on dirait une métaphore si cette notion n'était ici trop dérivée" (p. 274). The translation: "In every rhetorical definition of metaphor is implied not just a philosophical position, but a conceptual network within which philosophy as such is constituted. Each thread of the net in addition forms a turn of speech (we might say a metaphor, but that the notion is too derivative in this case)."

From this, two points: there is clearly cause to refrain from simply substituting "metaphor" for *tour*, since the latter is, as it were, more primitive, less precisely fixed in a delineated system; there is also cause, as we consider the difference the translation makes by specifying the sense of *tour* as "turn of speech," to reflect on the considerable spectrum described by the word's many meanings. Among these: turn, revolution, circuit, circumference; twist, twisting; trick, feat, skill; shape, outline, course; sweep, lap; sprain. Hence a gamut quite as rich as that of the etymologically parallel English word "turn" and often corresponding to it, and one that is subject, moreover, to anasemic connections with *retour* and *détour* that prove to be critical in Derrida's writing. What, then, is the force of *tour* that we might wish to preserve in translation?

On the strength of these two points alone, having to do with the meaning-capacity of *tour* and with its relations to adjacent notions, it would seem important to reckon with the relatively abstract, conceptually imprecise and flexible nature of the term. More particularly, the semantic load born by *tour*/"turn" prompts us to ask what seme makes for the amazing malleability that we grasp in its definition and multiple uses. Unsurprisingly the sense of "circular motion" that stands out in the etymology—the turning of the term "turn," we might say—is the key to its leverage: *tour* is one of those oscillatory nouns that can, depending on the context, designate a particular act, an ongoing activity, a fact, or a state—in other words, that can move across a continuum between active and passive poles or modes. Owing to its capacity as a conceptual shifter, the word can figure a wide range of representations that its semantic core, signifying an order of conversion and circumscription, enables it to hold in a state of potential relation or articulation. It is this articulatory power that a strong translation will seek to retain. In the case of the phrase we have underscored here, "le tour de plus devenant le tour de moins," the anasemic opposition "tour de plus"/"tour de moins" obviously tends, via the repetition of *tour,* to set off the term "turn" as it is distinct from the term "metaphor"; but this is more telling here because the present participle *devenant* is an active form pointing to the very process of turning, the circular movement of perpetual shifting that the phrase attributes to tropical supplementarity. In this connection, moreover, the use of the term "tropical," rather than "metaphorical," to modify supplementarity also becomes significant because "trope" (from the Greek *tropos*) also means "turn" or "change." *Tour* instantiates the tropical.

So tropical supplementarity is not, or not just, the two-sidedness of the metaphor of metaphor; it is the turning in language—

the very movement of difference insofar as it is not the relation of same/inside to other/outside but the turning of the same away from yet necessarily back to itself—that is designated and also, by dint of the temporizing/temporalizing introduced by the present participle "becoming," exemplified or performed by the turning of this phrase that circumscribes it. The linkage of the two turns, the extra one and the missing one, is not a simple identity but a ceaseless process of conversion in time. As the text bluntly asserts, the dehiscence of the supplement can never pass out of temporal process into the state of the complement. Thus the translation's suppression of the term "history" in the main clause of the sentence we have been worrying borders on the scandalous. The point is indeed that the extra/missing metaphor of metaphors cannot be the key to the taxonomy and history of philosophical metaphors, that for an account of metaphor in general it is rather necessary to appeal to tropical supplementarity.

After Translation

From the foregoing observations and examples (they could be extended indefinitely), it is clear that "White Mythology" fails to measure up to the standard for abusive fidelity in translation that we have brought to bear on it. The abuses in the French text are commonly lost; the translation rarely produces any telling effects of its own; the special texture and tenor of Derrida's discourse get flattened out in an English that shies away from abnormal, odd-sounding constructions. Yet it is only fair to recognize that a negative evaluation is hardly appropriate here for two closely allied reasons. A comparative examination of original and translation shows that (1) the translation does comply with the expectations established by Guillemin-Flescher's contrastive characterization of French and English and also that, in so doing, (2) the translation complies with the aim to anglicize that is enunciated in the translator's introduction. The introduction states and comments on that aim as follows: "Intelligible English render-

ings have generally been preferred to direct transfers into English of M. Derrida's suggestive exploitation of nuances of
French vocabulary. This results inevitably in some loss of the
force of the original." Indeed, some force and also some sense
get lost.

Yet the salient feature of the translator's introduction, which
reaffirms the value of natural, intelligible, idiomatic English precisely by setting it off against Derrida's tortuous, precious, lan-
guage-straining French, is that the translator begins by pointing
out quite explicitly that the essay, through its analyses and arguments, contests the very criteria and suppositions that nonetheless govern his translation. The reader of "White Mythology"
does get a reasonably direct re-presentation of the Derridean
critique that challenges the originary status of nature, the priority of the intelligible, the privileging of the semantic over the
syntactic, the hegemony of use-values, and so forth. Although
with lesser clarity and incision, the reader also gets something of
the analytic strategy designed to pinpoint, in the play of mimetic
particles, in processes of articulation, anagrammatism, semantic
displacement, in the aporias occasioned by supplementarity, the
work of heterogeneous factors that dislocate the conception of
metaphor, that undermine all attempts at theorizing metaphor,
that infest metaphoricity with the untamable energy of difference.

Integral to that analytic strategy are moves and moments, not
simply interrogatory, descriptive, or explanatory, that we might
loosely term demonstrative or even performative. These are moments at which the elements and processes of rhetoric and syntax that Derrida points out analytically, or the theses that he
articulates, are also put into play—are put on display, enacted,
actualized—in his writing. Such skids into performance are
wrought in a practice that, for example, makes visible the very
incidence of syntactic formations upon meaning-generation that
is being argued. To miss that performative dimension is not to
miss the message but, just as the translator's note indicates, to
miss or reduce its force by diminishing the energy devoted to

tightening the link between message and discursive practice. That is no small miss. What it leaves intact, by default, is a disparity—a form of dissension or contradiction—between saying and doing, between telling and showing, thesis and expression, program and performance, a disparity that "La mythologie blanche" moves at discrete moments, with timely abuses, to override. The translation thus tends to sap the strength of the thesis it restates by blocking off its enactment or enforcement by the statement and thereby allowing the contested values to prevail unshaken in the fabric of the very discourse that purports to contest them.

"La mythologie blanche" contains, in its discussion of the treatment of catachresis in Fontanier's rhetoric, a kind of tropical version of language-shaping abuse—"le coup de force d'une torsion qui va *contre l'usage*" (p. 307)—that exemplifies the practice we have envisioned for the translation of Derrida. The interest of catachresis in Fontanier's theory, as Derrida's analysis shows, is its intermediate status between irreducibly original inceptions of the signifying code and the standard taxinomy of usage. Exerting an abuse that estranges it from each order, the trope can circulate between the two of them, exercising both an irruptive and an integrative function. It exemplifies the double move that abusive translation has to pursue: both to violate and to sustain the principles of usage. Like the *tour*, it thus comes very close to metaphor, indeed more commonly taking a metaphoric rather than metonymic turn, without however being reducible to it. But for translation the significance of the catachretic figure in "La mythologie" doubtless lies less in the additional possibility it affords us for conceptualizing the work of translation than in the critical questioning that Derrida introduces through his discussion of Fontanier. At stake in the final section of the essay is the movement of domesticaton or recuperation by which rhetoric—and analogously, philosophy— bring the abusive force of catachresis back under the control of a reigning interpretation, of meanings supposed to be already present in the storehouse of language. Derrida's forceful remarks about both rhetoric and philosophy stand as a warning, scarcely mistakable, against the very recuperation we have observed in the translation of his essay, in the passage from French to English—a warning against what amounts to recuperation by the "natural language," as we deem it, in which the original is, as we venture incautiously to claim, rendered. That recuperation is the obvious risk that a strong translation must run and overcome.

Despite its explicit disputation of and overt resistance to certain forms of recuperation that do not have to be accepted as simply inevitable, despite the manifest implications for translation of its treatment of analogy and processes of substitution or of its vigorous critique of the subordination of syntax in the metaphorology of metaphysics, "La mythologie blanche" could be, has been, translated in dissonance with its own program. This fact is a sobering commentary on the staying power of classical concepts of translation. No doubt their domination is so well built into our languages and thus into the thoughts we are able to articulate through them that even the most concerted efforts to translate abusively are doomed to suffer under their hegemony. Yet this is by no means to concede that resistance to recuperation in translation is therefore impossible or unwarranted, only that recuperation can never be completely thwarted and thus that the resistance has to be disabused. For the translator, the question is simply to what extent the recuperative effects of translation can be controlled, to what extent the resistance the original puts up to the recuperations imposed by its own idiom can be remobilized in the language of the translation. In the case of Derrida, where that resistance is preeminently a matter of writing performance, the task of the translator is surely to work out a strategy that allows the most insistent and decisive effects of that performance to resurface in the translated text and to assume an importance sufficient to suggest the vital status of stratified or contrapuntal writing in the original.

The existence of weak, entropic translations surely depends in part on a time factor about which little can be done: the very possibility of translating strongly derives from that of reading insightfully, and the latter derives in turn from a familiarity that can only be gained over time. The closer a translation of a monumental text such as those of Derrida is to the original's date of publication, the more likely it is to be unduly deficient. Yet from the weak translation that is published and starts exerting influence well before the strong appreciation of the original has become possible, there remains an importance lesson to be learned. That lesson concerns not translation but commentary. The history of deconstruction in North America during the past decade or so has included something of a debate among various partisans of the critical endeavor concerning the form in which Derrida's work should be disseminated. At one pole, a purist view, holding an uncompromisingly as possible to the integrity of Derrida's philosophical project; at the other pole, an adaptivist view, allowing for a domesticated version of deconstruction that could, for example, be sketched out as a method usable for literary criticism. Since some recuperation is inevitable in any derived text, be it translation or commentary, and since, indeed, both translation and commentary are initially caught up in the same struggle to transmit the force of the original, the issue can only be a question of degree: to what lengths should we go in order to minimize the recuperation?

As I suggested much earlier, the existence of weak, misleading translations does have an effect on the commentator's conception of her task. Insofar as an interpretation of Derrida in North America has to reckon with such translations, commentary must attempt not simply to explain the intricacies of the French text and to suggest how we might describe them and understand them in English but also to reject and explain away the translations and the misconceptions they spawn. The translation thus becomes a special problem for the commentary, intervening in the relation between original text and commentary so as to complicate the task of interpretation. At the risk of an excessively schematic account, let us lay out the problem in the following way.

(1) Between the original French text and any commentary on it, there is a relation of supplementarity, that is, insofar as the

commentary is an addition to the original text, saying something the original does not say, it implies something missing in the original that it seeks to supply, so that "paradoxically" what supplies (makes up for) the lack also supplies (furnishes) it; and once this process is under way, the lack is forever to be supplied, commentary will forever pursue a fundamentally productive course as the continuance of an interrogation undertaken in the original.

(2) Between the translated French text and the commentary, there is a comparable relation of supplementarity, centered on the process of correction; the commentary strives to make up for what the translation states inadequately, recuperatively constituting the translation as a loss forever to be compensated in the ongoing history of that text's interpretations.

(3) When relation (1) is complicated by relation (2), the effect is not to to alter the supplemental relation between original and commentary in structure; it is simply to orient that relation toward an elemental task, that of a critical redress devoted rather more to describing the original—to pointing out what it really does and thereby says—than to saying what it does not say, to supplementing it in the strong sense.

Given this situation, the risk is then that the burden of lackluster translation will become an impedance to commentary, that it will interfere with the commentarial effort to respond strongly to the challenges of the original. The risk, we might say, is that commentary will be content to suggest what should come across in translation and will go no further. That would in fact be a failure to deal with the problem of recuperation as translation itself manifests it. For inadequate translation confronts the commentator with a dual necessity: on the one hand, it is clearly imperative to address critically the question of what the translation misses, to expose the crucial losses in the abusive and performative dimensions of the text; on the other hand, this very indictive/corrective operation makes it all the more essential for the commentary to supplement strongly with its own performance, to enact its own abuses, to regenerate the textual energy wasted in the translation. The increased difficulty of commentary stems from its having to dwell in the tension between these two responses, the one analytic, the other writerly, and somehow to program the former so that it will fecundate, rather than hold in check, the ploys of the latter.

As Derrida so clearly understands (his essay in this volume is one of many cases to the point), commentary does not have the option of ignoring the effects of translation, of pretending to be separable from translation. In the scheme we have outlined here, under the aegis of "free" translation, commentary is distinguished from translation above all by the former's opportunity to capture the abusive and performative dimensions of the original, not simply through reproduction, but also through invention. Relatively speaking, the translator's lot is an unhappy one because he plays an instrument more restrictively mimetic than that of the commentator. Translation imposes by default recuperations the commentator can reasonably seek to elude, entails limits on abuse and formulative discovery that she can studiously transgress. Yet the commentator's (pursuit of) translation still has to be valid, has to be rearticulable throughout the framework of her interpretation. The exigency of high fidelity never recedes. Thus, if commentary is to compensate in some measure for the recuperative losses occasioned by *us*able translations, it must meet the challenge of the original to supplement strongly, on a performative register, without forsaking the thankless task of the translator. Through the processes of supplementarity, the very demarcation of translation from commentary cannot help but become problematic. For commentary to supplement the translation is perhaps first to add to it, to correct it, simply to contest its recuperations by exposing them; but ultimately that move, if it is not to acquiesce to the very discursive order of the translation that it questions, *turns* into a replacement of the translation. So let us add, in all the senses of an elliptical phrase: commentary supplies the translation by doing other than translation. In the wake of translation, the mission of commentary is to translate in difference.

2

Paragon, Parergon: Baudelaire Translates Rousseau

CYNTHIA CHASE

Why does Baudelaire write "Morale du joujou"? Why set under a moral heading the essay from which he will detach the prose poem "Le joujou du pauvre"? Why not give it a title like "De l'essence du jeu," like "De l'essence du rire"?[1]

The essay's heading signals a recapitulation: Baudelaire's meditation on la morale du joujou repeats Rousseau's revery about the moral pleasure of offering gifts to children, the ninth of the *Rêveries du promeneur solitaire*. "Le joujou du pauvre" is first celebrated in the Neuvième Promenade. When Baudelaire repeats himself, he also repeats Rousseau: the prose poem he draws from the essay begins by recapitulating Rousseau's claim for the moral quality of a certain pleasure. "Je veux donner l'idée d'un divertissement innocent. Il y a si peu d'amusements

In an earlier version this essay was published in *Diacritics* 11:2 (Summer 1981), 42–51, and it is reprinted by permission of the editor.
[1]"De l'essence du rire et généralement du comique dans les arts plastiques," *Oeuvres complètes de Charles Baudelaire* (Paris: Gallimard, 1961), 975–93; first published in 1855. "Morale du joujou" was first published in 1853. Baudelaire transformed the twelfth through fourteenth paragraphs of this essay into a prose poem, "Le joujou du pauvre" (XIX in *Le Spleen de Paris),* first published in 1862.

qui ne soient pas coupables!"[2] In addition to this reference to the moral status of "diversion," Baudelaire's prose takes from Rousseau's revery its most peculiar motif: the edible toy. The toy as food figures decisively in the Neuvième Promenade, for Rousseau's *rêverie* consists largely in confuting the imagined charge that he is a "père dénaturé" by dwelling on his memories of offering gifts to children, gifts invariably edible: apples, rolls, cone-shaped wafers. Rousseau remembers other people's children receiving "pains de Nanterre" and "oublies"; Baudelaire pictures catlike children grinning together at the poor child's toy, a live rat. Baudelaire's text, and Rosseau's revery, could be titled not "A Child Is Being Beaten" (Freud's title for a fantasy turned moral, made reflexive), but "A Child Is Being Given a Toy to Eat."

How should we describe the way in which Baudelaire repeats Rousseau in "Morale du joujou"? This essay does not simply recapitulate the *themes* of the Neuvième Promenade or *reinterpret* Rousseau's revery. It repeats an angle, the moral angle, and a strange piece of material, the edible gift; the angle of the frame, the *morceau-cadeau*, are transported into another context. To put it emphatically, they are translated. To say that Baudelaire translates Rousseau is not to say that he reads and understands him. "For translation," as de Man writes, interpreting Walter Benjamin's choice of *Übersetzung* rather than reception or reading as the proper analogon for the "understanding" of a literary work, "translation is per definition intra-linguistic, not a relation between a subject and an object, . . . but between one linguistic function and another."[3] Baudelaire's writing does something other and more than reading: it reinscribes Rousseau's words in the language of Baudelaire's text: it does not reinterpret them but repeats them, with a difference. We must

[2]"Le joujou du pauvre," in *Oeuvres Complètes*, 255.
[3]Walter Benjamin, "Aufgabe des Übersetzers," *Gesammelte Schriften*, 4:1 (Frankfurt: Suhrkamp, 1972), 7–21. Benjamin wrote this essay as an introduction to his translation of *Les fleurs du mal*. Paul de Man, introduction to *Towards an Aesthetics of Reception*, by Hans Robert Jauss (Minneapolis: University of Minnesota Press, 1982).

think of these texts as written not just in a language (French) but also, each of them, in a language of its own, as every dream (every revery) is a text to decipher not through recourse to a universal language of dream symbols but by recreating the specific contingent associations that make up the unique language of a single dream.

One word in particular in "Morale du joujou" is best identified as a *translation* of a certain word in the Neuvième Promenade. I should like to make the claim in those terms, and so I shall make use—shall hazard an abuse—of Philip Lewis's directions "vers la traduction abusive."[4] Lewis invokes the strategy of a rigorously abusive translation, which would counter what is lost in the translation with an addition, a supplement. The translator commits an excess, performs an abuse—but not just anywhere. "The abusive move in the translation cannot be directed at just any element of the original; rather, it will bear upon a key operator or decisive textual knot that will be recognized by dint of its own abusive features. . . . The abusive work of translation will be oriented by specific nubs in the original, by points or passages that are in some sense forced."[5] Baudelaire's repetition of Rousseau is oriented like such an abusive translation. I shall focus on a word in Baudelaire's essay that reenacts a moment of excess or abuse in Rousseau's text—a word that rigorously if abusively *translates* a word in the Neuvième Promenade.

The eighth paragraph of "Morale du joujou" draws a contrast between slavish and imaginative imitation, or imitative and imaginative play. In the exclamation that divides the paragraph, Baudelaire celebrates the spontaneous creative power that children manifest in what is most genuinely play, not mimicry. But the name here for such play is also the name for devotion to work. The sentence makes sense in its immediate context only when we understand "l'éternel drame de la diligence" to refer,

---

[4]Intervention: Philip Lewis, "Vers la traduction abusive," in *Les fins de l'homme: A partir du travail de Jacques Derrida*, Cerisy Colloquium, July 23–August 2, 1980 (Paris: Galilée, 1981), 253–261.
[5]Lewis, pp. 255–56.

not to a drama of diligence, but to the recurrently enthralling stagecoach game played by imaginative children. Diligence, however, is named in the same breath. "La diligence" is what Riffaterre in *Semiotics of Poetry* calls a "dual sign"—"an equivocal word situated at the point where two sequences of semantic or formal associations intersect."[6] One set of associations comes from the sign's immediate context, its syntactical position. The other set of associations comes from a wider context, from themes active in the text as a whole, or, as Riffaterre puts it, from "another text" in the text. In the dual sign, a semiotic text located at the level of paradigms intrudes upon a mimetic text located at the level of syntax. But in this case, I would claim, the "semiotic text" within "Morale du joujou" is not the only "other text" to intrude upon the syntax of Baudelaire's paragraph. The other "other text" that intrudes is another dual sign that "diligence" *translates*. The "syntactical ungrammaticality" of Baudelaire's dual sign functions as a rigorously abusive translation of another such abuse in another text, Rousseau's Neuvième Promenade.

The abuse that occurs in the Neuvième Promenade is the defacement of a word's most resonant meaning. The word is *oublie*, which means waffle or wafer: cylindrical or cone-shaped wafers that could be gotten by buying chances from a vendor equipped with a sort of numbered wheel or turntable. These wafers figure as one of various fragile edible souvenirs of an encounter with Rousseau (like the apples bought for the little Savoyards in another episode recounted in the Ninth Promenade). Rousseau recalls presiding over the distribution of such oublies to a class of schoolgirls at the edge of the Bois de Boulogne.[7] That occasion, he tells us, is one of his fondest memories. Rousseau tells us he's remembering—and tells us of engaging an *oublieur*. Like *diligence*, *oublie* is a dual sign with

---

[6]Michael Riffaterre, *Semiotics of Poetry* (Bloomington: Indiana University Press, 1978), 86.

[7]See *Les rêveries du promeneur solitaire,* Neuvième Promenade, in *Oeuvres complètes de Jean-Jacques Rousseau* (Paris: Gallimard, 1959), 1090–91.

directly opposite sets of associations. Baudelaire celebrates play and writes a word that suggests work. Rousseau celebrates a memory and writes a word that sounds like forgetting. The reader is forced to forget the meaning of the word's sound in order to follow its function in the syntax of the anecdote. What the reader is forced to forget is forgetting. But at the same time the dual sign forces forgetting on the reader: *e* or no *e, oubli(e)* forces forgetting down our throat. Baudelaire's dual sign, too, forces forgetting on the reader. *Diligence* translates *oublie:* the translation's rigor lies in its reenactment of Rousseau's imposition on the reader. Rousseau's wording forces something down, and Baudelaire's reading forces that out. Baudelaire's *diligence*, like Rousseau's *oublie*, designates a thing—a game, a toy—with a word that also names an abstraction, a concept, and a concept *opposed* to the pleasure the same word designates.

Why is it *this* moment in the Neuvième Promenade that "Morale du joujou" repeats? Why does Baudelaire translate, and why this word? Baudelaire's dual sign repeating Rousseau's requires us to analyze the peculiarly inassimilable or compelling quality of oublies.

The prominence of oublies in a passage about a memory calls attention to the word's etymology and permits an archaeology of the sign. *Oublie* is a word whose meaning in the so-called semiotic text located at the level of themes or paradigms *names* the effacement, or oubli, of the etymology of its meaning in the mimetic text located at the level of syntax. For *oublie* derives from *oblata,* the Latin word for the consecrated host, the wafer consumed *in memory* of the sacrifice of the Word made Flesh. The forgetting of the "origin" of *oublie*—its etymology, its figural status, commemorating the disfiguration of "Flesh" fixed on a cross—leaves waffles, edible souvenirs to be consumed forgetfully. Thus the dual sign *oublie* at once reveals and defaces the effaced disfiguration that produces literal language, language that can be taken into the mouth without a special act of remembering. The etymology of *oublie* recapitulates the account in Rousseau's *Essai sur l'origine des langues,* where the postulate

"Que le premier language dut être figuré" is illustrated in a parable tracing the origin of the word "homme" from a forgetting of a figure for fear (initially the word *géant*).[8] Compacted in *oublies* is Rousseau's history of language as disfiguration. Such a sign might well prove indigestible.

The rest of Rousseau's Rêverie may be absorbed, diffused, by Baudelaire's essay; only the toy food and dual sign comes up as if he cannot keep it down. Rousseau's oublies may be hard to keep down because of the way he distributes them. The game of getting a wafer—buying a chance, watching the vendor spin his wheel—becomes part of a business of ensuring equal desserts. The little girls are made to line up, take turns, share, and plead their differences at what Rousseau gaily calls his "tribunal de justice." Taking pleasure in giving pleasure takes the form, here, of meting out justice. A kind of game gets an ethical framework; playing is bound up with ethical scheming.

Rousseau cites the scene with the oublieur as the kind of thing that induces the *contentement* he is concerned to analyze in the rest of this text. Contentement is a crucial category in the Neuvième Promenade. Rousseau distinguishes it from a more fleeting and less readable condition he calls *bonheur* and identifies it, explicitly, with reading: "le contentement se lit dans les yeux."[9]

Rousseau goes on to identify contentment as the condition inspired in him by the visible signs of other people's contentment. He makes two claims for this condition. It is, he insists, a physical pleasure in visible signs, a "plaisir de sensation." But he also insists that it has a "cause morale"; he has to know that the signs he reads signify other people's contentment in others' contentment, not in their suffering: "Quoique ce ne soit là qu'un plaisir de sensation il a certainement une cause morale et la preuve en est que ce même aspect, au lieu de me flater, de me plaire peut me déchirer de douleur et d'indignation quand je sais

---

[8]Jean-Jacques Rousseau, *Essai sur l'origine des langues* (Bordeaux: Ducros, 1970), 45–47. Compare Paul de Man, *Allegories of Reading* (New Haven: Yale University Press, 1979), 149–155.

[9]Rousseau, *Oeuvres complètes*, 1083.

que ces signes de douleur et de joye sur les visages des méchans ne sont que des marques que leur malignité est satisfaite."[10]

Rousseau thus locates contentement in the two modes of activity that are *excluded* from aesthetic pleasure by Kant: enjoyment of sensation, and moral reflection. Since *contentement* designates the activity of reading signs, Rousseau situates *reading* remote by definition from aesthetic activity or aesthetic pleasure.

That implication is one that the reader of literature must find it virtually impossible to assimilate, for both the practice of reading and the theory of literature need to invoke the realm of aesthetics to articulate the continuity between signifying procedures and significance, between poetics and hermeneutics. However, Rousseau insists: insists that he feels good when he feels *good*. This is as much as to insist that we do the same: the enjoyment is urged on us with the claim that it is caused by the signs' moral significance, and the moral interpretation is urged on us with the claim that it is a source of pleasure. We feel *forced* to enjoy.

Kant comments on this special effect in paragraph 48 of the Third Critique, "Of the Relation of Genius to Taste":

> Denn in dieser sonderbaren, auf lauter Einbildung beruhenden Empfindung der Gegenstand gleichsam, als ob er sich zum Genusse *aufdränge*, wider den wir doch mit Gewalt streben, vorgestellt wird: so wird die künstliche Vorstellung des Gegenstandes von der Natur dieses Gegenstandes selbst in unserer Empfindung nicht mehr unterschieden, und jene kann alsdann unmöglich für schön gehalten werden.[11]

> In this peculiar sensation, which rests on mere imagination, the object is represented as it were obtruding itself for our enjoyment while we strive against it. . . .And the artistic representation is no longer distinguished from the nature of the object itself in our sensation, and thus it is impossible that it can be regarded as beautiful.[12]

[10]Ibid., p. 1904.
[11]Immanuel Kant, *Kritik der Urteilskraft* (Frankfurt: Suhrkamp, 1979), 248.
[12]*Kant's Critique of Judgement*, trans. J. H. Bernard (London: Macmillan, 1931), 195.

Certainly Rousseau's contentement cannot be regarded as beautiful; but it is precisely not a matter of taste. Rousseau demands not that one exercise taste but that one take something in. He exacts an act of reading about the activity of reading signs. Rousseau situates that activity in the two instances that Kant excludes from the aesthetic, and he forces them together and insists on their coincidence. He urges his reader to swallow the notion of *moral gratification.*

A notion that would force one to enjoy in this way exceeds the limits of taste to produce the "peculiar sensation" analyzed by Kant and identified as (not distaste but) disgust. *Ekel*: the word is Kant's for that "peculiar sensation" excited by what cannot become an object of aesthetic judgment. Here Derrida intervenes. "Il faut s'assurer que le mot *dégout* (*Ekel*) ne désigne pas le répugnant ou le négatif en général. Il s'agit bien de ce qui donne *envie de vomir*" ("One must be assured that the word 'disgust' (*Ekel*) does not designate the repugnant or the negative in general. It is indeed a matter of that which makes one *want to vomit*)."[13] Forced to swallow Rousseau's moral gratification, forced to enjoy his contentment, a person wants, then, rigorously speaking, to throw up. As Baudelaire does: he throws up Rousseau's plaisirs, Rousseau's oublies, as a recognizably similar sign—la diligence.

But why throw up Rousseau's oublies rather than some other item on the menu of moral gratification? The reasons must lie in the context of that peculiar word, in the dimensions of that dual sign, *oubli(e)*. The more insistent *aur*al sense of *oubli* comes into the sentences that describe Rousseau's gratification at seeing the schoolgirls take pleasure in their equal desserts. "La gentillesse de quelques-unes," remarks Rousseau, "faisait oublier leur laideur."[14] I was not gloating over pretty little girls, he tells us. But the sentence says something else. It cites *forgetting* as the connection between a moral quality and an aesthetic one. Re-

[13]Jacques Derrida, "Economimesis," in *Mimesis: desarticulations* (Paris: Aubier-Flammarion, 1975), 91.
[14]Rousseau, *Oeuvres complètes.* 1901.

sponse to a moral quality *precludes* response to an aesthetic one;
they are separated by a moment of forgetfulness, of oubli. Kant
sets the same terms in a similar relation. We recall the so-called
"First Moment of the Judgment of Taste": "the satisfaction
which determines the judgment of taste is disinterested,"
whereas "the satisfaction in the good is bound up with interest."
Hence a pure judgment of taste involves a momentary forgetting
of the moral qualities of the object. Rousseau claims, instead, a
momentary forgetting of the object's aesthetic inadequacy,
thanks to its moral qualities. Rousseau's formulation calls attention to what he does not claim: disinterested aesthetic pleasure,
pleasure without interest. Forget that, the sentence says; forget
the forgetting entailed in making a judgment of taste: *this* oubli
forgets and forgoes that forgetting. In the situation Rousseau
imposes on us, the condition of the possibility of beauty, the
condition of aesthetic judgment, must be gone without.

What does Rousseau forgo forgetting? The *purpose* of the
scene he contemplates, the *end* of the process he presides over:
just enjoyment of equal desserts. The Neuvième Promenade is a
revery about the kind of satisfaction available to man in the
contemplation of man ("a man, a woman, or a child," says Kant;
or a schoolgirl, says Rousseau): sole object, says Kant, to have an
unforgettable end in itself, a purpose: humanity. (Man alone can
be the subject of a work of "ideal" beauty, which is not "free"
beauty, constituted by aesthetic detachment, by a forgetting of
one's interest in the subject represented, but rather a gratification of our "Reason's" interest, our ethical interest in the subject. So Kant writes in paragraph 17 of the Third Critique, "Of
the Ideal of Beauty.")[15] Thus the end is reached when the humanity of the oublies' recipients emerges in such a way that the
matter of their beauty is put in brackets. What is put in brackets,
then, is a certain bracketing. For beauty, free beauty, has this
condition: that the purpose of the object be bracketed, be momentarily forgotten. The condition of beauty is purposiveness

[15]Kant, *Kritik*, 149–54.

without purpose. The condition of Rousseau's contentment is purposiveness *without* the condition of being without purpose.

What "contents" Rousseau is an inversion, or negation, of purposiveness without purpose: not the contemplation of *purpose*, but the *suspension* of purposiveness without purpose. This is not simply because his object is the paragon, man, who has his purpose of his existence in himself, who therefore is alone capable of *ideal* beauty—and *not* capable of free beauty, not allowing the forgetfulness of its purpose that allows an object to be freely beautiful. It is rather because Rousseau formulates his contentment in terms that determine it as the deprivation of an exclusion.

But furthermore, the very idea of the paragon turns out itself to be determined in this way. For man, in his ideal beauty, turns out to be determined by a framework around a frame, the frame that separates the beautiful object from its purpose.

The integrity of Kant's critical system defining man's faculties depends upon the faculty analyzed in the Third Critique: "Judgement, which in the order of our cognitive faculties forms a mediating link between Understanding and Reason."[16] It turns out, furthermore, that Judgment must be analyzed as aesthetic judgment, for it is "mainly in those judgements that we call aesthetical, which concern the Beautiful and the Sublime," that it is possible to discover a cognitive process that neither contributes to the knowledge of the object nor confuses attendant feelings of pleasure or pain with the subject's will or motives (with what Kant refers to as "the faculty of desire, which has its principles *a priori* in concepts of reason").[17] Only aesthetic judgment, that is, may be sufficiently distinguished from the workings of the Understanding and the Reason to enable the identification of an independent faculty mediating between them.

The frame that separates the object from its purpose constitutes an object as aesthetic. From the "First Moment of the Judgement of Taste," aesthetic judgment is defined as a certain

[16]*Kant's Critique of Judgement*, 2.
[17]Ibid., p. 4.

bracketing, as the posing of a frame, the frame that presents an object as a figure, separated from purpose and so susceptible of being judged freely beautiful. Aesthetic judgment, taste, is then examined, in the "Analytic of the Beautiful," according to quality, quantity, relation to purposes, and modality, a categorial frame imported from the analysis of concepts in the First Critique. Judgment of the freely beautiful thereby becomes subordinated, finally, to the conception of an ideal of beauty. In the Third Critique, then, as Derrida puts it, the question of the frame is framed. It is set within a critical framework that sets it up as the link between man's understanding and his reason, the link that establishes his special status. That status is established by *framing* the free beauty that can never be man's: by presenting it as a matter of a frame, as a question of a "without," as a purposiveness-without-purpose forever less *ideal* than ideal beauty. The special status of man depends on the framing—the frame-up—of a frame.[18] The "man" of Kant's Third Critique originates as does the word "man" analyzed in Rousseau's *Essai*: as an initial act of framing becomes obscured. What is a frame? It may be an ornament, or an essential support, or an accessory, or a frame-up. What is a parergon? It is, for instance, a frame, writes Kant, writes Derrida. (Derrida is reading Kant's paragraph 14, "Elucidation by Means of Examples"; see "Parergon," *La vérité en peinture*.)[19] We may translate: the paragon is determined as the parergon of a parergon or the envelope of an hors

[18]On the frame as frame-up, see also Barbara Johnson, "The Frame of reference: Poe, Lacan, Derrida," in *Literature and Psychoanalysis, the Question of Reading: Otherwise*, Yale French Studies 55/56 (New Haven: Yale University, 1977), particularly part 4 (pp. 478–93), which opens with the following epigraph (from Mallarmé's "Sonnet en x"):

> Elle, défunte nue en le miroir, encore
> Que, dans *l'oubli fermé par le cadre*, se fixe
> De scintillations sitôt le septuor.
>
> [Italics added by Johnson]

Johnson's essay detects the framing of Lacan in Derrida's reading of Lacan's reading of Poe, in "Le facteur de la vérité" (*La carte postale—De Socrate à Freud et au-delà* [Paris: Flammarion, 1980]).

[19]Derrida, *La vérité en peinture* (Paris Flammarion, 1978), 66–89.

d'oeuvre. In Derrida's rendering, the Third Critique mixes not only with Rousseau's *Essai* but also with his Neuvième Promenade.

The Promenade connects with the passage in which Kant affirms man's ability to conceive an ideal of beauty (paragraph 17). As Derrida translates it, the condition of beauty, in the Third Critique, is "finalité-sans-fin." "C'est la finalité-sans-fin qui est *dite* belle." "It's purposiveness-without-purpose which is *said* to be beautiful. . . . It's the *without* that counts, then, for beauty, neither the purposiveness nor the purpose . . . , but the *without* of purposiveness without purpose."[20] "C'est donc le *sans* qui compte pour la beauté": the *sans*, not the *sens*; the "without," not the "sense"; not a sense to be enjoyed, not a sense to be understood, but rather a *sans*, a "without." Derrida's "sans" is a dual sign, resonant with the "meaning" it is "without." It translates the *ohne* of "Zweckmässigkeit ohne Zweck" in a way that displaces and reinscribes an abuse in the Kantian text, an abuse of the frame. "Ce *sans*-là, est-il traduisible?" And is it useable?—for instance, to translate what in Rousseau is translated by Baudelaire? The slide in the sense of "translation" here may be a matter for disgust. But sense itself is not without such sliding.

"It's the 'without' that counts, for beauty." Why then does *man* count so? "Il est seul capable d'un idéal de beauté. . . . Il [en] est capable . . . parce qu'il est doué de raison, ce qui veut dire, en langage kantien, apte à se fixer ses propres fins. [C'est le] Seul être dans la nature à se donner ses propres fins, à lever en lui le *sans*" ("He alone is capable of an ideal of beauty. He is capable [of it] because he is endowed with reason, which means, in Kantian terms, apt at determing his own ends. [He is] the only being in nature to give himself his own ends, to suspend in himself the 'without'").[21] Kant's paragon, in Derrida's "Parergon," is "the only being to *suspend* in himself the 'without'"— to do without being without. It's the additional "without" that counts for man's status as paragon.

[20]Ibid., p. 101.
[21]Ibid.

That "without" is also the sum of Rousseau's contentment. For concurrent claims to take pleasure in a sensation and to exercise ethical judgment cancel each other, and by the end of the Neuvième Promenade, Rousseau is calling up moments of physical discomfort and moral confusion. But what, exactly, does he go without? Going in for reading, Rousseau goes without aesthetic judgment, without beauty, without purposiveness without purpose. Yet he claims not one but both of the two modes of experience that the aesthetic excludes, moral judgment and sensual pleasure, which cannot as such condition each other. The double claim cancels itself out; what remains? Going without being without has to be gone without, too. It turns out, reading Rousseau, that one cannot have freedom *from* aesthetic activity any more than one can have aesthetic activity, freedom from moral and sensual responses.

In the process of writing, *oubli(e)* has a tendency to become forgoing forgetting, and "being without" to become "doing without being without," and "without" to become "without without," or *sans* "*sans* sans." "Ils jouent," writes Baudelaire, "sans joujoux."[22] How did this reiteration of negative syllables ever begin? Rousseau tells a story of how it began with a promise, his promise to the oublieur. "Faites tirer . . . et je vous paierai le tout."[23] He says that he will pay for the oublies; not that he will eat them. He guarantees vicarious consumption of oubli(es). Rousseau makes promises; but it is Baudelaire who eats Rousseau's words.

They cannot be kept down, they have to be thrown up. That proliferating sign, that sliding *sans*, disgusts us and eludes our comprehension; it makes one want to throw up. "Comment avoir *envie* de vomir?" presses Derrida. How could someone *want* to throw up? One wants to throw up to reverse the process, to draw the line, and "mettre la chose à la bouché."[24] So Baudelaire throws up—*la diligence*.

[22]Baudelaire, *Oeuvres complètes*, 525.
[23]Rousseau, *Oeuvres complètes*, 1091.
[24]Derrida, "Economimesis," 91, 93.

A dual sign, like *oublie, diligence* requires the reader to re-read. For even as it designates a supremely autonomous kind of play, it names a quality valuable for purposeful work. Baude-laire's dual sign engages us in construing the relevance of dili-gence in this ostensible celebration of play. We reread to create a context in which, to use Riffaterre's words, "the dual sign's second (or syntactically unacceptable) semantic allegiance can be *vindicated.*"[25] *La diligence* engages us in understanding that a name for a game, for a particular kind of play, also inscribes a conceptual framework that valorizes purposeful activity. Kant's "Critique of the Aesthetical Judgement" engages us along the same lines. Taste is conceived as a connection between man's purposeful activity (Understanding as a means of knowledge) and his purpose (his Reason). In inviting us to imagine a similar situation to warrant the senses of his dual sign, Baudelaire's inscription of *la diligence* would be truly Kantian. We are in-duced to conceive a framework that vindicates the sense of dili-gence; we are lured into complicity with a complicity between purposefulness and play.

Or are we lured into drawing a line between them? We are made to feel that the two senses of *la diligence* conflict; that in the immediate mimetic context the word means play free of purpose, whereas in the vaster semiotic context it means almost the reverse: commitment to purposeful activity. One meaning of the word points to something done without a purpose (the stage-coach game). Another meaning points to something done with a purpose (with diligence). The sharp opposition between the two senses of *la diligence* would seem to reinstall, then, the distinc-tion eroded by the sense of *oublie*—to reestablish the difference between forgoing playfulness and forgetting purposefulness. For Rousseau's "doing without being without" (or going without doing without being without), Baudelaire substitutes either doing without or else doing with a purpose.

Except how are we made to draw the line, to think that ei-

---

[25]Riffaterre, *Semiotics of Poetry*, 91.

ther/or? We are made to construe the framework in which *diligence* as diligence makes sense, in which the line is drawn between work and play, by bracketing, momentarily, the first appropriate sense. To make sense of the other sense, we have to do without the stagecoach game. We have to do without that play without purpose to get at the opposition between purposeful work and purposeless play. To draw the line, we have to do without the sense of doing without. Drawing the line, then, is a matter of adding *another* "without" to distinguish from "with" a "without" that was already there. Baudelaire reenacts the proliferation of *sans* of Rousseau's text in the very line he draws against it.

So it will come up again; it cannot be thrown up once and for all. It comes up again when Baudelaire introduces a distinction between his prose poem and his prose *prose,* where he substitutes one group of words for another in rewriting two paragraphs of "Morale du joujou" as the prose poem "Le joujou du pauvre." The prose poem follows the essay almost word for word except at one point. Where the essay describes the poor child as "one of those urchins who," and so forth, the prose poem introduces an analogy. Baudelaire compares the eye it takes to discover the child's beauty beneath the "patina of miserable poverty" with the eye it takes to divine "une peinture idéale sous un vernis de carrossier": an ideally beautiful painting obscured by coachmaker's varnish. Cheap varnish is the idea. But "coachmaker" points back to the stagecoach game, *carrossier,* to *diligence.* When Baudelaire rewrites his prose as prose poem, one of the words he writes recalls the word with which he translates Rousseau. *Carrossier* points back to *diligence,* and *diligence* translates *oublie*: where Baudelaire rewrites, he reinscribes a translation of Rousseau.

So the oublie comes up again, not just as the toy food, the *cadeau-morceau* contemplated by the catlike children, but in the words that name the film that can fill the frame of the ideal painting. "Vernis de carrossier"; *vernis de diligence?* We sense a frame in that reference to "une idéale peinture sous un vernis de

carrossier." Isn't the film of varnish a sort of frame effect, a sign
of an excessive diligence in desiring that the painting be thor-
oughly framed? Baudelaire's image tempts us to take it as a
reading of Kant and Rousseau.

To read is to make the sign come to rest in a meaning, to let it
be understood. In Baudelaire's text something else is under way.
The word *carrossier*—pointing to *diligence*—marks this moment of rewriting as a repetition not of reading but of translation,
Baudelaire's translation of Rousseau's *oublie. Carrossier* repeats
and remarks that gesture replacing one signifier-and-signified
with another, one sign with another whose *relations* must be
homologous. What does the rewritten version repeat or replace?
It replaces Baudelaire's essay with a prose poem—making the
essay prose prose (another sort of "without without"). And it
replaces a passage in the essay that describes a function that
could be regarded as not unlike the way in which Baudelaire
repeats Rousseau. This passage describes not vomiting but snot.
Where the prose poem describes the child's patina of poverty
analogically, the essay describes it literally: the child is "one of
those urchins upon whom *snot* slowly makes a pathway in the
dirt and dust" ("un de ces marmots sur lesquels *la morve se fraye
lentement un chemin* dans la crasse et la poussière").[26]
We would hesitate, perhaps, to say that this is a moment of
disgust. Baudelaire describes a snotty urchin. Something other
than disgust, other, in other words, than the desire to throw up,
makes this passage represent the way Baudelaire repeats Rousseau. The passage draws a line between negligibly different elements, marking the trace of "la morve . . . dans la crasse et la
poussière" and locating the snotty child "sur la route, entre les
chardons et les orties" ("between the thistles and the nettles").
This drawing of lines between minimally different conditions
characterizes the process by which Baudelaire translates Rousseau: a process of distinguishing *doing* without from doing *without* being without; of distinguishing one *sans,* and one *oubli(e),*

[26]Baudelaire, *Oeuvres complètes,* 527.

from another. But the sense of this image of snot making a line is that the line itself is one of those slippery *sans*. Instead of drawing a line against what disgusts, Baudelaire's repetition of his process of translation draws a slightly disgusting line.

Rousseau's *oublie* does not just come up again as *diligence; diligence* glides into "vernis de carrossier," and "vernis de diligence" slides into *morve*. *La morve* would seem to be a variant of *le vomi*, that is, of what Baudelaire throws up in the process of drawing a line between his text and Rousseau's. But snot can't be thrown up. It oozes down. Not just snot, perhaps, but its variants. And what we sense in Baudelaire's text, and in Rousseau's, is the variance. We can point to certain words, we can locate some substitutions. But if that localization seems other than sheerly arbitrary, it is only because the peculiar tendency shared by these dual signs (and their repetitions) is to shift locale and to evoke locations that are no more than multiplying localizations, places for drawing the line against drawing the line. What we sense in Baudelaire's text, and in Rousseau's, is not lines that disgust, and not the place of disgust, but rather the vicariousness of disgust. Baudelaire's repetition of Rousseau's dual sign does not exhaust disgust; it does not satisfy the desire to throw up. The reason could be that there lies, in Rousseau's text, what is "worse than the literally disgusting." I translate Derrida near the end of "Economimesis": "Il y a pire que le dégoutant littéral." "There is worse than the literally disgusting. And if there's worse it's because the literally disgusting is maintained, for security's sake, in the place of the worse. If not of something worse, at least of an 'in place of'; in place of a replacement without a proper place without a trajectory, without economic and circular return. In place of prosthesis."[27]

Prosthesis, then—an adding of artificial parts that remarks and perpetuates a disfiguration—characterizes Rousseau's text. For in Baudelaire's text it produces not only signs of satisfied disgust, but traces of vicariousness. But can prosthesis be said to *charac-*

[27]Derrida, "Economimesis," 93.

terize Rousseau's text, when the word evokes the fungibility of organic characteristics—the fungibility, say, of organic parts of Baudelaire's text and organic parts of Rousseau's?

We are reminded that another name can be attached to the practice of inserting prosthetic devices, of adding artificial organs to supply a deficiency. That is the process, for instance, of translation, of the surgically intrusive, rigorously abusive translation that replaces one device with another. A translation will be deficient in the force of the translated text: deficient at least in the forcings peculiar to it, such as the duality of its dual signs. But a translation may supply—not deny—that deficiency, in allowing other forcings to appear in place of those: not in their places, but in *other* places in the translation. These devices, these abuses, do then both signal and defend against what the translation must ward off: not the peculiar force of the translated text but its translatability.[28] Baudelaire's "Morale du joujou" responds to the intolerable translatability of Rousseau's Ninth Promenade.

[28]Walter Benjamin writes at the end of "Aufgabe des Übersetzers" ("The Task of the Translator") of the sense in which the text is *schlechthin übersetzbar*—absolutely translatable—in such a way that it radically endangers the translator. Benjamin's suggestion that such translatability is intolerable is reinforced in Maurice de Gandillac's translation of this essay (*Mythe et violence* [Paris: Denoël, 1971]) by a revealing mistranslation or felicitous *coquille*, noticed in a seminar of Derrida's that was using both the French and the German texts of Benjamin's essay: for *schlechthin übersetzbar*, the French reads, *purement et simplement* in*traduisible*.

3

"o'er-brimm'd"

> Dès son titre . . . Benjamin situe le *problème* . . .
> comme celui du traducteur et non de la traduction
> (ni d'ailleurs, soit dit au passage et la question n'est
> pas négligeable, de la traductrice).
> > JACQUES DERRIDA, "Des Tours de Babel"

That the field of literary criticism seeks to constitute itself *as* a field, with its own limits, identity, and coherence, is readily seen in the manner in which it deploys or disposes of its defining terms, words that we find, or do not find, in the glossaries at the ends of textbooks, such as "character," "plot," "figure," "meter," or "genre." In the grand edifice of literary studies, every term has its *place*, as guaranteed by a single architectonic principle, the law of identity declaring that a thing cannot be, and also not be, itself at the same time. Every term has a proper meaning and a proper function in the scheme of things: thus, for example, the term "meter" is not to be confused with the term "plot," or the term "character" with the term "metaphor," even if we can show that such terms overlap in their meanings and their etymologies. This essay, for instance, is on the topic of "translation," and in the conceptual system of literary criticism, "translation" is accorded a special and peculiar place: it is a genre, a minor genre, framed by the most careful, if always reworded, rules. Thus, translation takes place between two languages, each with its own identity; translation is of a work, as identified by its own textual limits; and, ideally, the work to be translated has an author, as does the translation itself, each author being identified by his or her own proper name. So placed and defined, the term "translation" serves in its turn to situate and define the terms of "language," "work," and "author" and thereby to guarantee the stability of the critical edifice as a whole.

But suppose that we let the word "translation" spread to a fuller semantic range, toward the limit (if such a limit indeed exists) of its semantic potential. Suppose we say, for example, that an author has translated a work from one language to another but that both of those languages are one and the same—in fact, the author's mother tongue—and that the work translated was originally written by the translator himself; and that the translated work, indeed, was nothing other than the very same work produced through the act of translation. To speak of translation in this way would invite the reproach of the field. . . .

This, I repeat, is an essay on translation, but it could just as well be an essay on "genre," "metaphor," "character," "plot," "meter," "criticism," "literature," "essay," or "on." Each term is open to the same semantic expansion and subject to the suppression of that semantic range. So menaced is literary criticism by the instability, the semantic unreliability of its own terms, that it spends the better part of its time and energy policing those terms, its techniques being those of the police in other fields, such as sudden arrests, solitary confinement, or deportation. "Translation," a famous suspect, has compiled a long and distinguished dossier. Two entries will suffice to characterize its file, the first of which was submitted some two centuries ago.

> The great pest of speech is frequency of translation. No book was ever turned from one language to another, without imparting something of its native idiom; this is the most mischievous and

comprehensive innovation; single words may enter by thousands, and the fabrick of the tongue continue the same, but new phraseology changes much at once; it alters not the single stones of the building, but the order of the columns. If an academy should be established for the cultivation of our stile, which I, who can never wish to see dependence multiplied, hope the spirit of *English* liberty will hinder or destroy, let them, instead of compiling grammars and dictionaries, endeavour, with all their influence, to stop the licence of translatours, whose idleness and ignorance, if it be suffered to proceed, will reduce us to babble a dialect of *France.*

It would be tempting to linger on this passage, on its pathos, its eloquence, its coherence, and its incoherence also. We could linger at length, indeed, on Dr. Johnson's *Dictionary of the English Langauge*, from the "preface" of which this particular paragraph has been drawn.[1] But we turn instead to a later entry in the dossier on "translation," recent, brutal, and brief:

The writer who is content to destroy is on a plane with the writer who is content to translate. Both are parasites.

It would be tempting to linger on *this* passage, and on the lifework of its author (Wallace Stevens), who rarely, if ever, dissents from the norms enunciated by Samuel Johnson.[2] But we shall turn instead to another pursuit, which is to put these police to the test of reading itself, to the test of reading a work of their choice, a work of "pure English" whose formal integrity is widely held to be "perfect" and whose author is absolutely secure in his identity and canonical standing. Such a poem would be "To Autumn" by John Keats:

It is because "To Autumn" is so uniquely a distillation, and at many different levels, that each generation has found it one of the most nearly perfect poems in English. We need not be afraid of

[1]*Samuel Johnson: "Rasselas," Poems, and Selected Prose*, ed. Bertrand H. Bronson (New York: Holt, Rinehart and Winston, 1960), 236.
[2]Wallace Stevens, *Opus Posthumous* (New York: Alfred A. Knopf, 1957), 165.

continuing to use the adjective. In its strict sense the word is peculiarly applicable: the whole is "perfected"—carried through to completion—solely by means of the given parts; and the parts observe decorum (for no other poem of the last two centuries does the classical critical vocabulary prove so satisfying) by contributing directly to the whole, with nothing dangling or independent. . . . the poem is entirely concrete, and self-sufficient in and through its concreteness. . . . Here at last is something of a genuine paradise, therefore.[3]

This judgment (pronounced by W. J. Bate) sums up a universal attitude toward the poem, there being (in the words of Paul de Man) a "clear consensus"[4] among all scholars who speak the "so satisfying vocabulary" of "classical criticism." Hence the value of the poem as a test case for the classical method: is "To Autumn," in a word, truly a "genuine paradise"? Is it free of destruction, pestilence, parasites, and French? Or is it, contrarily, the very setting of those imperfections, an *essay in translation?* If so, then the speakers of the "so satisfying vocabulary" are really lost on the plains of Shinar, even as their poet passes among them, incognito, to wander in the misty shades of Babel's tower.

To Autumn

1

Season of mists and mellow fruitfulness,
　　Close bosom-friend of the maturing sun;
Conspiring with him how to load and bless
　　With fruit the vines that round the thatch-eves run;
5　To bend with apples the moss'd cottage-trees,
　　And fill all fruit with ripeness to the core;
　　　　To swell the gourd, and plump the hazel shells
　　With a sweet kernel; to set budding more,
And still more, later flowers for the bees,
10　Until they think warm days will never cease,
　　For summer has o'er-brimm'd their clammy cells.

---

[3]Walter Jackson Bate, *John Keats* (Cambridge: Harvard University Press, 1963), 581.
[4]*The Selected Poetry of John Keats*, ed. Paul de Man (New York: New American Library, 1966), xxvi.

2

Who hath not seen thee oft amid thy store?
Sometimes whoever seeks abroad may find
Thee sitting careless on a granary floor,
15   Thy hair soft-lifted by the winnowing wind;
Or on a half-reap'd furrow sound asleep,
    Drows'd with the fume of poppies, while thy hook
        Spares the next swath and all its twined flowers:
And sometimes like a gleaner thou dost keep
20   Steady thy laden head across a brook;
Or by a cyder-press, with patient look,
    Thou watchest the last oozings hours by hours.

3

Where are the songs of spring? Ay, where are they?
Think not of them, thou hast thy music too,—
25   While barred clouds bloom the soft-dying day,
    And touch the stubble-plains with rosy hue;
Then in a wailful choir the small gnats mourn
    Among the river swallows, borne aloft
        Or sinking as the light wind lives or dies;
30   And full-grown lambs loud bleat from hilly bourn;
Hedge-crickets sing; and now with treble soft
The red-breast whistles from a garden-croft;
    And gathering swallows twitter in the skies.[5]

Intensive and concentrated as it is, "To Autumn" solicits a
lengthy, extensive reading; I shall try to confine my remarks to a
few points and to a few of their implications.

(1) As with a number of poems by Keats—sonnets, epistles,
and odes among them—"To Autumn" is written to an addressee;
but unlike some of those poems, which bear the headings of "To
———" or "To ****," the addressee in this instance has a proper name, the name, indeed, of "Autumn."[6]

[5]*The Poems of John Keats*, ed. Jack Stillinger (Cambridge: Harvard University Press, 1978), 476–77. All quotations of Keats's poetry are taken from this
edition. Line references appear in the text of my essay, and line references
alone are given.
[6]It is notable that Stillinger suppresses the "unaddressed" headings in his
edition, even though they have the authority of the copy text. This is a strange

(2) The identity of the addressee, the recipient (perhaps) of the poem, is complex. On the one hand the poet refers to it as a "season" ("Season of mists and mellow fruitfulness"), but on the other hand he also describes it as having a human figure (stanza 2) and apostrophizes it in the familiar, the intimate form ("thee," "thou"). More precisely, the poet represents the human figure of "Autumn" as a worker, as an artist working in a variety of materials, among them the flora of autumn (stanza 1), the products of harvesting (stanza 2), and something referred to as Autumn's "music" (stanza 3). As an artist, and apparently female—we say "apparently" because the poem is not *absolutely* explicit on this point and because some readers have gone to great lengths to ignore or deny the femininity of Autumn[7]—the addressee bears a family resemblance to a number of other woman artists in the poetry of Keats, among them Isabella, the "Belle Dame sans Merci," Madeline, and Lamia.

(3) The distinction between the addressee as a season and the addressee as a person plays on the fundamental distinction between common nouns and proper names. As a word referring to a season of the year, "autumn" functions as a common noun in the English language, a word with a definable (and translatable) semantic content. As a proper name, however (the name of the person apostrophized as "thee" and "thou"), the word "Autumn" refers to a singular, absolutely unique being, and as such it is undefinable, semantically ungeneralizable, and hence untranslatable as well, either into a foreign language, or into a common noun of the English language itself. For, as Derrida

---

violation of his own rules, which he justifies by a kind of "reason of state" or what he calls "practical considerations—mainly the need to provide distinctive titles that can be used for scholarly and critical reference" (ibid., p. 16). The suppression is strange inasmuch as scholars have done very nicely without such assistance.

[7]Bate, for example, refers to Autumn never as "she" but always as "it" or as "the deity" (*John Keats*, 581ff., passim). Reuben Brower, in *The Fields of Light* (Oxford: Oxford University Press, 1951), speaks of the "person" of Autumn but makes no reference to its sex (pp. 38–41).

repeatedly insists, the proper name, unlike the common noun, lies outside the semantic system of a language.[8]

(4) Just as the homonyms of "Autumn" (proper name) and "autumn" (common noun) are nonidentical, nonequivalent, and noninterchangeable, so the figure of "Autumn" and the forms comprising "autumn" are heterogeneous and different in kind. But there are links between the two, and those links are intricately joined. Although the forms of "autumn" are also the works of "Autumn," there is a distance between the two, and this distance, which is also a difference, is asserted in each of the three stanzas. Thus, in the first stanza, Autumn is said to "conspire with" the sun to produce the fruits of the season; but since the sun as such is beyond the limits of any given season (it is the agent itself of all seasons and days), the "conspiracy" of Autumn and sun, as an interaction between the two, must occur in some indeterminate dimension extending beyond the days and settings of "autumn." So too, in the second stanza, there is a distance between the figure of Autumn as harvester and the products comprising the harvest, and, in stanza 3, between the "music" of autumn and the figure of "Autumn" as its composer. On the other hand, however, the distance (the difference) between the figure "Autumn" and the fruits of autumn is marked by a tightly articulated affinity, a "twining" of worker and words. The fruits and songs of "autumn" belong to "Autumn" *only*, and they are also the *only* works of Autumn, who cannot lay claim to the works of "Winter," "Summer," or "Spring." Such, in part, is the attributive reasoning of stanza 3: "Where are the songs of spring? Ay, where are they? / Think not of them, thou hast thy music too. . . ."

(5) In a literal sense, the works of Autumn are translations, the changing of things into other things, as of raw fruit into ripe, of blossoms into flowers, of nectar into honey, of cereal into grain, of apples into "cyder," of cornfields into stubble plains, of

---

[8]See "Des Tours de Babel" in this volume.

newborn lambs into "full-grown" lambs. Correlatively, it is an instance of translation that a figure called "Autumn" should produce *autumnal* works, the instance of an attempt to translate the (untranslatable) proper name into a common noun.[9] More precisely, the fact that Keats should pose an undertaking of this kind is one indication, among others, that the challenge of translating the proper name—for example, the name of "John Keats" into the semantic field of the English language—is a major issue at play in the poem "To Autumn." (It would require a reading machine to sort out the letters and sounds of the proper name "John Keats," as scattered throughout the thirty-three lines of this text.)[10] Such an attempt is coextensive, indeed, with the concept of translation as a kind of transfer, or "rendering," or economic exchange: Autumn, in attempting to translate her name into her works, is also attempting to make of those works her own, her personal, signature. As in a contract with another party—by means of which, for example, a person pays off a debt and returns a favor—the artist is moved to put his (or her) proper name into circulation, to confer upon it the exchange value of a document properly signed. But since the proper name resists translation, it also remains exterior to the literary work and to the systems of exchange in which the work is meant to circulate, be they within the text itself (between proper name and common nouns) or between the text and some other text, composed by an author bearing another proper name.

(6) Autumn not only attempts to translate the works and days of nature, and, by analogy, her proper name into a common noun; she not only translates, that is, the visible and audible forms of a language devoid of semantic content—what Wordsworth calls an "inarticulate language"[11]—but also translates,

---

[9]Ibid., passim.

[10]Derrida sets this sort of task for a reading machine in *Signéponge/Signsponge* (New York: Columbia University Press, 1984.)

[11]The phrase occurs in "The Excursion," Book IV, 1, 1207 (in *Poetical Works*, ed. E. de Selincourt and Helen Darbishire [Oxford: Oxford University Press, 1949], V, 148).

into her own (inarticulate) language, the works of authors who happen to compose in the "articulate" languages of human discourse, languages endowed with a semantic content. Necessarily, she performs this task within the *limits* of her own language, by translating the "forms" of her human originals without recourse to their meanings, their communicable content. (She thereby becomes, from the viewpoint of Walter Benjamin, the model practitioner of translation.)[12] I will not attempt to enumerate the more or less infinite variety of human works that the scholars have found among the transformations wrought by Autumn but will confine my attention to her renderings of the works of Keats, though here, again, her citations and recitations of his poetry, at least from *Endymion* onward, are far too numerous to specify in the space of an article.[13] Suffice it to say that Autumn has read her Keats attentively, and has translated him with exceptional felicity and shrewdness, and in so doing has tried to fashion, in her own language, a gift that bears her own name, addressed to Keats (among others), in repayment for the gifts that Keats himself has given her. (This interchange bears a striking resemblance to the interchange between the poet and Moneta in *The Fall of Hyperion*.) This she does by repeating, miming, or duplicating the plots, characters, and settings scattered through Keats's poems. Some examples drawn from each stanza will convey the scope of Autumn's enterprise.

(a) When Autumn "conspires with the sun" to furnish forth the fruits of the first stanza, their collaboration repeats the conspiracy (the *artful* conspiracy) of Porphyro and Angela in *The*

[12]Walter Benjamin, "The Task of the Translator," in *Illuminations*, trans. Harry Zohn (New York: Harcourt Brace Jovanovich, 1968): "Translation must in large measure refrain from wanting to communicate something, from rendering the sense of the original" (p. 78). The relation that Benjamin then proceeds to spell out between "form" and "meaning" is, as Derrida shows in "Des Tours de Babel," supremely subtle and complex. Would Benjamin himself call Autumn a translator, and if so, how would he describe the place (or nonplace) of "meaning" in her translation? As of this writing, the answer to the question is well beyond me.

[13]For that matter, source studies on the whole poem are too numerous to be listed here in a note.

Eve of St. Agnes. In fact, the very fruits of Autumn are the fruits of Porphyro's feast (itself a translation of raw foods into cooked): where Porphyro brings out "a heap / Of candied apple, quince, and plum, and gourd" (ll. 264–65), Autumn "bend[s] with apples the moss'd cottage-trees" and "swell[s] the gourd, and plump[s] the hazel shells" (ll. 5, 7).

(b) The translations at work in the second stanza are the most complex and suggestive of the poem, and we will therefore read them at some length, emulating, as best we can, the "patient look" of Autumn herself. In this stanza, each image of Autumn reverses, fulfills, or revises the images of women in Keats who are figures of mourning or of unrequited desire. (The situation of these images, be it said in passing, is absolutely undecidable: the apparitions of Autumn could be figures of Autumn herself, *in propria persona*, or they could be a sequence of mirror images of the [absent] artist, as placed *en abîme* "amid the store" of her other works. Autumn is either an actress, assuming a range of poses with her own body, or a painter, figuring forth her person in the guise of the human body.) In translating the images of other women in Keats, Autumn rewrites the Keatsian script on the subject of translation itself. More precisely, the women who mourn in the original works do *not* engage in translation; but in the translations comprising the second stanza, the women do indeed engage in translation, with healthy consequences for all. Consider, for example, the first scene of the stanza:

> Sometimes whoever seeks abroad may find
> Thee sitting careless on a granary floor,
> Thy hair soft-lifted by the winnowing wind;

This passage translates, into an image of translation ("winnowing" the hair, itself a "translation" of grain or corn), a moment of mourning in *Isabella* where the heroine preserves (does not translate, but keeps or encrypts) the severed head of her dead lover, Lorenzo, by constantly "combing" his "wild hair":

In anxious secrecy they took it home,
  And then the prize was all for Isabel:
She calm'd its wild hair with a golden comb,
  And all around each eye's sepulchral cell
Pointed each fringed lash; the smeared loam
  With tears, as chilly as a dripping well,
She drench'd away:—and still she comb'd, and kept
Sighing all day—and still she kiss'd, and wept.

[ll. 401–408]

The second passage of the stanza revises a scene from *The Eve of St. Agnes,* where Madeline lies in an unrequited (and, in itself, unproductive) nighttime sleep, when the "poppied warmth of sleep oppress'd / Her soothed limbs" (ll. 237–38), and when the "tambour" and "lute" lay unemployed in the bedroom (ll. 174–75). Very much "translated" are the circumstances of Autumn's midday nap:

  Or on a half-reap'd furrow sound asleep,
    Drows'd with the fume of poppies, while thy hook
    Spares the next swath and all its twined flowers. . . .

the sleeping figure takes a break from the ongoing play, the transformations wrought by the reaping and cutting of her "hook."

Still more explicit, as the translation of a Keatsian scene into a scene of Autumnal translation, is the third passage of the stanza, whose gleaner is almost certainly drawn from the *Ode to a Nightingale.* There we encounter the mournful Ruth as she takes in the nightingale's song:

  Perhaps the self-same song that found a path
    Through the sad heart of Ruth, when, sick for home,
    She stood in tears amid the alien corn. . . .

[ll. 65–68]

Ruth, if I may put it so, enacts a scene of "nontranslation": she hears, weeps, and does nothing. She does not "glean" but merely "stands in tears amid the alien corn." Not so the gleaner in "To Autumn":

> And sometimes like a gleaner thou dost keep
> Steady thy laden head across a brook. . . .

Autumn has translated the earlier scene of sorrowful hearing, of mournful and unproductive imbalance, into a situation where the work itself of bearing the corn across the brook—of lifting it up and removing it from one place to another (*translatio*)—itself enables or causes the gleaner to "keep" her "laden head" "steady."

But the fourth figure of the stanza represents, perhaps, the most far-reaching and radical translation of all: it is the transformation of Lamia, who had herself been transformed from serpent into woman to win the love of Lycius. Fearful that Lycius will learn of this translation, which was deceitful and hence "improper" (the semantic and ethical registers being indistinguishable in this text), Lamia becomes "the lady every watchful, penetrant" (pt. 2, l. 35). She is "watchful" because she has had to preserve and protect a translation (herself) that is constantly menaced by the threat of its exposure and consequent return to a proper meaning, which is the very outcome, indeed, of the poem. *Lamia*, in a word, construes (and maybe evaluates) translation in terms of classical, or neoclassical, semantic values, for which all figures, all metaphors, and all translations are inherently "improper." All this is changed, however, with the last of the four figures in the second stanza of "To Autumn":

> Or by a cyder-press, with patient look,
> Thou watchest the last oozings hours by hours.

Here, "translation," as of apples into "cyder," certainly invites a certain watchfulness, but the watchfulness of one who has read the process of change without arresting that process or breaking off the gaze. Within this simple image, Autumn shows us how to take leave from the strictures of neoclassical decorum. Indeed, the tempo of the stanza, like the tempo of the poem as a whole, enacts the new and "patient look" of Autumn herself, watching the movement of autumn's own manifold translations.[14]

(c) As in the first two stanzas of the poem, Autumn composes a scene in stanza 3—the concert of evening sounds and "songs"— by citing, transposing, and altering sounds and songs from other settings and other seasons, to be found in "articulate" as well as "inarticulate" contexts. For example, the "wailful choir of gnats" recalls the "virgin-choir" in the *Ode to Psyche* and the "flies" in their "murmurous haunts" on the "summer eves" of the *Ode to a Nightingale:* the bleating lambs recall the sheep of *Endymion,* and the "hedge-crickets" point back to the sonnet "On the Grasshopper and the Cricket."[15] The evening scene itself, com-

---

[14]The *mise-en-scène* of the stanza, in which one person watches another through a sequence of different settings, repeats the opening passage of *Isabella,* where Lorenzo follows the figure of the heroine. Because the parallels to the situation of this poem are so striking, I give the second and third stanzas in full:

> With every morn their love grew tenderer,
>   With every eve deeper and tenderer still;
> He might not in house, field, or garden stir,
>   But her full shape would all his seeing fill;
> And his continual voice was pleasanter
>   To her, than noise of trees or hidden rill;
> Her lute-string gave an echo of his name,
> She spoilt her half-done broidery with the same.
>
> He knew whose gentle hand was at the latch,
>   Before the door had given her to his eyes;
> And from her chamber-window he would catch
>   Her beauty farther than the falcon spies;
> And constant as her vespers would he watch,
>   Because her face was turn'd to the same skies;
> And with sick longing all the night outwear,
> To hear her morning-step upon the stair.

[ll. 9–24]

[15]W. J. Bate usefully observes that the sound of the gnats "is no more confined to autumn alone than is the 'soft-dying' of any day, and, if the swallows are 'gathering,' they are not necessarily gathering for migration" (*John Keats,* 583). Harold Bloom, associating the closing lines of the poem with the closing lines of Coleridge's "Frost at Midnight," attributes the sounds, and notably the song of the red-breast, to "winter"

prising the whole of stanza 3, reenacts with its own variations, an earlier scene from the sonnet "After Dark Vapors," a scene of "autumn suns / Smiling at eve upon the quiet sheaves" (ll. 10–11).

(7) If I appear to overinsist, somewhat eccentrically and even repetitiously, that Autumn has translated Keats, and to refer those translations, somewhat rashly, to specific, and therefore debatable, sources (*Lamia? Isabella? The Eve of St. Agnes?*), I do so in order to advance, as forcefully as I can, a point that is always ignored by the classical readings of the poem: Keats, in his poem "To Autumn," has *translated,* into the English language, the works of a figure named "Autumn." He attempts in this way to render back *"To* Autumn" the many gifts that Autumn has furnished to his attention. (That those works also happen to be translations of works by Keats in no way alters the essential situation; for the works of Autumn, like the works of any other author, still call out for translation, through the very fact of their alien character.) Keats, we will recall, is something of a specialist at rendering thanks (renditions, translations) to authors, composers, artists, and works of art, whatever their language or their material happens to be. Passing over the incidental objects that fascinate him, such as the Elgin marbles, the Grecian Urn, the lock of Milton's hair, the anonymous lady at Vauxhall, a picture of Leander, the sea, or the song of the nightingale, we will simply provide a partial list of the names of those poets in the English language *alone* to whom (or to which) he has responded, rendering back their gifts to the best of his abilities: the list includes the names of Chaucer, Chapman, Spenser, Shakespeare, Milton, Chatterton, Burns, Leigh Hunt, Coleridge, Wordsworth, and Byron.

It is one thing, however, to translate the works of English into English and quite another to translate the inarticulate, silent, meaningless forms of Autumn. Much has been written about the

---

(*The Visionary Company* [New York: Doubleday, 1961], 455–56). Sources of the music, like the sexual identity of Autumn, are a subdued but continuous point of dispute among the commentators.

diction of this poem, about its "mimetic" tendency, its "cratylism," its attempt to fashion a language that mimes the shapes and sounds to which it refers. There is, for example, the prominence throughout the poem of the vowels "o" and "u," and of the liquids "l" and "r": that the fruits of autumn are liquid and rotund is something the poem intends to capture as best it can. (I would be willing to suppose, once again, that only a reading machine could sort out the sounds and letters of the word "autumn" as they are scattered throughout the poem.) Much has also been written about the minimal degree of "meaning," of semantic complexity, in the poem, and this too, I would argue, is another effect of translation. For Keats and Autumn have complementary, and symmetrically impossible, tasks: just as Autumn must translate his semantically loaded language into mute (or meaningless) forms, so Keats must translate her meaningless forms into language semantically loaded.

(9) What, then, to make of a poem that is structured thus, with Autumn translating Keats and Keats translating Autumn? To speak of some decisive "original" here ("original" language, "original" author, "original" text) is absolutely out of the question. The cherished values of originality and identity have given way to another system, where origins and identities are truly undecidable. Which is not to say, however, that the poem is in any sense unstructured or formless: the term of "invagination," referring at once to the sheathing of an object and the turning inside out of the sheath itself (or a glove, a sock, or a sweater), has recently been used by Jacques Derrida and Carol Jacobs to describe a structure of this kind.[16] In such a system, each text contains, or "sheathes," the other; and in such a system, the inner surface or limits of one text ("To Autumn," for example), becomes the outer surface of the other text (the works, for example, of Autumn), and vice versa. Thus, the "songs of Autumn" are indeed *inside* the poem "To Autumn," but the poem itself occurs among the songs *of* Autumn: for the poem declares itself

[16]Carol Jacobs, *The Dissimulating Harmony* (Baltimore: Johns Hopkins University Press, 1978), 125–26; Jacques Derrida, "La loi du genre," *Glyph* 7 (1980), 190–92.

to be situated in a here-and-now that is nothing other than an autumn landscape, the very landscape represented in the poem ("and *now* with treble soft / The red-breast whistles from a garden croft" [ll. 31–32]). Although the poem "To Autumn" contains within itself the very songs of which it is a part, somewhere, in the context of its own third stanza, the containing and embracing text entitled "To Autumn" is itself embraced, included, and contained among the songs of Autumn; somewhere, scattered among the "songs of Autumn," is a song that is sung, uttered, or inscribed by the poet John Keats. One part of the poem contains the whole of those songs of which the poem itself is a part, and it is therefore impossible, logically, to decide where *one* text, or *one* language, or *one* poet begins, and where the other leaves off.

Who, for that matter, *signs* and where, and how, and what? Two signers have been proposed, though their names appear, we hasten to add, only on the margins of the poem: that of "Autumn" in the title (as if the title were a kind of shorthand for the phrase "this work is attributed *to Autumn*") and that of John Keats on the title page of the volume of 1820. Both, in some way, are legitimate signatories of the poem and could even quarrel, perhaps, over the matter of its copyright, were it not for the fact that each one signs by signing the text *away*, in a gesture that Derrida has somewhere called the *exappropriation* of the signature. In stanza 3, for example, when the poet says to Autumn "thou hast thy music too," he signs away his rights, not only to the rest of stanza 3, but to the *whole* of the poem "To Autumn" (which, insofar as it is itself a song *of* autumn, is itself contained, *en abîme*, by its own third stanza). And Autumn does the same, when she performs, as her own work, renderings of the work of Keats. This movement of exappropriation could well serve as the basis of a new logic of exchange: we would no longer look upon translation as the faithful return of a debt (as in the transmission of a personal check that somehow fails to bounce) but would construe it instead as a process of mutual indebtedness, not to be resolved because the property can never be properly assigned in the first place. It is, instead, con-fused.

We can close this phase of the argument by putting in a good word, an *interested* word, for "confusion." According to Keats, there is a kind of confusion that attends the most rigorous exercise: he represents it as "mist," as in the phrase "Season of mists and mellow fruitfulness." Thus, when the poet in *The Fall of Hyperion* first comes upon the temple of Moneta, he describes it as having a "silent massy range / Of columns north and south, ending in mist / Of nothing" (canto 1, ll. 83–85). Mist, and the dislocation and disorientation that it brings, is apt to be found in high places—high like the Tower of Babel—places hard to ascend and dangerous in their footing. In a sonnet on the subject of mist, Keats has some things to say that bear upon the experience of becoming lost in translation, such as happens (or so we have found) in the poem entitled "To Autumn":

> Read me a lesson, Muse, and speak it loud
>   Upon the top of Nevis, blind in mist!
> I look into the chasms, and a shroud
>   Vaprous doth hide them; just so much I wist
> Mankind do know of hell: I look o'er head,
>   And there is sullen mist; even so much
> Mankind can tell of heaven: mist is spread
>   Before the earth beneath me; even such,
> Even so vague is man's sight of himself.
>   Here are the craggy stones beneath my feet;
> Thus much I know, that, a poor witless elf,
>   I tread on them; that all my eye doth meet
> Is mist and crag—not only on this height,
> But in the world of thought and mental might.

****

Polemical Overflow

If these remarks appear to overstate the place of translation in "To Autumn," or the place of "To Autumn" in an ongoing context of translation (the work of Keats), it may be due to the fact

that the link between "Keats" and "translation" has been traditionally understated . . . by way of ellipsis. For it is a fact that all
readings of the poem do, in the end, describe it in terms of
translation and that no one can read the poem without resorting
to the concept, however disguised, restrained, or "translated"
that concept may be: and when a reading understates the translational character of the poem, it necessarily, and also, resorts to a
more-or-less violent translation of translation at work in the
poem and hence of the poem as such.

I could lend force to this argument by reviewing, in detail, a
long and distinguished series of essays on the ode, by such devoted readers as Reuben Brower, Harold Bloom, Geoffrey
Hartman, and Helen Vendler. For the sake of brevity, I will
limit my comments to the most recent of these readings, as set
forth by Vendler in an article entitled "Stevens and Keats' 'To
Autumn.'" I quote at length from a key paragraph:

> Keats' goddess of autumn, nearer to us than pagan goddesses
> because, unlike them, she *labors in the fields* and is herself
> *threshed* by the winnowing wind, varies in her manifestations
> from careless *girl* to *burdened* gleaner to patient watcher, *erotic*
> in her abandon to the fume of poppies, intimate of light in her
> bosom friendship with the maturing sun, *worn* by her vigil over
> the last oozings. . . . Keats' season is an earth goddess whose
> *union* with the sun *makes her bear fruit; the sun, his part in
> procreation done, departs from the poem as the harvest begins,*
> and the season *ages* from the careless figure on the granary floor
> to the watcher over the last drops of the crushed apples. Finally,
> when she *becomes* the "soft-dying day," she is *mourned* by crea-
> tures *deliberately infantine,* as even full-grown sheep are repre-
> sented as bleating lambs: these creatures are *filial* forms, *grieving
> for the death of the mother.* [Emphasis added][17]

For Vendler, the "goddess" of autumn does not "vary in her
manifestations" in any random or accidental way: rather, those

---

[17]Helen Vendler, "Stevens and Keats' 'To Autumn,'" in *Wallace Stevens: A Celebration,* ed. Frank Doggett and Robert Buttell (Princeton: Princeton University
Press, 1980), 171–95. The quoted passage is to be found on pp. 178–79. Page
references to other citations appear in the text of my essay.

manifestations tell an eloquent and moving story, the tale of a distinctly human tragedy, with a beginning, a middle, and an end. Autumn sets forth, so to speak, as a "careless girl," then enters into a "union with the sun" that "makes her bear fruit"; the sun, having "done his part," then "de" (-) "parts," leaving the scene to the goddess, who is now translated from girlhood into a tragic version of motherhood: she is "burdened," she "labors," is "threshed," and is "worn" by her motherly "vigils," "ages," and finally dies ("becomes the 'softy-dying day'"). Sad as this sequence is for the goddess, it is absolutely catastrophic for the offspring, small children still ("deliberately infantine"), who "grieve for the death of the mother" and quite understandably so, having become, at this point in the story, orphans in need of adoption.

What happens in Vendler's paragraph? Hers is no ordinary paraphrase, for she has skewed and invented things in order to fill out the story: thus ,the "conspiracy" of the first stanza is made into a sexual "union" (would the same be said of the conspiracy between Porphyro and Angela?); the sun is said "to depart from the poem as the harvest begins," though the sun is in fact never absent (its setting is the setting, or scene, of stanza 3); no one is "threshed"; no one "labors," nor is the gleaner "burdened," merely "laden" (by bearing her burden "steadily," on the head, she relieves the load of its burden); no one is "worn out" by any "vigil"; the goddess no more "becomes the 'soft-dying day'" than she becomes any other of her works; hence she does not "die"; and what little "mourning" there is in the third stanza (only the gnats mourn) is not addressed *to* anyone, least of all to a mother, or by a brood of her orphaned offspring.

What happens, then, in the paragraph? If it is not a conventional paraphrase, is it, perhaps, a translation? If so, what kind of translation might it be? What are the principles of translation at work here? Vendler herself provides us with a helpful hint at another point in the essay, when she speaks of the "method of the ode": "Keats' ode is spoken by one whose poetic impulse arises from a recoil at the stubble plains; the method of the ode is

to adopt a reparatory fantasy whereby the barren plains are 'repopulated' with fruit, flowers, wheat, and a providential goddess" (p. 180).

Perhaps "recoil[ing] at the stubble plains" of the ode, which
are certainly "barren" of human pathos and suffering, Vendler
has herself "'repopulated'" the poem with the "fruit, flowers,
wheat" of another poem, perhaps of another poet. If so, of which
poem and of which poet? Vendler again provides a hint; "Keats'
ode," she tells us, "borrows from Shakespeare's image of 'the
teeming autumn, big with rich increase, / Bearing the wanton
burden of the prime, / Like widow'd wombs after their lord's
decease' (Sonnet XCVII)" (pp. 178–79). In effect, Vendler has
translated Shakespeare into Keats, or Keats into Shakespeare,
producing a work that could best be signed by "Keatspeare," the
nom de plume, perhaps, of Helen Vendler herself, since it is her
"method," in this particular instance, to "adopt the reparatory
fantasy" and to "'repopulate'" the poem with a disintegrating
family scene, as if the poem itself were an infant in need of
adoption, orphaned by the very absence of such a scene (by the
absence of an absent mother). . . . *But it is not her method
alone;* which, for us, is the main pertinence to the ode of her
reading; it provides, by imitation, an insight into the workings of
the poem itself. At numerous points throughout "To Autumn,"
there seems indeed to be a "reparatory fantasy" at work and at
work as a method of translation. If Autumn, for example, has
indeed translated, into the tableau vivant of the girl whose "hair"
is "soft-lifted by the winnowing wind," the passage from *Isabella*
in which the heroine combs the hair on the severed head of
Lorenzo, then her translation not only repairs the death of
Lorenzo but does so "fantastically" (the "wind" becomes a lover)
and in the form of a "reparation" (the wind "winnows" the hair of
the girl in return for Isabella's combing). Furthermore, to construe this passage as a translation of *Isabella* may itself be a
"reparatory fantasy" on our own part, "recoiling," as we seem to
do, from the mere thought that Autumn may *not* be engaged in
translation.

We nonetheless have a basic reservation about Vendler's reading: we cannot agree that "reparatory fantasy" and "'repopulation'" are "*the* method of the ode." For just as there are many motives for fantasy ("reparation" is only one of these) and many kinds of reparation ("fantasy" is only one of these), so there are many kinds, *innumerable* kinds, of translation (and "'repopulation'" is only one of these). Others include a conventional paraphrase, or a word-for-word translation, or the sort of dizzying mirror play that occurs when an author translates back into his (or her) mother tongue a work that he (or she) composed in a foreign language; or translates his (or her) own original from his (or her) mother tongue into a foreign one; or translates the translated original back into his (or her) mother tongue once again. The term "reparatory fantasy" could not do justice to these different kinds of translation, which, I hasten to add, can all coexist within the so-called "single" work at one and the same time. "Reparatory *reality*" may come closer to the mark, it being a reality, in a work like "To Autumn," that many (real) languages do co-occur at one and the same time, as do their many forms of translation. It is the aim of "To Autumn," we would argue, to realize

> the being-language of the language, tongue or language *as such,*
> l'être-langue de la langue, la langue ou le langage *en tant que tels,*
> that unity without any self-identity which makes for the fact that
> cette unité sans aucune identité à soi qui fait qu'il y a des langues,
> there are languages and that they are languages.
> et que ce sont des langues.[18]

[18]"Des Tours de Babel."

4

On the History of a Mistranslation and the Psychoanalytic Movement

ALAN BASS

Kite, Vulture, Eagle

The image of the psychoanalyst as a translator is a familiar one, bequeathed to us by Freud. In fact, Freud often compared his initial discoveries to triumphs of translation. During the 1890s he frequently maintained that he had found the means to translate hysterical symptoms and dreams into ordinary language, thereby claiming for science what had once been considered incomprehensible or trivial. This is one reason why Freud more than once compared symptoms and dreams to hieroglyphics and his own work to that of François Champollion, whom he called "the first man to succeed in reading hieroglyphics."

Thus, for example, in 1896 Freud wrote that previous investigations of hysteria resembled the work of explorers who come upon ruins with unfamiliar inscriptions on them. The "explorers" content themselves with inspecting and describing these inscriptions—an obvious reference to the descriptive psychiatry that cataloged symptoms without attempting to understand them. After the explorers, however, come the archaeologists who seek the code that will decipher, will *translate,* the inscriptions—an obvious reference to Freud himself. Pursuing the comparison, Freud writes: "The many inscriptions, which by good luck may be bilingual, reveal an alphabet and a language, and when deciphered and translated may yield undreamed-of information about the events of the past."[1] And soon Freud came to postulate that dreams and hysterical symptoms were purposefully baffling, in order to disguise the "unacceptable" ideas and wishes into which they must be translated. Thus we find Freud pursuing the comparison of psychoanalysis to translation in *The Interpretation of Dreams: "The productions of the dream-work, which, it must be remembered, are not made with the intention of being understood*, present no greater difficulties to their translators than do the ancient hieroglyphic scripts to those who seek to read them."[2]

What, then, is a mistaken translation in psychoanalysis? Is it a failure to find the right code, the code that transforms previously baffling inscriptions into everyday language? Is psychoanalytic theory an attempt to find more and more efficient means of translation? What do such questions have to do with translation in general?

Jacques Derrida has often investigated this question of "translation in general." Discussing metaphysics's endless quest for what he calls a "transcendental signified," that is, a concept outside of language, a concept uncontaminated by a distorting *vehicle* of representation, Derrida acknowledges that this quest is implied by "everything that links our language, our culture, our 'system of thought' to the history and system of metaphysics." However, he goes on to insist, that statement does not mean that such a quest, and all the concepts it has produced (for example, those of the sign, the signifier, and the signified), can simply be abandoned, even if their logic can be taken apart.

[1]"The Aetiology of Hysteria," in *The Standard Edition of the Complete Psychological Works of Sigmund Freud* (London: Hogarth Press, 1955), III, 192. Henceforth all references to the *Standard Edition* will appear with a roman volume number and an arabic page number.

[2]*The Interpretation of Dreams*, V, 341; italics in Freud's original.

Speaking specifically of the opposition of signified and signifier, Derrida says, and here we turn to questions of translation in general:

> That this opposition or difference cannot be radical or absolute does not prevent it from functioning, and even from being indispensable within certain limits—very wide limits. For example, no translation would be possible without it. In effect, the theme of a transcendental signified took shape within the horizon of an absolutely pure, transparent, and unequivocal translatability. In the limits to which it is possible, or at least *appears* possible, translation practices the difference between signified and signifier. But if this difference is never pure, no more so is translation, and for the notion of translation, we would have to substitute a notion of *transformation*: a regulated transformation of one language by another, of one text by another. We never will have, and in fact never have had, a "transport" of pure signifieds from one language to another, or within one and the same language, that the signifying instrument would leave virgin and untouched.[3]

As both psychoanalyst and translator I often wonder how Derrida's remarks about translation as transformation might affect Freud's comparisons of psychoanalysis to translation. Do not psychoanalytic translations (interpretations) aim at transformation? Does not every analyst know that he never makes a pure translation, that using the unconscious as a "signifying instrument" means that the analyst neither leaves "virgin and untouched" the material he translates nor is left virgin and untouched by it? That translating also transforms the analyst? What, then, is a mistaken translation in psychoanalysis?

Putting these questions to myself, I have been drawn back again and again to a text of Freud's in which there is a mistaken translation *and* in which a key psychoanalytic concept is once again compared to a hieroglyph. In reading this text I will demonstrate a previously unnoticed relation between the mistaken

---

[3]Jacques Derrida, *Positions*, trans. Alan Bass (Chicago: University of Chicago Press, 1981), 20.

translation and the hieroglyph, a relation that bears upon both Freud's and Derrida's notions of translation in ways that affect psychoanalytic history, theory, and technique.

The text is Freud's well-known monograph *Leonardo da Vinci and a Memory of His Childhood*,[4] published in 1910. James Strachey succinctly describes the mistake in his editor's introduction to the *Standard Edition* translation of the work, which is by Alan Tyson: "A prominent part is played by Leonardo's memory or phantasy of being visited in his cradle by a bird of prey. The name applied to this bird in his notebooks is '*nibio*,' which . . . is the ordinary Italian word for 'kite.' Freud, however, throughout his study translates the word by '*Geier*,' for which the English can only be 'vulture.' Freud's mistake seems to have originated from some of the German translations which he used" (p. 61).

Ernest Jones, in his biography of Freud, has called this mistake "a singular lapse in Freud's knowledge of natural history. Kites were as common in Italy as vultures in Egypt."[5] (Why Jones should speak of Egypt in this context will become clear as we proceed.) The mistake becomes even more singular when Jones tells us that, although of all his works Freud thought most highly of *The Interpretation of Dreams*, the *Three Essays on the Theory of Sexuality*, and *Totem and Taboo*, "perhaps the one for which he had the greatest personal affection was his book on Leonardo."[6] Moreover, Jones thinks that, in the Leonardo study,

> Freud was expressing conclusions which in all probability had been derived from his self-analysis and are therefore of great importance for the study of his personality. His letters of the time make it abundantly clear with what exceptional intensity he had

[4]*Standard Edition*, XI. Page numbers in my text signal further references to the Leonardo study. All German interpolations are taken from the *Gesammelte Werke* (London: Imago, 1940), VIII.

[5]Ernest Jones, *The Life and Work of Sigmund Freud* (New York: Basic, 1955), II, 348.

[6]Ibid., p. 401.

thrown himself into this particular investigation. . . . much of
what Freud said when he penetrated into Leonardo's personality
was at the same time a self-description; there was surely an extensive identification between Leonardo and himself.[7]

We will read some of Freud's letters shortly, in order to trace
the relations between his interest in Leonardo and the history of
psychoanalysis. For the moment, though, let us remain with the
history of the error. In a 1955 article entitled "A Retrospect of
Freud's *Leonardo*," Richard Wohl and Harry Trosman state:
"This error has had quite a remarkable history of its own. It has
passed, unnoticed and unquestioned, from translator to translator; and more remarkably still, it has produced a special literature devoted to amplifying and reinforcing it. . . . Marie Bonaparte, for example, while otherwise extremely scrupulous in
her documentation, renders the word quite faithfully, following
Freud, as *le vautour*."[8] What is even more "singular" (Jones) or
"remarkable" (Wohl and Trosman) about the error's history is
the following letter to the editor of a London art journal called
the *Burlington Magazine*. The letter was published in the January 1923 issue, not long after the publication of the English
translation of the Leonardo study, and is entitled "Leonardo in
the Consulting Room"; the author is Eric Maclagan.

> SIR—In view of the prominence given to Dr. Freud's little book
> on Leonardo in the Editorial Article of the December number of
> *The Burlington Magazine*, I think it may be worthwhile to point
> out on what very inadequate grounds his theories are built up. I
> refer throughout to the 2nd German edition . . . from which the
> English translation at which I have only been able to glance, was
> no doubt made. . . . Dr. Freud devotes pages to the Egyptian
> symbolism of the vulture, and any impartial reader will admit that
> he makes it the main basis of his argument. But Leonardo never
> mentions a vulture at all. He tells the story of a kite (nibio) and
> the Italian text is actually printed by Dr. Freud (p. 21, note 2)

[7]Ibid., pp. 78 and 432.
[8]Richard Wohl and Harry Trosman, "A Retrospect of Freud's *Leonardo*," in
Psychiatry 18 (February 1955), 33.

though none of his admirers seem to have taken the trouble to read it.[9]

We will take up later Maclagan's point about how the mistranslation affects Freud's arguments. For now, let us note the historical fact that Maclagan's letter appeared two years *before* the Leonardo study was reprinted in the *Gesammelte Schriften* in 1925. Jones himself had written the preface to the first edition of the book to appear in England (in 1922), the edition referred to in the letter. Why was this letter never brought to Jones's attention? If it had been, he surely would have communicated its contents to Freud in time for the 1925 edition of the book to be corrected. To make this oversight stranger still, we know from Jones himself that he was *already* familiar with the *Burlington Magazine*. Concerning the events of 1921, Jones writes: "In May I sent Freud a copy of the *Burlington Magazine* which contained a description of a bronze statue of Moses made by Nicholas of Verdun in the twelfth century. It was cast in the intermediate posture that Freud had assumed must have preceded the final one depicted by Michelangelo. Freud was highly gratified at this confirmation of his interpretation, though his only comment in a letter was 'Should I be right after all?'"[10]

Wohl and Trosman, who have reviewed the error's "remarkable history," are also unaware of Maclagan's letter,[11] thus making incorrect *their* assertion that the error has passed "unnoticed and unquestioned." Which thereby inscribes their own efforts in the chain of the error's "remarkable history." Their account of this history, which also has a remarkable relation to the history of the psychoanalytic movement, is nonetheless informative. Their most interesting finding is the following one, again a question of mistranslation. "The most recent contribution to this rather

[9]Eric Maclagan, "Leonardo in the Consulting Room," in *Burlington Magazine* 42 (January 1923), 51–54.

[10]Jones, II, 79.

[11]Meyer Schapiro, in his "Leonardo and Freud: An Art Historical Study" (*Journal of the History of Ideas* 17 [April 1956]), also makes this point (p. 178, n. 109).

bizarre erudition [that is, the 'special literature devoted to amplifying and reinforcing' Freud's mistake] consists of a seemingly learned article which praises Freud's monograph most enthusiastically, but systematically refers to the bird in question as an 'eagle.'"[12] Let us cite this learned article, both for the way in which it takes mistranslation to new ornithological heights and for its synopsis of Freud's argument. Each time that "eagle" appears in italics one should recall that Freud is speaking of a vulture (*Geier*) and Leonardo of a kite (*nibio*):

> In his manuscripts there is a passage in which Leonardo describes an infantile memory. An *eagle* opened his mouth by pushing his tail many times against it. It (the memory which Freud treats as a fantasy) is linked to an *eagle* because *eagles* were thought to be females only; a scientific fairy tale which goes back to the bisexual Egyptian goddess Mut, represented as an *eagle* and a mother symbol. Though Leonardo may not have known that the Egyptian god Mut was bisexual, he may well have been familiar with the Christian aspect of this fable, where the *eagle* is a female, as he was a great reader and Milan was a book center. . . . Leonardo too, was like an *eagle* child, having a mother without a father. . . . The fact that his mother is supplanted by an *eagle* shows that the child missed his father when he found himself alone with his mother. . . . Freud has been criticized for overlooking what does not fit in with a preconceived interpretation. Such is not the case here, as his treatment of the *eagle* fantasy indicates. Freud deals rather carefully with this point, as it represents an important link in his argument. Unless the *eagle* were feminine, there would have been no reason for identifying it with Leonardo's mother.[13]

The Use of Leonardo at Odd Times

To appreciate the effects of the mistaken translation, and its bearing on the history of the psychoanalytic movement, we must

---

[12]Wohl and Trosman, 33.

[13]Erwin Christensen, "Freud and Leonardo da Vinci," *Psychoanalytic Review* 31 (April 1944), 155 and 162; my italics.

trace both the history of Freud's interest in Leonardo and the history of the theoretical issues raised in the Leonardo study. This is the context in which we will place our first reading of the vulture.

The history of Freud's interest in Leonardo begins for us in the late 1890s, the period of his self-analysis. Both Jones and Strachey observe that Freud "identified" with Leonardo, and Jones contends, as we saw above, that much of Freud's analysis of Leonardo was derived from his self-analysis. Although Jones does not say *why* he thinks so, the evidence is available in the letters to Fliess.

In the late fall of 1897 Fliess told Freud about his theory of innate bisexuality. Freud's reaction to Fliess's theory was ambivalent, for Fliess had linked bisexuality to bilaterality, the left side being feminine, the right masculine. Thus, Freud wrote to Fliess on December 29, 1897: "What I want now is plenty of material for a mercilessly severe test of the left-handedness theory. I have got the needle and thread ready. Incidentally the question that is bound up with it is the first for a long time on which our ideas and inclinations have not gone the same way."[14]

Fliess's response to this letter must have been unhappy, for one week later, on January 4, 1898, Freud wrote to him:

> It interests me that you should take it so much amiss that I am still unable to accept your interpretation of left-handedness. I shall try to be objective—I know well how difficult that is. . . . I seized eagerly on your notion of bisexuality, which I regard as the most significant for my subject since that of defence. If I had had some aversion on personal grounds, because I am a bit neurotic myself, it would certainly have taken the form of aversion to the idea of bisexuality, which we hold to be responsible for the inclination to repression. It seems to me that I object only to the identification of bisexuality and bilateralism which you demand. . . . It also occurred to me that you may have considered me to be partially left-handed; if so, you should tell me, for there

[14]*The Origins of Psychoanalysis*, ed. M. Bonaparte, A. Freud, and E. Kris (New York: Basic, 1954), 241.

would be nothing hurtful to me in such a piece of self-knowledge.[15]

And then, ten months later (on October 9, 1898), we find the following, which seems intended to conciliate: "Leonardo, of whom no love affair is recorded, was perhaps the most famous case of left-handedness. Can you use him?"[16]

What is at stake in the first two letters is the issue of a psychological, rather than a biological, explanation of bisexuality. Fliess's view grounds bisexuality in biology, however strange the explanation may seem (two hands, two sexes). Freud is beginning to elaborate a theory of bisexuality based upon the idea of identification, the child's identifications with both mother and father. Thus, very much in the mode of the patient who anticipates the analyst's painful interpretation, Freud claims that he would not be hurt by Fliess's view of him as "partially left-handed," that is, somewhat feminine. Freud "identifies" with Leonardo, then, because of what his self-analysis has led him to see as his own femininity. And twelve years later, the Leonardo monograph will explain the genesis of homosexuality in terms of identification with the mother. What deserves emphasis here also, is the peculiar way in which Freud's interest in Leonardo intertwines with the history of psychoanalysis. In 1897–98 the "psychoanalytic movement" is indistinguishable from Freud's transferential relation to Fliess ("Can you use him?"), and from the first question on which their "ideas and inclinations have not gone the same way." Further, this shift in Freud's relation to Fliess is indistinguishable from the major theoretical shift in Freud's thinking at this time, the constitution of psychoanalysis as a discipline that would explain neurosis in terms not of innate biological mechanisms (bisexuality-bilaterality), of neurophysiology (as in the *Project*), or of real traumatic events (the seduction theory of history, which Freud first began to give up only in October 1897, two months before the letter expressing his

[15]Ibid., pp. 242–43.
[16]Ibid., p. 268.

doubts about the "left-handedness theory"). And yet, Freud offers Leonardo to Fliess for possible confirmation of the left-
handedness theory. Much later, we will see the vulture, the
mistaken translation in the analysis of Leonardo, play a role
similar to the one Leonardo plays in the Fliess letters: the mutual complication of transference and theoretical advance that is so
intrinsic to the history of psychoanalysis.

Although the theme of Leonardo's left-handedness appears
only briefly at the end of Freud's monograph (p. 136), he does
allude to it in an undated letter to Jones, presumably from the
period of the study's composition. The letter recapitulates,
twelve years later, the conflicts expressed in the Fliess letters. "I
think L. was 'bimanual,' but that is about the same thing as left-
handed. I have not inquired further into his handwriting, because I avoided by purpose all biological views, restraining myself to the discussion of the psychological ones."[17] Jones explains
Freud's curious inclusion of Leonardo's handwriting under the
heading of biology as a reference to Fliess and to Leonardo's
practice of mirror writing. Although the latter is indeed not
mentioned in the study, this is far from the case for the (biological?) question of writing itself. The Leonardo study is replete
with references to traces, hieroglyphs, the writing of history, and
the art of printing. Freud's frequent comparisons of psychic
events to various forms of writing are, of course, well known.
What we shall see is that in the Leonardo study *all* these comparisons are related to the "vulture." To understand how this
situation arose, we shall have to read three more letters, two to
Jung and one to Abraham. These letters reveal a revision of the
theory of sexuality that concerned Freud as he was thinking
about Leonardo in 1909.

In 1909 Jung was still very much Freud's chosen successor.
Freud's letters to him at the time are filled with talk of the
potentially triumphant prospects of psychoanalysis. In a letter
dated October 17, 1909, Freud writes that psychoanalysis must

[17]Jones, II, 347.

conquer not only the field of mythology, as Jung had already done, but also the field of biography. Freud will attempt to do so via his work on Leonardo, and feels that he has already

> solved the riddle of L.'s character. But the material concerning L. is so sparse that I despair of demonstrating my conviction intelligibly to others. I have ordered an *Italian* work on his youth and am now waiting eagerly for it. . . . Do you remember my remarks in the "Sexual Theories of Children" . . . to the effect that children's first primitive researches in this sphere were bound to fail and that this first failure could have a paralysing effect? . . . Well, the great Leonardo was such a man; at an early age he converted his sexuality into an urge for knowledge and from then on the inability to finish anything he undertook became a pattern to which he had to conform in all his ventures.[18]

The italics in the quoted passage are mine. They are meant to emphasize the point made by Eric Maclagan in his 1923 letter to the *Burlington Magazine*: Freud had the Italian text concerning the "vulture" (kite) at his disposition. The point that Maclagan does not raise, however, a point in fact not raised in *any* of the literature on Freud's maintenance of a mistranslation, is the link between the mistranslation and the theory of sexuality. We will watch this link reveal itself in the next two letters; let us keep in mind the references to the *Italian* work on Leonardo and the sexual theories of children.

One month later (November 21, 1909) we find the following to Jung:

> Quite by accident I recently hit on what I hope is the ultimate secret of foot-fetishism. In the foot it has become permissible to worship the long lost and ardently longed for woman's penis of the primordial age of infancy. Evidently some people search as passionately for this *precious* object as the pious English do for the ten lost tribes of Israel. . . . I do wish I could show you my

[18]*The Freud/Jung Letters*, ed. William McGuire, Bollingen Series 94 (Princeton: Princeton University Press, 1974), 255.

analysis of Leonardo da Vinci. . . . I am coming to attach more
and more importance to the infantile theories of sexuality.[19]

Again we find Freud thinking about Leonardo in conjunction
with the infantile sexual theories, specifically the theory of the
woman's (mother's) penis. And we also find a major shift in
psychoanalytic theory: until this time Freud (and Abraham) had
thought that foot fetishism was to be explained by a return of the
repressed pleasure in smell from the anal period. This letter, I
believe, represents Freud's first postulation that the "secret" of
fetishism lies in the infantile sexual theory of the mother's penis.
(This idea was to find its full elaboration in the 1927 paper
"Fetishism," although Freud incorporated his finding into the
1910 edition of the *Three Essays on the Theory of Sexuality*;
compare *Standard Edition*, VII, 155, n. 2.) Let us remember
throughout the following discussion that this letter places the
Leonardo study in the history of Freud's theory of fetishism—
again, the point not raised in the literature on the mistranslation.

During the years 1908–10 both Freud and Abraham had analyzed cases of fetishism. In a letter from September 1909, (about
the same time as the two letters to Jung just cited), Freud had
promised Abraham his notes on one of these cases. On February
22, 1910, Abraham mentioned in a letter that he was preparing a
paper on fetishism and reminded Freud of his promise. Two
days later Freud responded: "It must be emphasized that the
female foot is apparently a substitute for the painfully missed,
prehistorically postulated female penis. The plait too must be a
substitute for this. Cutting off plaits thus stands for castration of
the female, 'making' female, since it is by castration that females
are 'made.' I have not analysed glaring cases of fetishism. I am
now writing Leonardo *at odd times*."[20] The italicized words appeared in English in the original. Fetishism and Leonardo are

[19]Ibid., p. 265; italics added.
[20]*The Letters of Sigmund Freud and Karl Abraham*, trans. Bernard Marsh
and Hilda Abraham (New York: Basic, 1965), 87.

mentioned one on the heels of the other; in fact, Freud almost literally transposed the statements in this letter into the Leonardo study itself, which was completed about two months later (April 1910):

> The fixation on the object that was once strongly desired, the woman's penis, leaves *indelible traces* ["unauslöschliche Spuren"] on the mental life of the child, who has pursued that portion of his infantile sexual researches with particular thoroughness. Fetishistic reverence for a woman's foot and shoe appears to take the foot merely as a *substitutive symbol [Ersatzsymbol]* for the woman's penis which was once revered and later missed; without knowing it, *coupeurs de nattes* play the part of people who carry out an act of castration on the female genital organ. [P. 96]

The italics here are mine again. And as in the October letter to Jung, Freud uses the mistranslation, the vulture, to represent the "indelible trace" left by the fantasy of the maternal phallus in Leonardo's unconscious and does so with (implicit or explicit) reference to the question of fetishism. The title of this paper, for reasons that will become clearer as we proceed, could equally have been "mistranslation and fetishism."

Our reading of the vulture sequence itself, then, will be guided by Freud's words in these letters, that is, that he was "coming to attach more and more importance to the infantile theories of sexuality" as he was composing the Leonardo study. The paper "On the Sexual Theories of Children," published in 1908, may thus be viewed as part of the history of the Leonardo study, and we will turn to it briefly. In 1908 Freud introduced his problem in this way:

> If we could divest ourselves of our corporeal existence, and could view the things of this earth with a fresh eye as purely thinking beings, from another planet for instance, nothing perhaps would strike our attention more forcibly than the fact of two sexes among human beings, who, though so much alike in other respects, yet mark the difference between them with such obvious external

signs. But it does not seem that children choose this fundamental fact in the same way as the starting point of their researches into sexual problems. [IX, 211–12]

In other words, a "purely thinking being" would first tackle the problem of sexual differentiation from the point of view of perception, that is, by observing the "obvious external signs" which would "strike our attention." The equation of what Freud here calls "pure thought" and perception is not surprising, for both perception and logical thought belong to consciousness, or the "secondary process." The implication is clear: infantile sexual theories will follow the laws of the "primary process," that is, of the unconscious. Thus, these "theories" will show the same characteristics as all productions of the unconscious (dreams, slips, hallucinations, and so forth). They will be divisible into a manifest and a latent content, the manifest content being a puzzling distortion of the latent, like an untranslated hieroglyph. Infantile sexual "theories" will be understood as typical infantile *fantasies* about the origin of sexual difference.

Freud prepares the ground for a "fantastic" theory by examining the emotional nature of the young child's search for knowledge, an idea that will be particularly important in the Leonardo paper. Either the actual arrival of a new baby or the idea that one might possibly arrive prompts the child to come to grips with the "first, grand problem of life"—where do babies come from? However, this problem is not approached by the child in the spirit of idle speculation. "The question itself is, like all research, the product of a vital exigency, as though thinking were entrusted with the task of preventing the recurrence of such dreaded events" (IX, 213). This driven search for knowledge, along with the unwelcome discoveries it brings, is kept secret and has the same destiny as many of the child's other fantasies: it is "repressed and forgotten."

The necessarily repressed "theory" (fantasy) "starts out from the neglect of the differences between the sexes on which I laid stress at the beginning of this paper as being characteristic of children. It consists in *attributing to everyone, including fe-males, the possession of a penis,* such as the boy knows from his own body" (IX, 215; italics in the original). Since this "theory" is necessarily repressed, Freud goes on to explain, it can return in the dreams of adult life: "The dreamer, in a state of nocturnal sexual excitation, will throw a woman down, strip her and pre-pare for intercourse—and then, in place of the female genitals, he beholds a well developed penis and breaks off the dream and the excitation" (IX, 216).

In essence, this is the situation Freud will analyze in the vulture sequence of the Leonardo study: a manifest content of a female figure with a penis that disguises infantile wishes directed toward the phallic mother. Manifest content is puzzling, accord-ing to Freud, because it is a regressive means of representation. It works the way children do when they construct their infantile sexual theories, that is, *pictorially.* This is also the way the ear-liest forms of writing work, according to Freud, which is why, again, both the manifest content of the dream *and* the infantile sexual theories, although "not made with the intention of being understood, present no greater difficulties to their translators than do the ancient hieroglyphic scripts to those who seek to read them."

Let us consider a final historical point before we turn to the Leonardo study itself. In the autumn of 1909, that is, at the time of the letters to Jung that I cited above, when he felt that his findings on the infantile sexual theories had permitted him both to "solve the riddle of Leonardo's character" and "to hit on. . .the ultimate secret of foot-fetishism," Freud *also* discovered Karl Abel's 1884 pamphlet "The Antithetical Meaning of Primal Words." Freud published a short article on Abel's work in 1910, the same year as the publication of the Leonardo study. Abel was concerned with questions of Egyptian philology, and Freud was pleased to find that Abel's investigations of ancient language formation confirmed many of his own hypotheses about the for-mation of the manifest dream content.

The Value of a Mistranslation

Leonardo da Vinci and a Memory of His Childhood is based upon what Freud claims to be the only passage in Leonardo's scientific notebooks in which the artist-scientist gives any information about his childhood. The *Standard Edition* gives the passage in question as follows, including a prefatory sentence by Freud:

> In a passage about the flight of vultures he suddenly interrupts himself to pursue a memory from very early years which had sprung to his mind: "It seems that I was always destined to be so deeply concerned with vultures; for I recall as one of my very earliest memories that while I was in my cradle a vulture came down and opened my mouth with its tail, and struck me many times with its tail against my lips." [P. 82]

The passage actually cited by Freud is a German translation of excerpts from Leonardo's notebooks. This translation contains more than one mistake, and the *Standard Edition* has rendered the mistakes into English for the sake of consistency. Freud, however, was careful also to cite the Italian original version of this passage in a footnote that immediately follows the citation of the (German) translation; Maclagan refers to this in his letter to the *Burlington Magazine*. Freud himself had found the Italian text in the extracts from Leonardo's notebooks presented by Smiraglia Scognamiglio in his 1900 study of Leonardo's childhood. (This is the "Italian work" to which Freud referred in the letter to Jung of October 17, 1909.) Scognamiglio's source, in turn, was the notebooks themselves, which are to be found in the Ambrosian Library in Milan as the *Codex Atlanticus*. The *Standard Edition* not only maintains Freud's citation of the Italian text in a footnote but also adds an editor's note that points out the errors in the German text cited by Freud. As we know already, in Italian the bird is *nibio*, kite, whereas the German reads *Geier*, or vulture. Moreover, the preposition translated into German as "against"—"struck me many times with its tail *against* my lips"—is actually *dentro,* "within" or "inside," in the Italian text.

Before proceeding to interpret his vulture as a symbolic representation of the phallic mother, Freud first establishes the ground rules for the kind of interpretation he wishes to make. No matter what sort of bird this is, the scene described by Leonardo, as Freud says, is clearly "improbable and fabulous." It cannot be an actual memory. Rather, it must follow the same pattern as many other so-called childhood memories: it is actually a fantasy formed at a later date and transposed back to childhood.

In order to illustrate how such fantasy memories function, Freud compares them to history in the various ways that it comes to be written. (In an editor's note Strachey points out that the comparison between the formation of screen memories and the writing of history was first made in a 1907 addition to *The Psychopathology of Everyday Life.*)[21] The comparison is regulated, as always in Freud, by the distinction between conscious and unconscious material. In order to demonstrate that Leonardo's memory contains unconscious material, Freud first states that unlike the *conscious* memories of adulthood, childhood memories are not registered at the moment of experience. "Childhood" memories are to be understood, here, as memories that may become unconscious. "Registration" is inscription of a memory such that it is available to consciousness. It is only after childhood that such memories are elicited. They "are put into the service of later trends, so that generally speaking they cannot be sharply distinguished from phantasies. Their nature is perhaps best illustrated by a comparison with the way in which the writing of history originated among the peoples of antiquity" (p. 83).

21The practice of comparing memories containing unconscious material to a process of inscription or registration, however, dates as far back as the *Project* of 1895 and culminates in the "Note on the Mystic Writing Pad" of 1925, as Derrida has shown in "Freud and the Scene of Writing" (in *Writing and Difference,* trans. Alan Bass [Chicago: University of Chicago Press, 1978]).

In a nation's early days, says Freud, it has to struggle in order to survive and leaves very few traces of itself. This is like the period of early childhood which is usually subject to amnesia. Then, when the nation's struggle for survival is over, comes an age of reflection, when a record of current events is kept. This period is comparable to a person's conscious memories of maturity. Finally, and for mostly tendentious reasons, a nation seeks to reinterpret the few remaining traces of its earliest days in terms of its current beliefs and recorded history. Thus, histories of the nation's earliest days come to be written, and such histories distort whatever traces are available from those days in terms of current needs. This is comparable to the way in which the supposed memories of early childhood, such as the one in Leonardo's notebook, are formed (p. 83). We must keep in mind—although Freud does not state the point explicitly here, as he does in "On the Sexual Theories of Children"—that the comparison also implies a relation of repression between the earliest traces and the recorded history. There are so few of the early traces because most of them have been erased—repressed into the general amnesia of early "history." Furthermore, the earliest traces are not necessarily memories in the sense of inscriptions of actual events but may be traces in the sense of inscriptions of pictorial unconscious fantasies—for example, the fantasy of that which can only be represented in a picture because it *is not*: the fantasy of the mother's penis. These "fantastic" traces are both indelible *and* necessarily subject to repression, or at least to attempted repression.

Having established through his comparison to the writing of history that Leonardo's memory must be understood in relation to unconscious material—thus making it subject to the same kinds of distortions as all unconscious material—Freud proposes to treat it like a dream. If we follow the rules of dream interpretation, then "we may venture to *translate [übersetzen]* the phantasy from its own special language into words that are generally understood. The translation [*Übersetzung*] is then seen to point to an erotic content" (p. 85; emphasis added). This is the usual procedure of translating the confusing, pictorial manifest content of a dream into the comprehensible latent language of wish fulfillment, like the translation of puzzling picture writing into ordinary language.

But, in order to be sure that his translation of the manifest into the latent content of the fantasy is correct, Freud turns to the Italian text twice. First he notices the word *coda*, the tail, the bird's tail. He states: "A tail, *'coda,'* is one of the most familiar symbols and substitutive expressions [*Ersatzbezeichnungnen*] for the male organ, in Italian no less than in other languages." Then—and here we must imagine Freud turning from the German translation to the Italian text—he notices that the tail is placed *inside* the child's lips, "dentro alle labbra," even though the German reads that the tail is placed *against* the child's lips, "gegen meine Lippen gestossen." This observation allows Freud to complete his sentence: "A tail, *'coda,'* is one of the most familiar symbols and substitutive expressions for the male organ, in Italian no less than in other languages; the situation in the phantasy, of a vulture opening the child's mouth and beating *inside* it virogously with its tail, corresponds to the idea of an act of fellatio" (p. 86; italics added).

The question then becomes: why does Leonardo have unconscious fellatio fantasies? Remarking on the passivity of the infant in the fantasy (the child in the cradle), Freud traces Leonardo's apparently homosexual fantasy to what he calls "the first source of pleasure in our life," which "doubtless remains indelibly printed ["unzerstörbar eingeprägt"] on us" (p. 87). This is the pleasure of taking the mother's nipple into the mouth. Thus, says Freud, Leonardo's assertion that the scene with the "vulture" belongs to his suckling period means that the fantasy conceals a memory of pleasure at his mother's breast. As an adult, Leonardo transformed this trace of his earliest life into a passive homosexual fantasy. Like the "mature" nation concerned with its archives, Leonardo has reinterpreted an obscure piece of early history—which is nevertheless "indelibly printed" in unconscious memory—to make it conform to the trends of his later sexual history. Let us note that at this point the traces of earliest history seem to be traces of real events—the obscure memory of real pleasure at the breast. The discussion that follows, however, not only attempts to make inferences about real events in Leonardo's early life but also makes unconscious fantasy, the fantasy of the maternal phallus, the crux of the analysis. This will be the moment of the *hieroglyphic* vulture.

Having proved that the "memory" is a fantasy, Freud is now concerned with what he called "considerations of representability" in *The Interpretation of Dreams*. He wants to know why a particular symbol has been chosen by the unconscious to "rewrite," in distorted form, the indelibly printed text of early memory. In other words, why does the latent content become this particular manifest content? Why does Leonardo's fantasy replace his mother with a *vulture*? What is the specificity of the vulture here?

Freud has an answer ready, but he introduces it with a gesture which we can only call cautionary or defensive:

> We interpret Leonardo's phantasy as one of being suckled by his mother, and we find his mother replaced by—a vulture. Where does this vulture come from and how does it happen to be found in its present place?
>
> At this point a thought comes to the mind from such a remote quarter that it would be tempting to set it aside. ["Einfall bietet sich da, so fernab liegend, dass man versucht wäre, auf ihn zu verzichten."] [P. 88]

Freud's gesture here might be viewed at first as a rhetorical request for the reader's indulgence. Its "manifest content" expresses his comprehension of the reader's situation. It is as if he were saying that he too would reject the material he is about to present if he were reading it for the first time. Thus, he is asking the reader to follow him for the time necessary to fill in what seem to be logical gaps.

But what if there were no way to fill in these gaps? In other words, what if there were a "latent" content to Freud's desire to set aside his own thought, that is, a desire to express this thought even if it does not fulfill its assigned role in his argument? When Freud says that "a thought comes to the mind from such a remote quarter that it would be tempting to set it aside," he is surely echoing the "fundamental rule" of psychoanalysis, that is, the injunction that the patient make an effort not to censor his thoughts, that he give voice to the kind of thoughts one usually suppresses: precisely whatever "comes to the mind from such a remote quarter that it would be tempting to set it aside." Furthermore, any analyst would be struck if a patient, in seeming compliance with the fundamental rule, hesitated to say something and then proceeded to give *mis*information. Which is just what Freud is about to do: we know that the bird is not a vulture, and that the very detailed explanation he is about to give— preceded by a gesture of hesitation about its "remoteness"—is irrelevant to his analysis of Leonardo. Like the analyst, then, we will read this passage for what it expresses despite itself:

> At this point a thought comes to the mind from such a remote quarter that it would be tempting to set it aside. In the hieroglyphics of the ancient Egyptians the mother is represented by a *picture* of a vulture. The Egyptians also worshipped a Mother Goddess, who was represented as having a vulture's head, or else several heads, of which at least one was a vulture's. This goddess's name was pronounced *Mut*. Can the similarity to the sound of our word *Mutter* be merely coincidence? There is then some real connection between vulture and mother—but what help is that to us? For have we any right to expect Leonardo to know of it, seeing that the first man who succeeded in reading hieroglyphics was François Champollion? [P. 88, italics added]

It takes Freud several pages of the most intricate scholarship to establish the connection between vulture and mother in Leonardo's fantasy. In summarizing the argument, which is dense, even dizzying, we will be able to locate the "latent" content of his defensive gesture and to show that the vulture does play a role different from the one Freud intends. (In order to follow the summary, the reader must have the text in hand.)

Freud begins by asking why the Egyptians chose the vulture as a symbol for motherhood. Thus, he turns to several scholarly texts, primarily Leemans's 1835 edition of a Greek study of uncertain date attributed to Horapollo and entitled *Hieroglyphica*. Leemans's work presents the original *Greek* version of Horapollo's study with a *Latin* commentary. Although the *Standard Edition* provides translations of the Greek and Latin passages cited by Freud, these passages are *left untranslated* in *all* the German editions of the Leonardo study, including the *Gesammelte Schriften*. We see Freud at his most scholarly here, citing Leonardo in Italian, Horapollo in Greek, and Leemans in Latin, making it difficult to imagine him working without dictionaries. Above we saw that Freud even corrected one mistake in the German translation of Leonardo's memory by going back to the Italian text (*gegen* for *dentro*).

The crux of Freud's argument (for which he finds support not only in Horapollo, but also in a sentence from Aelian as cited by Römer and again cited in Greek), is that the Egyptians believed that only female vultures existed. A counterpart to this belief was the idea that only male scarab beetles existed. Freud annotates this last piece of information with a Latin sentence attesting to the Egyptians' parallel beliefs in the exclusive femaleness of vultures and the exclusive maleness of scarab beetles. This sentence is attributed to Plutarch, but Strachey points out that Freud has "inadvertently attributed to Plutarch a sentence which is in fact a gloss by Leemans on Horapollo" (p. 89, n. 1). Thus a mistaken reference attributes a Latin sentence perfectly understood by Freud to a source perhaps more authoritative than the actual one.

Next, Freud asks how the Egyptians explained the reproduction of vultures if they were all supposed to be female. He claims that this point is covered by Horapollo: according to the latter, the Egyptians believed that at a certain time the vulture paused in mid-flight, opened her vagina, and was impregnated by the wind. Freud annotates this information by citing another Greek sentence from Horapollo. He prefaces the citation with this phrase: "The words that refer to the vulture's sex run." The Greek phrase which Freud then cites does in fact assert that the vulture is "a mother, because in this race of creatures there are no males." Strachey then adds, in an editor's note: "It seems as though the wrong passage from Horapollo is quoted here. The phrase in the text implies that what we should have here is the myth of the vulture's impregnation by the wind." I think that Strachey has missed the point, which is that all of Freud's learned citations—from Aelian, "Plutarch" (actually Leemans), and Horapollo—serve the same purpose: they prove that in antiquity the vulture was a mother symbol.

Freud has not yet explained why Leonardo's fantasy "replaced" his mother with a favored mother symbol from ancient times, but an overview of the formal apparatus up to this point will be useful. Freud has checked the Italian text of Leonardo's memory, leading him to place the word *coda* in its linguistic context (Italian slang), and to correct the mistranslation of *dentro* by *gegen*. He has cited Greek in Greek, and Latin in Latin, with no mistakes in comprehension. And yet he never checked the translation of the one word on which all this careful scholarship depends: *nibio*. And a glance through the rest of the Leonardo study will show that almost every time Freud cites a work in a foreign language he leaves it untranslated. Is this a display of erudition? Does the display conceal Freud's failure to check the translation of the *one* word that has generated all his learned Greek and Latin citations? Let us keep this question in mind as we follow the rest of the analysis of the vulture, keeping in mind also the following points: first, Freud has stated his hesitation to pursue this line of thought; second, the aim of the analysis is to explain the transformation of the latent content of the fantasy into its distorted, pictographic manifest content; and third, that Freud is also concerned with how personal "history" "rewrites" "indelible traces" that are necessarily subject to repression.

When we left off, Freud had established that the Egyptians used the vulture as a mother symbol because of their belief in the vulture's exclusive femaleness. How could this knowledge have come into Leonardo's hands? Freud has two answers, the first again complicated by writing and the second again left untranslated in Latin. Here is the first answer:

> It is quite possible that Leonardo was familiar with the scientific fable which was responsible for the vulture being used by the Egyptians as a *pictorial representation* of the idea of the mother. ["Leonardo kann das wissenschaftliche Märchen, dem es Geier verdankt, dass die Ägypter mit seinem Bilde den Begriff der Mutter schrieben (that the Egyptians wrote the concept of mother with its picture), sehr wohl gekannt haben."] He was a wide reader and his interest embraced all branches of literature and learning. In the Codex Atlanticus we find a catalogue of all the books he possessed at a particular date, and in addition numerous jottings on other books that he had borrowed from friends; and if we may judge by the extracts from his notes by Richter, the extent of his reading can hardly be overestimated. Early works on natural history were well represented among them in addition to contemporary books; and all of them were already in print at the time. *Milan was in fact the leading city in Italy for the new art of printing.* [P. 89; italics added]

The Latin answer is another citation from Leemans. The following is the translation provided by the *Standard Edition*, but *not* by Freud in the German editions of his works, although he has obviously understood the text: "This story about the vulture was eagerly taken up by the Fathers of the Church in order to refute, by means of a proof drawn from the natural order, those who denied the Virgin Birth. The subject is therefore mentioned in almost all of them" (p. 89).

Thus, Freud has given Leonardo ample opportunity to read the literature on Egyptian vulture symbolism, supporting his argument with the catalogs of Leonardo's books, Milan's role as the center of the "new art of printing," and Latin citations concerning the Fathers of the Church. Inherent throughout this discussion is the analogy to the writing of history: the church, like a latter-day nation in Freud's analogy, seizes on traces from the past that it can use in order to write its own tendentious history. And in Milan, in Leonardo's time, technology had made this rewriting of the "indelible trace" of early history available to a wider audience than ever via the printing press. But—*nibio*.

In pursuit of undreamed-of information about Leonardo's history, Freud next asserts that the replacement of the mother by a vulture in the fantasy indicates Leonardo's awareness that as an infant he was alone with his mother (p. 90). After referring to the few known facts about Leonardo's earliest years that tend to confirm this hypothesis,[22] Freud goes on to wonder what effect this absence of his father must have had on Leonardo's infantile sexual researches. Indeed, Leonardo himself traces his own adult preoccupation with the flight of birds and with flying machines to this early "memory." What we still do not know, Freud points out, is why Leonardo should have endowed a mother symbol with the "distinguishing mark of masculinity," given that the bird's tail cannot represent anything except a penis, "according to the usual way in which language makes use of substitutes" (p. 93). Returning to his Egyptian sources—and now Freud is looking at an *Italian* dictionary of Egyptian mythology compiled by Lanzone—Freud notes the equally puzzling fact that the vulture-headed mother goddess was usually represented with a phallus. Instead of explaining this further coincidence by once more proving how likely it is that Leonardo should have read or heard about this peculiarity of hieroglyphics, Freud states that it is "more plausible to trace the correspondence back to a common factor operative in both cases" (p. 94).

Freud's "plausible" explanation of this common factor rests on the assumption that the origin of intellectual curiosity in children must recapitulate the origin of thought in general, since "the

[22]Much of the controversy generated by the Leonardo study centers on this issue. Even the psychoanalysts who have written on the Leonardo study, including Kurt Eissler (in his *Leonardo da Vinci: Psychoanalytic Notes on the Enigma* [New York: International Universities Press, 1961]), have turned to the same Florentine censuses, tax records, marriage and birth certificates, and so forth as other Leonardo scholars, in order to prove or disprove the point. Although this scholarship is not without its own value, it overlooks the "internal" reading of the Leonardo study that I am attempting here. For this reason such readings have not noticed the "logic" that produced the vulture.

individual's mental development repeats the course of human development in an abbreviated form" (p. 97). Here Freud applies directly his findings from the paper "On the Sexual Theories of Children." There he showed, as we saw above, that the young child's search for knowledge has an emotional basis. The child constructs "theories" (fantasies) about where babies come from and about sexual difference in order to account for such dreadful realities. Thus, given Freud's constant assumption that infantile equals primitive in the ontogenetic repetition of phylogeny, he is looking for parallels between the child's fantastic explanations of procreation and the mythological explanations of creation in general. This brings us onto familiar ground. The paper on the infantile sexual theories had demonstrated that the boy's first infantile sexual "theory" attributes the penis to his mother. The parallel situation in mythology is "the addition of a phallus to the female body . . . intended to denote the primal creative force of nature" (p. 94).

For this reason, Freud says, the manifest content of Leonardo's "memory" disguises the latent content with the "vulture." As an adult, Leonardo is alleged to have known about Egyptian vulture (mother) symbolism, which is supposed to have become associatively linked to his own infantile sexual "theory" that his mother once possessed a penis. (This scenario is very much like the dream situation described in the paper on infantile sexual theories: the male dreamer beholds a penis "in the place of the female genitals.") Every individual, however, uses the "indelible trace" of the fantasy of the maternal phallus to rewrite his *own* sexual history, as the Fathers of the Church used ancient vulture symbolism to rewrite history in support of the idea of virgin birth. For Leonardo, according to Freud, the question was one of an early exclusive attachment to his mother, leading to a particular kind of sublimated homosexuality in adult life. This is why the manifest content of the fantasy condenses an experience of pleasure at the breast with a passive fellatio fantasy. Freud develops this idea in the rest of the Leonardo study, using it to explain both Leonardo's ambivalent attitude toward painting and his preoccupation with scientific research, particularly with the project for a flying machine modeled on birds' flying mechanism. The "memory" then, for Freud, is a good example of the rewriting of history that reinterprets indestructible pictures of early fantasies in terms of current needs. It is a screen memory that encapsulates the interplay of Leonardo's infantile sexuality and his career as artist and scientist.

Why the *vulture* then? The question becomes even more compelling when we find that Freud's display of erudition concerning vulture symbolism also overlooks other facts about the kite—*nibio*. Meyer Schapiro, consulting Leonardo's notebooks, has found that Leonardo noted the memory, which does purport to account for his lifelong fascination with flight, on the back of a sheet that contained various scientific observations on this topic. The kite is mentioned more than any other avian species. According to Schapiro, Leonardo was particularly interested in the kite—"as common in Italy as vultures in Egypt," as Jones said—because the rudderlike movements of its forked *tail* "offer some hints for the design of a flying machine."[23] Yet Leonardo had more to say about kites. In his allegorical animal fable "Envy," Leonardo has the kite peck the sides of her children, who are too fat. Several authors have noted the hostile quality of this mother kite, the bird that "visits" Leonardo in his cradle, and have reinterpreted the "memory" accordingly.[24]

---

[23]Schapiro, 151. I do not know if Scognamiglio, who provided the excerpts from the notebooks that Freud cited, also provided Leonardo's observations on the flight of the kite. In addition, I wonder whether Marie Herzfeld—who was first responsible for the mistranslation—spoke of this point in her book on Leonardo, which Freud cites repeatedly. Unfortunately I have not yet been able to consult either book.

[24]See Wohl and Trosman, 36; Schapiro, 151; and especially Eissler, p. 83. Another essay could be written on Freud's lack of attention to Leonardo's tale of the kite (in his fable *Envy*) in conjunction with Eissler's interpretation of Leonardo's drawing "The Allegory of *Envy* and Virtue." Eissler interprets the drawing: "The female tries to castrate the male. The abundance of penis symbols . . . in the female is striking. From analytic observation it is justified to conclude that this type of symbolism refers to the pre-oedipal mother, who, in the child's imagination, is endowed with a male genital. Freud, in his analysis of Leonardo's cover memory, conjectured such symbolism to have been active in

All of this to emphasize that the vulture, so painstakingly documented, cannot play the role Freud intended. In essence, the "latent" content of Freud's hesitation to use his thought from a remote quarter is his desire to compare the fantasy of the phallic mother to a hieroglyph, to *Egyptian picture writing*. Why? We recall first Freud's comparison of manifest dream content to an untranslated hieroglyph, a puzzling piece of picture writing. Then we recall what we found in Freud's letters: his simultaneous preoccupation with the infantile sexual theories, the question of fetishism, and Leonardo. These three are bound together by the fantasy of the maternal phallus, which, as an infantile fantasy that can return in the adult's dreams or fantasies, must be both indelible and pictorial, that is, "hieroglyphic." Thus Freud's carefully prepared references to the *Egyptians'* practice of representing the mother by a "*picture* of a vulture" (p. 88), to "the vulture being used by the *Egyptians* as a *pictorial* representation of the idea of mother" (p. 89). "Pictorial" in Freud, from *The Interpretation of Dreams* onward, means regressive, infantile, difficult to translate, indelible. And "Egyptian" means the same.

We must now turn to Freud's happy discovery of Abel's pamphlet "The Antithetical Meaning of Primal Words," which occurred at the same time that he was thinking about fetishism and Leonardo (1909). In the brief article published soon after the Leonardo study (1910), the bulk of Freud's citations from Abel seek to demonstrate that Egyptian language shares with manifest dream content a disregard for contradiction: in both, the same word often expresses opposing ideas. Freud states that according

---

him. The Allegory is almost an illustration of this very interpretation." To which Eissler adds in a footnote: "The avian species is immaterial to this interpretation" (pp. 132–133). Our entire topic here is the ambiguity of Eissler's note. We could successfully argue that he is both right and wrong, right because Freud's interpretation stands, and in fact is corroborated, if the bird is a kite, which Leonardo *does* use as a mother-symbol and which *is* connected to his fascination with flight because of the peculiarities of its *tail*; and wrong because the avian species *is* material to the interplay of sexual theory and unconscious use of language that is intrinsic to the history of psychoanalysis.

to Abel "it is in the 'oldest roots' that antithetical double meanings are found" (XI, 158). How are such words to be translated? Freud cites Abel: "'If the Egyptian word '*ken*' is to mean 'strong,' its sound, which is written alphabetically, is followed by the *picture* of an upright armed man; if the same word has to express 'weak,' the letters which represent the sound are followed by the *picture* of a squatting, limp figure. The majority of other words with two meanings are similarly accompanied by explanatory *pictures*'" (XI, 158; italics added). For Freud, then, "Egypt" represents the moment in the course of human development that is repeated by individual development when the child creates the kind of indelible pictorial fantasies that may return, for example, in the manifest content of dreams or in fetishism; in a similar way the Fathers of the Church rewrote history using remainders of the Egyptian past. Here is the conclusion of Freud's article on Abel:

> In the correspondence between the peculiarity of the dream-work mentioned at the beginning of the paper and the practice discovered by philology in the oldest languages, we may see a confirmation of the view we have formed about the regressive, archaic character of the expression of thought in dreams. And we psychiatrists cannot escape the suspicion that we would be better at understanding and *translating* [übersetzen] the language of dreams if we knew more about the development of language. [XI, 161; italics added]

The vulture, then, cannot, and does not, work the way Freud literally intends it to in the analysis of Leonardo. His invocation of the fundamental rule before embarking on the vulture sequence, when placed in the entire context just described, reveals the "latent" content of Freud's hesitation to pursue the matter. The mistranslation of *nibio* by *Geier* (vulture) was too *precious* to be given up. It encapsulates, via the Egyptian picture of the phallic vulture-headed goddess, all of Freud's ideas at the time about the infantile fantasy of the maternal phallus; about the use of archaic (pictorial) language in the formation of such fantasies and in the formation of manifest dream content; about the indelibility of such "inscriptions," whose survival impels the psychoanalyst-archaeologist to seek the code with which to translate them; and finally, about the recapitulation by individual development of a moment in human development when not only were such fantasies as the phallic mother current, due to the primitive organization of thought, but were also, at this same moment of history, recorded forever in pictures: the infantile-pictorial-Egyptian-hieroglyphic sexual "theories." The "vulture," then, is a mistranslation as precious as the "precious object" for which the fetishist searches so passionately (letter to Jung of November 21, 1909, cited above).

Reproduction

"It [painting] does not beget
infinite progeny like printed books"
("Questa non fa infinite figliuoli,
come fa li libri stampati").[25]

The Leonardo study is in six sections, with the analysis of the vulture occupying the second and third of them. Freud reproduces the Mona Lisa on the page facing the beginning of the fourth section and opens with this sentence: "We have not yet done with Leonardo's vulture phantasy'" (p. 107). In the end, we will have to make this statement into a question and ask if it ever will be possible to be done with the "vulture," with the effects of mistranslation in psychoanalysis. For there is more to the question of the "vulture" than the sober explanation just provided via the letters, articles, and theoretical issues that surround the Leonardo study. In its role as too good an illustration to be given up, the vulture is also exuberant, fecund. Its indel-

[25]Leonardo, *Trattato della pittura*, cited in Eissler, 229.

ibility is not stationary: the vulture works and moves. As Wohl and Trosman said: "This error . . . has *produced* a special literature." The emphasis, henceforth, will be on *production*, on the production of *literature*, the begetting of "infinite progeny like printed books," in Leonardo's phrase. For has not Freud told us that the "first, grand problem of life" concerns the origin of babies? And has he not remarked that Milan was "the leading city in Italy for the new art of printing"?

In the fourth section of the Leonardo study Freud sets himself the grand problem of giving the definitive interpretation of the Gioconda smile, with special attention not only to the Mona Lisa itself but also to the painting of the Madonna and Child with St. Anne. Let us backtrack for a moment. Freud had concluded the third section with a discussion of Leonardo's choices of sexual object. In early childhood, Freud believes he has found, Leonardo had an overly intense relationship with his mother. Narcissistic identification with her led the adult Leonardo to choose the same kinds of sexual objects that he believed she did, namely boys like the young Leonardo. It is worth noting that this is Freud's first elaboration of the role of narcissism in homosexuality and that the vulture once more provides the code with which to *translate* the previously puzzling "inscription," the "riddle" of Leonardo's character:

> It would appear that Leonardo's erotic life did really belong to the type of homosexuality whose psychical development we have succeeded in disclosing, and the emergence of the homosexual situation in his phantasy of the vulture would become intelligible to us: for its meaning was exactly what we have already asserted of that type. We should have to *translate* it thus: "It was through this erotic relation with my mother that I became a homosexual." [XI, 106; italics added]

Freud continues this line of thought in the fourth section. When he finds that Leonardo also endowed handsome young men with the famous smile, he states that this "cannot fail to remind us of the two kinds of sexual objects that we have inferred from the analysis of his vulture-phantasy" (p. 111), that is, his mother and himself. The Gioconda smile, then, was original- ly his mother's smile,[26] which is why it can also be given to young men. In the painting of Anne with her daughter Mary and Mary's son, *both* women have the smile:

> After we have studied this picture for some time, it suddenly dawns on us that only Leonardo could have painted it, just as only he could have created the phantasy of the vulture. The picture contains the synthesis of the history of his childhood. . . . St. Anne, Mary's mother . . . is here portrayed as being perhaps a little more mature and serious than the Virgin Mary, but as still being a young woman of unfaded beauty. . . . both are endowed with the blissful smile. . . . Leonardo's childhood was remarkable in precisely the same way as this picture. He had two mothers: first, his true mother Caterina, from whom he was torn away when he was between three and five, and then a young and tender step-mother, his father's wife, Donna Albiera. [Pp. 112– 13]

This is how the most striking episode of the vulture's tale, of the vulture's striking tail, begins. The second (German) edition of the Leonardo study was published in 1919, nine years after the first. Freud added a very long footnote to the analysis of the St. Anne painting in the second edition, and in this note, he once more expresses some hesitation about the vulture, although not as much hesitation as on the occasion of its introduction. We must cite at length; all the emphasis here is Freud's except for the words "without reserve" and "outlines," which I have italicized:

> A remarkable discovery has been made in the Louvre picture by Oskar Pfister, which is of undeniable interest, even if one may not feel inclined to accept it *without reserve.* In Mary's curiously

[26]On the entire issue of attributing something *in* a painting to a person or thing *outside* the painting, see Derrida, "Restitutions," in *La vérité en peinture* (Paris: Flammarion, 1978). This issue *inevitably* raises the question of fetishism, as it will here; Derrida has discussed this matter in "Restitutions." The formula is: to restore by seeing what is not there.

arranged and rather confusing drapery he has discovered the *outline of a vulture* ["die Kontur des Geiers"] and he interprets it as an *unconscious picture-puzzle:*

"In the picture that represents the artist's mother *the vulture, the symbol of motherhood,* is perfectly clearly visible.

"In the length of blue cloth, which is visible around the hip of the woman in front and which extends in the direction of her lap and her right knee, one can see the vulture's extremely characteristic head, its neck and the sharp curve where its body begins. Hardly any observer whom I have confronted with my little find has been able to resist the evidence of this picture puzzle."

At this point the reader will not, I feel sure, grudge the effort of looking at the accompanying illustration, to see if he can find in it the *outlines* of the vulture seen by Pfister. . . .

Pfister continues: "The important question however is: How far does the picture-puzzle extend? If we follow the length of cloth, which stands out so sharply from its surroundings starting at the middle of the wing and continuing from there, we notice that one part of it runs down to the woman's foot, while the other part extends in an upward direction and rests on her shoulder and on the child. The former of these parts might more or less represent the vulture's wing and tail, as it is in nature; the latter might be a pointed belly and—especially when we notice the radiating lines which resemble the outlines of feathers—a bird's outspread tail, whose right-hand end, *exactly as in Leonardo's fateful childhood dream [sic], leads to the mouth of the child, i.e. of Leonardo himself.*" [Pp. 115–16, n. 1; Pfister's article, entitled "Kryptolalie, Kryptographie und unbewusstes Vexierbild bei Normalen," first appeared in the 1913 number of the *Jahrbuch für Psychoanalytische und Psychopathologische Forschungen*]

Freud's maintenance of a mistranslation has now been (mis)translated into Leonardo's painting. This is one of the more famous gaffes in psychoanalytic history. Pfister, the true disciple, sees proof of the master's words everywhere, even if the master is wrong. Before simply laughing this off, with bemusement, embarassment, or malice, depending on individual "theoretical" orientation, let us once more wonder about Freud's reserve, his continued hesitation to use a thought concerning the vulture. Again, the "manifest" content is obvious. Freud's reserve says that Pfister's "find" is probably too good to be true. It is not verifiable in any case, so let us treat it as an amusing coincidence to be placed at the end of a long footnote where it can do no harm. If Pfister is wrong, nothing is changed. If he is right, how extraordinary! Such is the obvious reading of Freud's reserve.

The history of the psychoanalytic movement, however, gives a twist to Freud's gesture here. Who was Pfister? A pastor from Zurich, Pfister was one of the founding members of the Swiss Psychoanalytic Society in 1910, the society headed by his fellow Zuricher Jung. In 1914 the Swiss society seceded from the International Psychoanalytic Association, marking Jung's "definitive break" with Freud. Pfister, however, did not follow Jung, and thereby became Freud's main representative in Zurich. By 1919—the year of the second edition of the Leonardo study— Pfister (along with Oberholzer) had founded a new Swiss Society for Psychoanalysis. Was Freud thanking Pfister for his loyalty by incorporating his "find" into the Leonardo study? After all, has not Pfister (once more) resolutely followed Freud along a difficult pathway, one that Freud himself had hesitated to follow because of its remoteness?

There is more. In 1910, when the Leonardo study was first published, Freud and Jung were still on good terms. On April 22, 1910 Freud had written to Jung: "I am now reading the proofs of the Leonardo; I am very curious to know your impression of it."[27] On June 17, 1910 Jung wrote to Freud:

> *Leonardo* is wonderful. Pfister tells me he has *seen* the vulture in the picture. I *saw* one too, but in a different place: the beak precisely in the pubic region. One would like to say with Kant: play of chance which equals the subtlest lucubrations of reason. I have read *Leonardo* straight through and shall soon come back to it again. The transition to mythology grows out of this essay from inner necessity, actually it is the first essay of yours with whose inner development I felt perfectly in tune from the start.[28]

[27]*The Freud/Jung Letters*, 311.
[28]Ibid., p. 329; italics added.

What are we to make of Freud's Zurich disciples competing to *see* what is not there?

On June 19, Freud wrote back to Jung: "I was overjoyed at your interest in *Leonardo* and at your saying that you were coming closer to my way of thinking. I have read your essay with pleasure the day it arrived; I have been thinking about it and will write you more soon. . . . I identified your vulture only today, undoubtedly under the influence of your letters; but it isn't as 'neat and beyond doubt' as Pfister's."[29] The essay of Jung's that Freud is referring to is a lecture on mythological symbolism: recall Jung's pleasure that in the Leonardo study the "transition to mythology grows . . . from inner necessity," thus making it the "first (!) essay of yours with whose inner development I felt perfectly in tune from the start." Hindsight makes it easy to see in these statements the issues that soon would come to divide Freud and Jung. Indeed, Freud's next letter to Jung contains a detailed critique of the essay mentioned in the June 19 letter; the remarks grow most critical over Jung's treatment of sexuality and his acceptance of the content of myths at face value.

In 1919, then, with the refounding of the Swiss Psychoanalytic Society by Pfister, Freud could not have failed to think also of Jung's vulture—never as "'neat and beyond doubt' as Pfister's"—when he incorporated Pfister's find into the Leonardo study. This too, must have contributed to Freud's reserve, which we might read as follows: Pfister was with me all along. He saw the vulture as I did. Jung's placement of the beak in the pubic region is upside down and shows his hostility to my sexual theories. How strange that even when we were supposedly on good terms Jung *had* to see a vulture other than the one loyal Pfister saw. How right I was to question it!

But there is more still. My reading of the vulture has shown that Freud could not give it up because it illustrated *too well* all his thoughts at the time about the maternal phallus, fetishism, and the use of archaic, pictographic language in dream and fan-

[29]Ibid., pp. 331–32.

tasy formation. The maternal phallus, we saw, can only be "seen" in the way dreams are seen: it is a fantastic mistranslation of sexual difference. Thus we have what Freud calls the "secret" of fetishism: the motivated need to *see* what is not there, what never has been there. Freud's mistranslation, then, is itself a fetish: Freud has continued to maintain that he sees what was never there—the vulture—for motivated reasons, that is, because it fits in too well with the related theories of the infantile sexual theories and of "Egyptian" language formation. And this fetishistic mistranslation itself has made theory into a fetish: Freud, not without reservations, has chosen Pfister's fetishization of his theories, Pfister's way of *seeing* what was never there, over Jung's. The theory of the fetish has been fetishized and indeed in both the economic and the sexual senses of fetishism. The debt to Pfister is "paid" when his fetish is put into wider circulation in the second edition of the Leonardo study; Jung's fetish, thereby, is taken out of circulation, devalued, declared counterfeit. There follows a repetition of the sexual sense of fetishism when Freud requests that we "see" along with him: "The reader will not, I feel sure, grudge the effort of *looking.*"

Thus, the mistranslation is the vehicle that turns the theory of the fetish back on itself, making it into a fetish. The vulture, the precious mistranslation, has *produced,* has *begotten* another vulture, another mistranslation that has to be *seen:* Freud reproduces the drawing of the St. Anne with Pfister's "vulture" outlined and shaded in (p. 116). Just as the child claims to see what is not there, and seeks validation for his precious, anxiety-relieving representation, so do Freud, Pfister, and Jung. (But have they not also proven Leonardo wrong? Has not a painting, the St. Anne, begotten progeny "like printed books," a "special literature" that repeats the mistranslation, reprints the hieroglyph?) What, then, is a mistaken translation in psychoanalysis?

Perhaps it is transference. An analyst might maintain that we are confusing the issues of transference and fetishism here. The theory of fetishism is one thing, the analyst might say, and the transferential relations of Freud, Jung, and Pfister quite another.

After all, Freud's theory of fetishism has stood up well, and it is probably no more than a historical curiosity that Freud maintained a mistranslation because it fit in so well with his ideas about the infantile sexual theories and hieroglyphics. And that this mistranslation should have led Freud, Pfister, and Jung to see what is not there in Leonardo's painting, and then to debate about it, only shows the power of transference—Pfister's overt positive transference and Jung's growing negative one—and yes, shows also the necessity of analyzing one's own countertransferences: if Freud had not always set up relationships with men conforming to his early pattern of "beloved friend, hated enemy," as he did by his own admission, he probably would not have overestimated Jung in the first place and would have been more suspicious of Pfister's "find" in the second. What more could there be to say on the matter?

We can add two things, at least. First, transference itself has to do with translation and mistranslation. *Übertragen* (to transfer) and *übersetzen* (to translate) can both mean "to translate" in German. For the same reason, "translate" and "transfer" have the same derivation in English, from the Latin *translatus, latus* being the suppletive past participle of *ferre,* to bear, to carry, whence trans-*fer. Tragen,* of course, means the same, that is, to carry, to bear. *Übertragen, übersetzen,* to transfer, to translate: to bear across, to carry over—implying some form of trans*port,* which is again the "same" word: from *portare,* to carry. This is why Freud can say with clinical and etymological accuracy that transference is the *vehicle* of success in psychoanalysis, as it is in any other form of treatment ("The Dynamics of the Transference," published in 1912; XII, 105). This coincidence of clinical principles and etymology is even more striking in German, where Freud uses the word *Trägerin* to describe transference as a vehicle. In its relation to *tragen, Trägerin* can be understood as "carrier"; thus, carrying over (*Übertragung,* transference) is the carrier (*Trägerin,* vehicle) of psychoanalysis. Translation, or rather mistranslation, the inevitable miscontruing that is unconsciously repeated in human relations, is the vehicle that moves analysis.

Second, mistranslation as a means of transport, as a vehicle, is also mechanical, works like a machine. We would have to turn to the entire history of Freud's well-known mechanical metaphors, his search for a way to represent psychic functioning as a machine that runs by itself. In "Freud and the Scene of Writing" Derrida has demonstrated the interdependence of Freud's scriptural and mechanical metaphors. The question of writing (history, hieroglyphs, traces), as we have seen, appears throughout the Leonardo study. What about machines? There is a twofold problematic of machines in the Leonardo study, which we can now bring into conjunction: Leonardo's own explanation of his lifelong preoccupation with building a flying machine via his "memory" and Freud's fleeting reference to the invention of the printing press in the vulture sequence ("Milan was in fact the leading city in Italy for the new art of printing").

The printing press and fetishism as *vehicles* of mistranslation pull together the threads of our argument in an unlikely weave. All the transferences ("carriers") at work in the history of the psychoanalytic movement (here Freud, Jung, Pfister), including Freud's transferential "identification" with Leonardo, which harkens back to his own transference to Fliess (which in turn—), along with Freud's frequent scriptural and mechanical metaphors and the theory of the maternal phallus as an indelible pictographic fantasy, have all been condensed into a mistranslating machine, a machine that began to run by itself in its automatic reproduction of fetishes, in the "debate" over the "vulture" in painting. Can we not take this one step further, and say that the mistranslating machine, in its production of "literature," its reproduction of transferences and fetishes like "printed books," runs psychoanalysis? How else are we to understand the role of transference (mistranslation), as the return of repressed-indelible pictographic fantasies (mistranslations) in the history of psychoanalytic theory and technique?

The sketch of the St. Anne with the "vulture" outlined and shaded in remains behind as evidence of the (re)productiveness of *Übertragungen*—transference as mistranslation and mistranslation as transference. We began with Freud's comparisons of psychoanalysis to translation and Derrida's remarks about translation as transformation. I believe that psychoanalytic translation-transformation can be understood in terms of what the mistranslating machine leaves behind, its "vultures," its precious counterfeits. This Derrida calls the "unanalyzed remainder" in a passage that I would like to cite in conclusion:

> Suppose that there is a male or female founder of psychoanalysis, a first analyst. Let us take the name Freud, for the sake of purely provisional convenience, as the index of such a function. Let us pretend that Freud had no analyst, another provisional convenience. . . . Suppose now that this founder, the so called institutor of the analytic movement, needed a supplementary "piece" [*tranche*] of analysis. . . .
> Then this unanalyzed remainder which in the last analysis relates the analytic movement to its absolute exterior will not play the role of a border, will not have the form of a limit *surrounding* the psychoanalytic, that to which the psychoanalytic, as theory and practice, would alas have had no access, as if it still had ground to gain. Not at all. This unanalyzed will be, will have been, that upon which and surrounding which the analytic movement will have been constructed and mobilized: everything will have been constructed and calculated so that this unanalyzed may be inherited, protected, transmitted intact, suitably bequeathed, consolidated, encysted, encrypted. This is what structures the movement and its architecture.
> Given these conditions, the decrypting can no longer come from the simple and alleged interior of what is still provisionally called psychoanalysis.[30]

Nor will it come from the simple and alleged exterior of psychoanalysis, given that the mistranslating machine leaves behind an unanalyzed remainder, a fetishized fetish, that is indistinguisha-

---

[30]"Du tout," in *La carte postale—De Socrate à Freud et au-delà* (Paris: Flammarion, 1980), 547.

bly transference-translation, which is the vehicle of psychoanalysis—the flying-writing-machine skywriting the "remarkable history" of the "singular error" that "has passed" (almost)
"unnoticed and unquestioned" ("inherited, protected, transmitted intact") "from translator to translator."

5

Taking Fidelity Philosophically

BARBARA JOHNSON

While the value of the notion of fidelity is at an all-time high in
the audiovisual media, its stocks are considerably lower in the
domains of marital mores and theories of translation. It almost
seems as though the stereo, the Betamax, and the Xerox have
taken over the duty of faithfulness in reproduction, leaving the
texts and the sexes with nothing to do but disseminate. This is
perhaps the inevitable result of the intersection between contemporary psychoanalytical, Marxist, and philosophical critiques
of consciousness, on the one hand, and modern technology, on
the other. When computers, automated assembly lines, and
photocopiers advantageously replace human memories and
hands, and when language, ideology, and the unconscious are
aptly compared to machines of which we are the puppets, it is
difficult to know what to do with that defensive excrescence
called consciousness. From that point of view, the crisis in marriage and the crisis in translation are identical. For while both
translators and spouses were once bound by contracts to love,
honor, and obey, and while both inevitably betray, the current
questioning of the possibility and desirability of conscious mas-
tery makes that contract seem deluded and exploitative from the

start. But what are the alternatives? Is it possible simply to renounce the meaning of promises or the promise of meaning?

Fortunately, I must address translation, not matrimony. Yet the analogy between the two is extremely far-reaching. It might, however, seem that the translator ought, despite or perhaps because of his or her oath of fidelity, to be considered not as a duteous spouse but as a faithful bigamist, with loyalties split between a native language and a foreign tongue. Each must accommodate the requirements of the other without their ever having the opportunity to meet. The bigamist is thus necessarily doubly unfaithful, but in such a way that he or she must push to its utmost limit the very capacity for faithfulness. Yet in the realm of translation, it is precisely today that, paradoxically enough, at the moment when the strictures of this double alliance are being made rigorously explicit, the notion of fidelity itself is being put in question. Both these movements come to a large extent from the work of Jacques Derrida, about whose relation to translation I would like now to make a few brief remarks.

It seems, in retrospect, as though literary criticism in the United States had long been on the lookout for someone to be unfaithful with. All signs seem to indicate that, in some strata, it has chosen Derrida, perhaps because he is such a good letter writer. Yet paradoxically enough, what seems to be happening to the seductive foreignness of Derrida's thought in this country is that it begins, as Rodolphe Gasché has recently pointed out,[1] to bear an uncanny resemblance to our own home-grown New Criticism. It is as though, through our excursion into the exotic, we had suddenly come to remember what it was that appealed to us in what we were being unfaithful to. This transferential bigamy or double infidelity thus indicates that it is not bigamy but rather incest that is at stake in the enterprise of translation. Through the foreign language we renew our love-hate intimacy with our mother tongue. We tear at her syntactic joints and semantic flesh

[1] Rodolphe Gasché, "Deconstruction as Criticism," *Glyph* 6 (1979), 177–215.

and resent her for not providing all the words we need. In translation, the everyday frustrations of writing assume an explicit, externally projected form. If we are impotent, it is because Mother is inadequate. In the process of translation from one language to another, the scene of linguistic castration—which is nothing other than a scene of impossible but unavoidable translation and normally takes place out of sight, behind the conscious stage—is played on center stage, evoking fear and pity and the illusion that all would perhaps have been well if we could simply have stayed at home.

But it is the impossibility of staying home with the mother tongue that is precisely at the core of the philosophy of Jacques Derrida. For Derrida's work, in fact, has always already been (about) translation. His first book was a translation of Husserl's "Origin of Geometry." Derrida's theory and practice of *écriture,* indeed, occupy the very point at which philosophy and translation meet. To gauge the extent of Derrida's subversive intervention in the history of philosophy, let us first quote from a translator's note that typifies the classical attitude toward the relations between philosophy and translation. The note introduces an English edition of Hegel's *Encyclopedia:*

To translate the world's worst stylist literally, sentence by sentence, is possible—it has been done—but it is perfectly pointless; the translation, then, is every bit as unintelligible as the original. But the world's worst stylist is, alas, also one of the world's greatest thinkers, certainly the most important for us in this twentieth century. In the whole history of philosophy there is no other single work which could hold a candle to his *Logic;* a work incomparable in its range, depth, clarity of thought, and beauty of composition—but it must be decoded.

The attempt must be risked, therefore, to rescue its grandeur from its abstruse linguistic chaos. . . . This is like detective work: what Hegel means, but hides under a dead heap of abstractions, must be guessed at and ferreted out. I have dared to translate—not the ponderous Hegelian jargon, which is as little German as it would be English—but the thought. My "translation," then, is a critical presentation or rendition; it is not a book about Hegel because it faithfully follows the order and sequence of his paragraphs.[2]

Presiding over classical notions of philosophy and translation are thus the separability of style and thought and the priority of the signified over the signifier, whose only legitimate role is to create order and sequence. Faithfulness to the text has meant faithfulness to the semantic tenor with as little interference as possible from the constraints of the vehicle. Translation, in other words, has always been the translation of *meaning*.

Derrida's rearticulation of philosophy and translation is obviously not designed to evacuate meaning entirely. But his concept of textuality displaces the very notion of *how* a text means. What goes on in every text far exceeds what can be reduced to so-and-so's "thought." Derrida's own ingenious translations, such as that of Hegel's *Aufhebung* by *la relève,* are attempts to render all the often contradictory meanings of a term in such a way that crucial logical complexities are not oversimplified. It is quite often by finding the pressure points previously lost in translation that Derrida rearticulates philosophy with itself. The most striking example is the Platonic word *Pharmakon*, which can mean both "poison" and "remedy" and thus makes problematic any statement in which it occurs. Previous translators had chosen to render one side or the other of its ambivalence at a time, thus deciding what in Plato remains undecidable. I quote from my own translation of Derrida's remarks in *La dissémination:*

> In our discussion of this text we have been using an authoritative French translation of Plato, the one published by Guillaume Budé. In the case of the *Phaedrus*, the translation is by Léon Robin. We will continue to refer to it, inserting the Greek text in parentheses, however, whenever it seems opportune or pertinent to our point. Hence, for example, the word *pharmakon*. In this way we hope to display in the most striking manner the regular,

[2]*Hegel's Encyclopedia of Philosophy*, trans. and annot. Gustav Emil Mueller (New York: Philosophical Library, 1959), 1.

ordered polysemy that has, through skewing, indetermination, or overdetermination, but without mistranslation, permitted the rendering of the same work by "remedy," "recipe," "poison," "drug," "philter," etc. It will also be seen to what extent the malleable unity of this concept, or rather its rules and the strange logic that links it with its signifier, has been dispersed, masked, obliterated, and rendered almost unreadable not only by the imprudence or empiricism of the translators, but first and foremost by the redoubtable, irreducible difficulty of translation. It is a difficulty inherent in its very principle, situated less in the passage from one language to another, from one philosophical language to another, than already, as we shall see, in the tradition between Greek and Greek; a violent difficulty in the transference of a non-philosopheme into a philosopheme. With this problem of translation we will thus be dealing with nothing less than the problem of the very passage into philosophy.[3]

It is thus precisely the way in which the original text is always already an impossible translation that renders translation impossible. Interestingly, the passage I have just quoted, in making explicit the problem of translation, presents an insoluble dilemma to the English translator. Since its point hangs on a French translation to which the English no longer directly refers, the translator must either transpose the point onto English translations—which, incidentally, bear it out equally well—thus fictively usurping the status of original author, or retain the reference to French, thus fictively returning to the original language. This difficulty, indeed, perfectly illustrates the point it conveys: the more a text is worked through by the problem of translation, the more untranslatable it becomes.

Derrida's entire philosophic enterprise, indeed, can be seen as an analysis of the translation process at work in every text. In studying the *différance* of signification, Derrida follows the misfires, losses, and infelicities that prevent any given language from being *one*. Language, in fact, can only exist in the space of its own foreignness to itself. But all of Western philosophy has

---

[3]Jacques Derrida, *Dissemination*, trans. Barbara Johnson (Chicago: University of Chicago Press, 1981), 71–72.

had as its aim to repress that foreignness, to take a text that is "as little German as it would be English" and to make it into the transparent expression of a great philosophic thought. Not only, however, is this self-différance the *object* of Derrida's attention: it is an integral part of the functioning of his own écriture. The challenges to translation presented by Derrida's writing have continually multiplied over the years. From the early, well-bred neologisms to a syntax that increasingly frustrates the desire for unified meaning, Derrida has even, in *Living On*[4]—first published in English—gone so far as to write *to* the translator *about* the difficulties he is in the act of creating for him, thus figuratively sticking out his tongue—his mother tongue—at the borderline between the translated text and the original.

It is thus a greatly overdetermined paradox that the translation of Derrida's writings should have become such a thriving industry in the United States today. The translator faces the impossibility and the necessity of translation on four fronts: within the text Derrida is reading; within what Derrida says about it; within the way Derrida says it; and within the very notion of translation that all of these areas imply. Indeed, the radicality of the revolution in the relations between signifiers and signifieds makes the project of separating these four fronts impossible. Yet the violence implied by classical faithfulness to the spirit at the expense of the letter cannot be avoided by simple faithfulness to the letter of any text. For it is necessary to be faithful to the violent love-hate relation *between* letter and spirit, which is already a problem of translation within the *original* text. If the original text is already a translatory battle in which what is being translated is ultimately the very impossibility of translation, then peacemaking gestures such as scrupulous adherence to the signifier are just as unfaithful to the energy of the conflict as the tyranny of the swell-footed signified. The translator must fight just as hard against the desire to be innocent as against what we today consider the guilty desire to master the text's message. It is, indeed,

[4]Jacques Derrida, "Living On," in *Deconstruction and Criticism* (New York: Seabury Press, 1979).

at the moment of translation that the textual battle comes into its own. Translation is a bridge that creates out of itself the two fields of battle it separates. Heidegger could have been talking about translation when he wrote of the bridge:

> It does not just connect banks that are already there. The banks emerge as banks only as the bridge crosses the stream. The bridge designedly causes them to lie across from each other. One side is set off against the other by the bridge. Nor do the banks stretch along the stream as indifferent border strips of dry land. With the banks, the bridge brings to the stream the one and the other expanse of the landscape lying behind them. It brings stream and bank and land into each other's neighborhood.[5]

The bridge of translation, which paradoxically releases within each text the subversive forces of its own foreignness, thus re-inscribes those forces in the tensile strength of a new neighborhood of otherness. Yet all travelers on that bridge are answering a summons that repulses them at every step, a summons reminiscent of the sign Lautréamont sets up in front of Maldoror, containing a warning that is received just a moment too late to be heeded: "Vous, qui passez sur ce pont, n'y allez pas." "You who are crossing over this bridge, don't get to the other side."

[5]Martin Heidegger, "Building Dwelling Thinking," in *Poetry, Language, Thought,* trans. Albert Hofstadter (New York: Harper and Row, 1971), 152.

6

What Did Archimedes Mean by 'χρυσός'?

ROBERT J. MATTHEWS

The traditional requirement that adequate translations be mean-ing-preserving has exercised a profound effect upon philosoph-ical theories of meaning. Determinacy of translation would seem to require determinacy of meaning, for otherwise there fails to be a determinate meaning that is either preserved or lost in translation. Our apparent ability to distinguish better and worse translations seemingly endorses traditional theories according to which meanings are not simply determinate but also "present to mind" in the sense of being known to speakers of a language. For if meanings are not present to mind, how could we know whether translations satisfied the requirement that they pre-serve meaning? According to some critics of traditional theories of meaning, the notion of translation is so inextricably bound to the fortunes of these theories, and in particular to the assump-tions of determinacy and presence to mind, as to require its abandonment. Jacques Derrida puts the matter this way in his *Positions:*

> Within the limits of its possibility, or its *apparent* possibility, translation practices the difference between signified and sig-

149

nifier. But, if this difference is never pure, translation is even less so, and a notion of *transformation* must be substituted for the notion of translation: a regulated transformation of one language by another, of one text by another. We shall not have and never have had to deal with some "transfer" of pure signifieds that the signifying instrument—or "vehicle"—would leave virgin and intact.[1]

What is surprising here is not the criticism of the traditional notion that translation is a matter of transferring a determinate semantic cargo from one phonetic vehicle to another but rather the suggestion that the notion of translation must be replaced by one of transformation. The suggestion is surprising because the notion of transformation carries with it precisely the same suggestions of determinacy and presence to mind. More surprising still is Derrida's suggestion that the inevitable intercourse between signifier and signified impugns the very possibility of translation. Derrida apparently believes it to be necessarily true that translation is an affair in which pure signifieds are transferred from one signifier to another, so that if what we take to be translation is not an affair of transference, there is, strictly speaking, no translation. But how can he know this to be so unless the meaning of the term 'translation' is itself determinate and furthermore present to mind?

A similar question can be put to Hilary Putnam, who in the course of setting out and defending an influential account of the meaning of natural kind terms claims that Archimedes meant by 'χρυσός' what we mean by 'gold'.[2] It is surprising that Putnam would make such a claim, since on his account it is very probable, inductively speaking, that we do not know what is meant by the word 'gold'. Indeed, it is very probable that we do not know

---

[1]*Positions* (Paris, 1972), 31. (The translation is from Gayatri Spivak's preface to her translation in Derrida's *Of Grammatology* [Baltimore: The Johns Hopkins University Press, 1976], lxxxvii.)

[2]"The Meaning of 'Meaning'," in his *Mind, Language, and Reality* (Cambridge: Cambridge University Press, 1975), 215–71.

the meaning of many words in our language. Meanings, according to Putnam, are simply not present to mind. Yet, surely, if we do not know the meaning of our own word 'gold', then we can hardly know, or properly claim to know, that Archimedes meant by 'χρυσός' what we mean by 'gold'. So how can Putnam possibly claim to know this fact about Archimedes?

Whether it is Derrida's concern with the notion of translation or Putnam's concern with the translation of Archimedes' term 'χρυσός', the problem is the same: how can we abandon the traditional assumptions that meanings are determinate and furthermore present to mind without thereby impugning the very possibility of translation? I shall attempt to explain, or at least explore, this point in the following pages. More specifically, I shall attempt to explain why translation has little, if anything, to do with meaning, at least as it is traditionally conceived. This explanation should be of interest to those who endorse Derrida's criticism of traditional theories of translation but nevertheless believe in the possibility of translation, since the assumption that there is an intimate relation between meaning and translation apparently underlies his doubts about the possibility of translation.

My reason for raising these questions about meaning and translation is in part to provide a pretext for discussion of an issue more germane to the focus of the present conference volume, namely the reception of Derrida's work in this country. The simple fact is that Derrida is largely ignored by American philosophers, much to the consternation of purveyors of contemporary French culture. Why in American translation he should suffer this fate is no doubt a question for the sociology of ideas, but it is equally a question regarding certain fundamental differences among the diverse enterprises that are commonly collected under the rubric of 'philosophy'. Attention to questions regarding meaning and translation may shed light on differences between French and American philosophy that help to explain Derrida's fate in translation.

1

Consider the following question: How can we know that someone means by 'gold' what we mean by 'gold'? Or more generally,
how can we know that he means what we mean by our terms?
The fact that we share the same vocabulary hardly decides the
question, as any amateur cryptographer would be quick to point
out. A crucial consideration would seem to be this: if the individual means what we mean, then a homophonic translation of
his utterances should lead to successful prediction of his behavior. Utterances that under the homophonic translation appear to
express beliefs about what we call 'gold', for example, should
figure appropriately in predictions of behavior that would presumably be predicated on those beliefs. If the homophonic translation leads to such predictive success, then by something akin to
Peircean abduction (that is, an inference to the best explanation),
we can conclude that this person means what we do by our
terms. We can claim to know this fact with no less confidence
than we can claim to know the results of other sorts of empirical
theorizing.

Because the choice of translation scheme depends crucially on
assumptions regarding the psychology of the person whose utterances we are attempting to translate, and not simply on observations of his behavior, we will typically have to raise questions
both about the appropriate translation of his utterances and
about the appropriate characterization of his beliefs, intentions,
and desires. In cases where our predictions fail, there will arise
the obvious difficulty of apportioning responsibility for this
failure between our psychological characterization of the individual, on the one hand, and our translation scheme, on the
other. If, for example, we translate a person's utterance as an
assertion to the effect that it is raining outside, but then see this
person intentionally leave behind both raincoat and umbrella, it
will not be possible in the absence of further evidence to decide
whether the translation is mistaken; perhaps this person has
peculiar beliefs and desires. Some philosophers have concluded

from such cases that translation is indeterminate; behavioral evidence is said to underdetermine the choice of psychological characterization and translation scheme so severely as to make it impossible to apportion responsibility between the two in any determinate fashion. For any proposed characterization-scheme pair there supposedly exists an alternative pair that will predict the observed behavior with equal accuracy. That there is often fairly wide agreement on the appropriate translation of a given set of utterances is said to reflect the workings of convention.

Yet claims of this sort notwithstanding, it is simply false that we are unable to bring behavioral evidence to bear on questions of translation independently of questions of belief, intention, and desire. We are able to do so because we can often develop a reasonably good psychological characterization of an individual independently of any understanding of his utterances. If such a characterization were not possible, translators would have no idea where to begin in their attempts to translate utterances from an unkown language, nor could we ever recognize a case in which actions belied a person's words. I do not deny that available behavioral evidence underdetermines the choice between alternative pairs of psychological characterization and translation scheme; however, the degree of underdetermination need not be any greater here than elsewhere in the empirical sciences. Knowledge claims regarding translations need be no less well founded than knowledge claims about other sorts of empirical matters. Of course, in point of fact the evidential underdetermination in matters of translation is typically greater than elsewhere, which explains the need for a rhetoric rather than a logic of translation.

From the perspective of the translator, translation is clearly determinate: relevant behavioral evidence, if available to the translator, would uniquely determine his choice of translation scheme for a set of utterances. Whether translation is determinate in some absolute, metaphysical sense would seem to depend on the existence of a uniquely correct psychological theory, inasmuch as the choice of a characterization-scheme pair is dictated not simply by behavioral evidence but also by the prevailing psychological theory in terms of which this evidence is interpreted. Whether in fact there is a uniquely correct psychological theory depends on the truth of realist claims about convergence in science, and in particular in psychology. But given the apparent interest relativity of existing psychological theory as well as the generally acknowledged untenability of psychophysical reductionism,[3] I am rather skeptical of the claim that there is such a theory. Thus, I suspect that translation is determinate only relative to a given psychological theory, so that while for any translator (or group of translators sharing a single psychological theory) there is a uniquely correct translation scheme for any given set of utterances, there is no absolutely correct scheme. I do not mean that in matters of translation anything goes: the choice of translation scheme must still accord with available evidence. Nor are we deluded in thinking that we can distinguish better translations from worse, correct translations from incorrect. It is just that correctness in these matters is a local, theory-relative notion. Of course, this locale may be quite large if there happens to be widespread acceptance of a single psychological theory. (Perhaps another way of putting the point would be to say that the notion of correctness is *internal* to the actual practice of translation.)

2

Sameness of meaning in the sense of sameness of extension is often taken to be a necessary, if not sufficient, condition for the intertranslatability of terms. And properly so, it would seem, for if you and I mean different kinds of things by the word 'gold', for example, then my word is not intertranslatable with yours. More generally, determinacy of translation is presumed to entail de-

---

[3]For a discussion of the interest relativity of psychological explanation, see Putnam, *Meaning and the Moral Sciences* (London: Routledge and Kegan Paul, 1978), esp. lecture 4.

terminacy of meaning, since otherwise the requirement that intertranslatable terms be coextensive would seemingly find no
application. Yet, if, as I have argued, the choice of translation
scheme turns on features of the *use* of the terms to be translated
rather than on their meaning, then this presumption may well be
mistaken. Translation may be determinate, at least in the local,
theory-relative sense, even if meaning is not. That this seems in
fact to be the case can be seen by examining Putnam's criticism
of and proposed alternative to traditional theories of meaning.

Traditional theories of meaning rest on two basic assumptions:
(1) that knowing the meaning of a term is just a matter of being in
a certain psychological state (where 'psychological state' is construed narrowly so as not to presuppose the existence of any
individual other than the subject to whom that state is ascribed);
and (2) that the meaning of a term determines its extension (in
the sense that sameness of intension entails sameness of extension).[4] Putnam's argument against theories incorporating these
assumptions involves showing that it is possible for two speakers
to be in exactly the same psychological state yet for the extension
of a term in the idiolect of one speaker to be different from the
extension of that same term in the idiolect of the other.[5] Putnam
asks us, for example, to perform the following thought experiment: suppose that there is a place, call it 'Twin-Earth', which is
indistinguishable from Earth except that what Twin-Earthians
(including our Doppelgängers) call 'water' is some complicated
chemical compound XYZ rather than H_2O. Putnam contends,
correctly I believe, that we would not translate their term 'water'
by our own term 'water', for (by hypothesis) these two terms do
not mean the same kind of thing. Yet clearly we and our Doppelgängers have the very same beliefs (narrowly construed) regarding what we respectively call 'water'; we are psychologically

---

[4]"The Meaning of 'Meaning'," 219.

[5]Putnam's argument applies equally well to both Platonist and "psychol-
ogistic" versions of traditional theories of meaning; Frege's and Husserl's accounts of meanings as abstract entities that are intuited or perceived by an act of
mind are equally committed to the assumptions that Putnam criticizes.

indistinguishable, yet we mean different things by our words. This difference of meaning (that is, extension) would be reflected in our choice of translation scheme.

The examples that Putnam adduces evidence the indexical character of so-called natural kind terms in our language: the extension of these terms depends crucially on features of the contexts or environments in which they are used. 'Gold', for example, refers to anything relevantly similar to our recognized paradigms of gold. The theory dependency of the extension of these terms is to be discovered in the a posteriori specification of what counts as the relevant similarities that instances must bear to the paradigms (and the paradigms to each other). For example, our best theory of the microstructural properties of paradigmatic examples of gold determines what are to count as the relevant similarities.

It is the a posteriori character of the specification of extension that leads Putnam to his realist construal of natural kind terms: it is, he says, the actual nature of things rather than our concepts that determine the extensions of our terms. Or, to put it another way, what we mean by our words depends on the way the world is. Yet this way of putting the matter is misleading, because it suggests that Putnam's account is applicable only to terms that have determinate extensions fixed by Nature. In fact the account need not presume determinacy of extension. If we are interested in theorizing about certain entities, and if part of the interest of the theory is to specify the class of entities in question, then we do not want this specification to be tied to any particular theory, much less to the criteria that serve initially to pick out in rough fashion the entities about which we wish to theorize. Rather we will take any particular theory (or set of criteria for the use of the term in question) to provide only a *provisional* specification of the class of entities in question, one that is always open to rational revision. Realist talk to the effect that through empirical research we can come to know the true extensions of natural kind terms expresses our willingness to revise our theories and beliefs about their extensions. Claims to the effect that Nature determines the extensions of these terms reflects the crucial role of experiment and observation in science: predictive failures provide the principle rationale for revising our specification of their extensions.

Once we recognize the import of Putnam's realist construal of natural kind terms, we are led to consider the possibility that there are terms that differ from natural kind terms only in the *sort* of reasons that will occasion revision of our theories and beliefs as to their extensions. There will surely be many such terms, since there are many circumstances in which for one reason or another we consider it important that we come to agree both on the precise extension of a term and on the important properties of the entities included within that extension. Thus, for example, it is important to viewers of contemporary art that they agree on what is art, both in the sense of the extension of the term 'art' and in the sense of the important properties of artworks. In such cases as these, especially when there is sharp disagreement, indexical terms of the sort exemplified by natural kind terms can provide a form of expression that permits us to refer to the objects of our disagreement in a way that makes reasoned argument possible. So long as there is agreement as to the paradigms, discussion can proceed. The use of indexical terms does not presuppose that these terms have a determinate extension; nor does it presuppose that we can reach agreement on what we will accept as the extension of these terms. There need not be convergence of any sort. Rather their use presumes only that the discussants consider agreement on the issues sufficiently important to warrant use of a form of expression that will facilitate the collective search for agreement, even if such agreement may never be forthcoming.[6]

[6]For a further elaboration of these points, see my "traditional Aesthetics Defended," *Journal of Aesthetics and Art Criticism* 38 (1979), 39–50, and "Literary Works and Institutional Practices," *British Journal of Aesthetics* 21 (1981), 39–49.

3

Putnam could have abandoned the traditional assumption according to which meanings are determinate while nonetheless preserving determinacy of translation. The reason that he does not abandon this assumption has to do not with the matter of translation but rather with the 'picture' of science that he wishes to preserve. Putnam regards Archimedes' theory of χρυσός and our theory of gold as "two approximately correct descriptions of some fixed realm of theory-independent entities. . . . our theory is a *better* description of the *same* entities that Archimedes was describing."[7] In construing the differences in our respective uses of 'χρυσός' and 'gold' as reflecting differences of belief about one and the same set of theory-independent entities, Putnam chooses to view Archimedes as sharing with us certain interests, concerns, and purposes that we believe to be important. Archimedes could have been brought to abandon certain of his mistaken beliefs about these entities; he could have been brought to recognize our theory of gold as an improvement over his own. Such confidence would hardly be warranted if one believed that we meant different things by our terms. Putnam's talk of the eventual convergence of our theories on the correct description of this realm of entities underscores the notion that we are engaged in a common intellectual enterprise, one that he is confident will prove successful. There is, to put it simply, an entire picture of this history of science contained in Putnam's claim that Archimedes meant by 'χρυσός' what we mean by 'gold'. This picture is made possible by Putnam's account of meaning according to which the meaning of a term is determinate though not present to mind. Without the assumption of determinacy, such a picture would not be possible, because no sense could be made of the claim that Archimedes and contemporary researchers were theorizing about the same thing. Our theoretical endeavors would lack a history; there would be no

---

[7]"The Meaning of 'Meaning'," 236.

room for notions of progress or improvement. We would not be better than our forefathers, simply different from them. There could, in Putnam's words, be no convergence.

4

Traditional theories of meaning fail to recognize the need for, indeed the possibility of, terms whose extensions are fixed only provisionally by their associated concepts (or intensions). Putnam's account of natural kind terms represents an important, though regrettably incomplete break with traditional theories. He insists on the provisional character of any particular theory as to what falls within the extension of such terms, but he then goes on to reinstate the traditional assumption that terms have determinate extensions. Our provisional theories are said to be converging on some ideal theory that does in fact correctly specify the extensions of natural kind terms. Putnam does not therefore abandon the traditional notion that meanings are both determinate and furthermore present to mind as much as he *displaces* the moment of presence to the end of science. The epistemological import of this displacement should be clear: traditional epistemology, which is wedded to these assumptions about meaning, is not thereby abandoned; rather the task of epistemology is now to demonstrate the possibility of knowledge-in-the-limit. For knowledge would now seem to be the potential possession of a completed science rather than of existing individuals.

Derrida's discussion of Walter Benjamin's essay "The Task of the Translator" is fortunate, for there is a striking affinity between Putnam's account of meaning and Benjamin's account of translation. Benjamin rejects traditional theories according to which translation is a matter of conveying or transmitting meaning from one language to another. He rejects these theories, because for him, as for Putnam, meanings are not present to mind. Rather their moment of presence is displaced into the future: "In the individual, unsupplemented languages, meaning is never found in relative independence, as in individual words or sentences; rather it is in a constant state of flux—until it is able to emerge as pure language from the harmony of all the various modes of intention. Until then, it remains hidden in the languages."[8] The translator is for Benjamin what the natural scientist is for Putnam, namely, the means or agency by which this pure language of meaning will be realized: in translating works from one language to another the translator transforms the individual, unsupplemented languages, progressively releasing or liberating fragments of the pure language which, according to Benjamin, is intended (or aimed at) by each individual language. Like Putnam, Benjamin insists on the provisional character of attempts to reveal the meaning hidden in these unsupplemented languages; and like Putnam, he also expresses confidence in an eventual convergence on what he describes as "the predestined, hitherto inaccessible realm of reconciliation and fulfillment of languages."[9]

There are, to be sure, certain differences: Putnam envisions convergence on the correct description of some fixed realm of theory-independent entities in terms of a series of increasingly accurate approximations. For Benjamin, on the other hand, convergence is achieved through supplementation rather than refinement: "A translation . . . must lovingly and in detail incorporate the original's mode of signification, thus making both the original and the translation recognizable as fragments of a greater language."[10] Moreover, there is an aspect of *recovery* present in Benjamin's account but not in Putnam's. Yet these differences should not be overestimated: both are committed to essentially eschatological accounts of meaning and translation that preserve determinacy of meaning while displacing the moment of presence of meaning into the future. Benjamin acknowledges this displacement in a way that reveals clearly the epistemological

[8]"The Task of the Translator," in his *Illuminations* (New York: Harcourt Brace Jovanovich, 1968), 74.

[9]Ibid., p. 75.

[10]Ibid., p. 78.

motive that underlies their respective accounts: "If there is such a thing as a language of truth, the tensionless and even silent depository of the ultimate truth which all thought strives for, then this language of truth is—the true language. And this very language, whose divination and description is the only perfection a philosopher can hope for, is concealed in concentrated fashion in translations."[11] Given the failures of traditional epistemology, Benjamin is surely right: this is the only perfection the modern epistemologist can hope for; present perfections have proven chimerical. Epistemology must now be practiced in the limit, if it is to be practiced at all; for given that the meanings of our words are arguably not present to mind but rather displaced into the future, the justification of knowledge claims that incorporate these words must be similarly displaced into the future.

5

When Derrida suggests that the notion of translation must be replaced by one of transformation, he must intend to draw our critical attention to influential theories of translation that have presumably drawn their inspiration from the etymological roots of the term 'translation'. The fact that we can imagine discovering that translation is *not* an affair of transference, as surely it is not, testifies to the revisability of our conception of translation; it is not necessarily true, as Derrida seems to suggest, that translation is an affair in which pure signifieds are transferred from one signifier to another. What is jeopardized by Derrida's observation is not the notion of translation but rather these traditional theories of translation. For the meaning of the term 'translation' is secured by (and to) the various paradigm examples of translation, not by its Latin etymon.

The attractiveness of these traditional theories is to be located in the prominent *criterial* role that they accord to meaning; they

[11]Ibid., p. 77.

foster the illusion that putative translations are assessed by ascertaining the degree to which they preserve something called 'meaning'. In point of fact, it is translatability that is a criterion of synonymy: meaning, almost by definition, is what good translations preserve. The desire to cast meaning in a criterial role for translation is motivated primarily by epistemological considerations. The traditional assumptions that meanings are both determinate and present to mind, when coupled with the notion that translations preserve meaning, provide an often-used strategy for epistemological justifications. The strategy is this: one justifies knowledge claims couched in a language L_1 by showing that these claims can be translated by claims in a second language L_2 that are presumably more easily justified, if not simply self-justifying. The success of this strategy requires the existence of a translation scheme that preserves under translation the supposedly determinate content (or meaning) of the knowledge claims couched in L_1. The strategy further requires that the author of these knowledge claims possess the translation scheme, thereby ensuring that this person is justified (and not merely correct) in his claims. The recourse to meaning plays a crucial role here: the meaning of knowledge claims couched in L_1 is analyzed in terms of statements in L_2, and the author of claims in L_1 is presumed to know this analysis in virtue of having learned L_1. To know the meaning of claims in L_1, it turns out, is just to possess (in the relevant sense) the translation scheme in question.

It would be difficult to exaggerate the prominence that the strategy described above has enjoyed in modern philosophy. Indeed, the history of modern philosophy could well be described as one of repeated attempts to employ one or another version of the strategy in an epistemological justification of modern science. These attempts received added impetus at the beginning of this century from the development of formal logic. The newly available logical tools seemed to promise a quick conclusion to the epistemological program outlined by Descartes, Locke, and other seventeenth-century philosophers of science. Unexpectedly, however, logical empiricist attempts to provide a "criterion for empirical (or cognitive) significance" soon ran into problems that, depending on the observer's perspective, either betoken the eventual failure of the program or show the technical difficulties to be more formidable than was first imagined. The history of modern Anglo-American analytic philosophy since the appearance of Carnap's *Der logische Aufbau der Welt* (1928) has been one of the progressive retrenchment of the epistemological program in the face of criticism to the effect that even substantially weakened versions of the strategy described above are untenable. Attempts to translate the theoretical claims of physics and other sciences into a phenomenal (or even observational) language have been largely abandoned in favor of much weaker reductionist goals.[12]

An obvious consequence of the continuing preoccupation with these epistemological issues has been a lively interest in the notions of meaning, synonymy, translation, and so on, that underpin the epistemological program. For these notions will require careful investigation if we are to determine the feasibility of this program. The relative neglect that Derrida's work has suffered in the hands (or bookshelves) of American philosophers is to be explained in part by his seeming disinterest in the epistemological questions that are so central to the Anglo-American tradition. To be sure, Derrida's work exhibits a strong interest in notions of meaning, translation, and the like; however, the interest does not seem epistemological. Unlike Putnam's work on natural kind terms, Derrida's does not seem to grow out of an antecedent interest in traditional epistemological questions. There has, of course, been a determined effort on the part of some writers, notably Richard Rorty, to find in Derrida's work a developed view on these questions. In the hands of such people Derrida turns out to be an American pragmatist *dépaysé!* These attempts to situate Derrida within our own epistemological tradition are rather strained, for they trade largely on the fact that

---

[12]For a comprehensive account of these developments, see Frederick Suppe's critical introduction to his book *The Structure of Scientific Theories* (Urbana: University of Illinois Press, 1977), 1–232.

Derrida occupies a critical position within his own philosophical tradition analogous to the one that these neopragmatists would claim to occupy within their own epistemological tradition. Yet this is hardly sufficient to make of Derrida a pragmatist of any sort. Better we should simply admit that *la philosophie,* even in translation, is not philosophy, which is not to say that each tradition may not profit from a greater familiarity with the other.

7

Des Tours de Babel

Translated by Joseph F. Graham

"Babel": first a proper name, granted. But when we say "Babel" today, do we know what we are naming? Do we know whom? If we consider the sur-vival of a text that is a legacy, the narrative or the myth of the tower of Babel, it does not constitute just one figure among others. Telling at least of the inadequation of one tongue to another, of one place in the encyclopedia to another, of language to itself and to meaning, and so forth, it also tells of the need for figuration, for myth, for tropes, for twists and turns, for translation inadequate to compensate for that which multiplicity denies us. In this sense it would be the myth of the origin of myth, the metaphor of metaphor, the narrative of narrative, the translation of translation, and so on. It would not be the only structure hollowing itself out like that, but it would do so in its own way (itself *almost* untranslatable, like a proper name), and its idiom would have to be saved.

The "tower of Babel" does not merely figure the irreducible multiplicity of tongues; it exhibits an incompletion, the impossibility of finishing, of totalizing, of saturating, of completing something on the order of edification, architectural construction, system and architectonics. What the multiplicity of idioms actu-

165

ally limits is not only a "true" translation, a transparent and adequate interexpression, it is also a structural order, a coherence of construct. There is then (let us translate) something like an internal limit to formalization, an incompleteness of the constructure. It would be easy and up to a certain point justified to see there the translation of a system in deconstruction.

One should never pass over in silence the question of the tongue in which the question of the tongue is raised and into which a discourse on translation is translated.

First: in what tongue was the tower of Babel constructed and deconstructed? In a tongue within which the proper name of Babel could also, by confusion, be translated by "confusion." The proper name Babel, as a proper name, should remain untranslatable, but, by a kind of associative confusion that a unique tongue rendered possible, one thought it translated in that very tongue, by a common noun signifying what *we* translate as confusion. Voltaire showed his astonishment in his *Dictionnaire philosophique*, at the *Babel* article:

> I do not know why it is said in *Genesis* that Babel signifies confusion, for *Ba* signifies father in the Oriental tongues, and *Bel* signifies God; Babel signifies the city of God, the holy city. The Ancients gave this name to all their capitals. But it is incontestable that Babel means confusion, either because the architects were confounded after having raised their work up to eighty-one thousand Jewish feet, or because the tongues were then confounded; and it is obviously from that time on that the Germans no longer understand the Chinese; for it is clear, according to the scholar Bochart, that Chinese is originally the same tongue as High German.

The calm irony of Voltaire means that Babel means: it is not only a proper name, the reference of a pure signifier to a single being—and for this reason untranslatable—but a common noun related to the generality of a meaning. This common noun means, and means not only confusion, even though "confusion" has at least two meanings, as Voltaire is aware, the confusion of tongues, but also the state of confusion in which the architects find themselves with the structure interrupted, so that a certain confusion has already begun to affect the two meanings of the word "confusion." The signification of "confusion" is confused, at least double. But Voltaire suggests something else again: Babel means not only confusion in the double sense of the word, but also the name of the father, more precisely and more commonly, the name of God as name of father. The city would bear the name of God the father and of the father of the city that is called confusion. God, the God, would have marked with his patronym a communal space, that city where understanding is no longer possible. And understanding is no longer possible when there are only proper names, and understanding is no longer possible when there are no longer proper names. In giving his name, a name of his choice, in giving all names, the father would be at the origin of language, and that power would belong by right to God the father. And the name of God the father would be the name of that origin of tongues. But it is also that God who, in the action of his anger (like the God of Böhme or of Hegel, he who leaves himself, determines himself in his finitude and thus produces history), annuls the gift of tongues, or at least embroils it, sows confusion among his sons, and poisons the present (*Gift*-gift). This is also the origin of tongues, of the multiplicity of idioms, of what in other words are usually called mother tongues. For this entire history deploys filiations, generations and genealogies: all Semitic. Before the deconstruction of Babel, the great Semitic family was establishing its empire, which it wanted universal, and its tongue, which it also attempts to impose on the universe. The moment of this project immediately precedes the deconstruction of the tower. I cite two French translations. The first translator stays away from what one would want to call "literality," in other words, from the Hebrew figure of speech for "tongue," where the second, more concerned about literality (metaphoric, or rather metonymic), says "lip," since in Hebrew "lip" designates what we call, in another metonymy, "tongue." One will have to say multiplicity of lips and not of tongues to name the Babelian confusion. The first translator, then, Louis Segond, author of the Segond Bible, published in 1910, writes this:

> Those are the sons of Sem, according to their families, their tongues, their countries, their nations. Such are the families of the sons of Noah, according to their generations, their nations. And it is from them that emerged the nations which spread over the earth after the flood. All the earth had a single tongue and the same words. As they had left the origin they found a plain in the country of Schinear, and they dwelt there. They said to one another: Come! Let us make bricks, and bake them in the fire. And brick served them as stone, and tar served as cement. Again they said: Come! Let us build ourselves a city and a tower whose summit touches the heavens, and let us make ourselves a name, so that we not be scattered over the face of all the earth.

I do not know just how to interpret this allusion to the substitution or the transmutation of materials, brick becoming stone and tar serving as mortar. That already resembles a translation, a translation of translation. But let us leave it and substitute a second translation for the first. It is that of Chouraqui. It is recent and wants to be more literal, almost *verbum pro verbo*, as Cicero said should not be done in one of those first recommendations to the translator which can be read in his *Libellus de Optimo Genera Oratorum*. Here it is:

> Here are the sons of Shem
> for their clans, for their tongues,
> in their lands, for their peoples.
> Here are the clans of the sons of Noah for their exploits,
> in their peoples:
> from the latter divide the peoples on earth, after the flood.
>
> And it is all the earth: a single lip, one speech.
> And it is at their departure from the Orient: they find a canyon,
> in the land of Shine'ar.
> They settle there.
> They say, each to his like:
> "Come, let us brick some bricks.

> Let us fire them in the fire."
> The brick becomes for them stone, the tar, mortar.
> They say:
> "Come, let us build ourselves a city and a tower.
> Its head: in the heavens.
> Let us make ourselves a name,
> that we not be scattered over the face of all the earth."

What happens to them? In other words, for what does God punish them in giving his name, or rather, since he gives it to nothing and to no one, in proclaiming his name, the proper name of "confusion" which will be his mark and his seal? Does he punish them for having wanted to build as high as the heavens? For having wanted to accede to the highest, up to the Most High? Perhaps for that too, no doubt, but incontestably for having wanted thus to *make a name for themselves,* to give themselves the name, to construct for and by themselves their own name, to gather themselves there ("that we no longer be scattered"), as in the unity of a place which is at once a tongue and a tower, the one as well as the other, the one as the other. He punishes them for having thus wanted to assure themselves, by themselves, a unique and universal genealogy. For the text of Genesis proceeds immediately, as if it were all a matter of the same design: raising a tower, constructing a city, making a name for oneself in a universal tongue which would also be an idiom, and gathering a filiation:

> They say:
> "Come, let us build ourselves a city and a tower.
> Its head: in the heavens.
> Let us make ourselves a name,
> that we not be scattered over the face of all the earth."
>
> YHWH descends to see the city and the tower
> that the sons of man have built.
> YHWH says:
> "Yes! A single people, a single lip for all:
> that is what they begin to do! . . .
> Come! Let us descend! Let us confound their lips,
> man will no longer understand the lip of his neighbor."

Then he disseminates the Sem, and dissemination is here deconstruction:

> YHWH disperses them from here over the face of all the earth.
> They cease to build the city.
> Over which he proclaims his name: Bavel, Confusion,
> for there, YHWH confounds the lip of all the earth,
> and from there YHWH disperses them over the face of all the earth.

Can we not, then, speak of God's jealousy? Out of resentment against that unique name and lip of men, he imposes his name, his name of father; and with this violent imposition he opens the deconstruction of the tower, as of the universal language; he scatters the genealogical filiation. He breaks the lineage. He *at the same time* imposes and forbids translation. He imposes it and forbids it, constrains, but as if to failure, the children who henceforth *will bear* his name, the name that *he* gives to the city. It is from a proper name of God, come from God, descended from God or from the father (and it is indeed said that YHWH, an unpronounceable name, *descends* toward the tower) and by him that tongues are scattered, confounded or multiplied, according to a descendance that in its very dispersion remains sealed by the only name that will have been the strongest, by the only idiom that will have triumphed. Now, this idiom bears within itself the mark of confusion, it improperly means the improper, to wit: Bavel, confusion. Translation then becomes necessary and impossible, like the effect of a struggle for the appropriation of the name, necessary and forbidden in the interval between two absolutely proper names. And the proper name of God (given by God) is divided enough in the tongue, already, to signify also, confusedly, "confusion." And the war that he declares has first raged within his name: divided, bifid, ambivalent, polysemic: God deconstructing. "And he war," one reads in *Finnegans Wake*, and we could follow this whole story from the side of Shem and Shaun. The "he war" does not only, in this place, tie together an incalculable number of phonic and semantic threads, in the immediate context and throughout this

Babelian book; it says the declaration of war (in English) of the
One who says I am the one who am, and who thus was (*war*); it
renders itself untranslatable in its very performance, *at least in
the fact* that it is enunciated in more than one language at a time,
at least English and German. If even an infinite translation exhausted its semantic stock, it would still translate into *one* language and would lose the multiplicity of "he war." Let us leave
for another time a less hastily interrupted reading of this "he
war," and let us note one of the limits of theories of translation:
all too often they treat the passing from one language to another
and do not sufficiently consider the possibility for languages to
be implicated *more than two* in a text. How is a text written in
several languages at a time to be translated? How is the effect of
plurality to be "rendered"? And what of translating with several
languages at a time, will that be called translating?

Babel: today we take it as a proper name. Indeed, but the
proper name of what and of whom? At times that of a narrative
text recounting a story (mythical, symbolic, allegorical; it matters
little for the moment), a story in which the proper name, which
is then no longer the title of the narrative, names a tower or a
city but a tower or a city that receives its name from an event
during which YHWH "proclaims his name." Now, this proper
name, which already names at least three times and three different things, also has, this is the whole point, as proper name the
function of a common noun. This story recounts, among other
things, the origin of the confusion of tongues, the irreducible
multiplicity of idioms, the necessary and impossible task of translation, its necessity *as* impossibility. Now, in general one pays
little attention to this fact: it is in translation that we most often
read this narrative. And in this translation, the proper name
retains a singular destiny, since it is not translated in its appearance as proper name. Now, a proper name as such remains
forever untranslatable, a fact that may lead one to conclude that
it does not strictly belong, for the same reason as the other
words, to the language, to the system of the language, be it
translated or translating. And yet "Babel," an event in a single

tongue, the one in which it appears so as to form a "text," also has a common meaning, a conceptual generality. That it be by way of a pun or a confused association matters little: "Babel" could be understood in one language as meaning "confusion." And from then on, just as Babel is at once proper name and common noun, confusion also becomes proper name and common noun, the one as the homonym of the other, the synonym as well, but not the equivalent, because there could be no question of confusing them in their value. It has for the translator no satisfactory solution. Recourse to apposition and capitalization ("Over which he proclaims his name: Bavel, Confusion") is not translating from one tongue into another. It comments, explains, paraphrases, but does not translate. At best it reproduces approximately and by dividing the equivocation into two words there where confusion gathered in potential, in all its potential, in the internal translation, if one can say that, which works the word in the so-called original tongue. For in the very tongue of the original narrative there is a translation, a sort of transfer, that gives immediately (by some confusion) the semantic equivalent of the proper name which, by itself, as a pure proper name, it would not have. As a matter of fact, this intralinguistic translation operates immediately; it is not even an operation in the strict sense. Nevertheless, someone who speaks the language of Genesis could be attentive to the effect of the proper name in effacing the conceptual equivalent (like *pierre* [rock] in *Pierre* [Peter], and these are two absolutely heterogeneous values or functions); one would then be tempted to say *first* that a proper name, in the proper sense, does not properly belong to the language; it does not belong there, *although and because* its call makes the language possible (what would a language be without the possibility of calling by a proper name?); consequently it can properly inscribe itself in a language only by allowing itself to be translated therein, in other words, *interpreted* by its semantic equivalent: from this moment it can no longer be taken as proper name. The noun *pierre* belongs to the French language, and its translation into a foreign language should in principle transport its meaning. This is not the case with *Pierre*, whose inclusion in the French language is not assured and is in any case not of the same type. "Peter" in this sense is not a *translation* of *Pierre*, any more than *Londres* is a translation of "London," and so forth. And *second*, anyone whose so-called mother tongue was the tongue of Genesis could indeed understand Babel as "confusion"; that person then effects a *confused* translation of the proper name by its common equivalent without having need for another word. It is as if there were two words there, two homonyms one of which has the value of proper name and the other that of common noun: between the two, a translation which one can evaluate quite diversely. Does it belong to the kind that Jakobson calls intralingual translation or rewording? I do not think so: "rewording" concerns the relations of transformation between common nouns and ordinary phrases. The essay *On Translation* (1959) distinguishes three forms of translation. *Intralingual* translation interprets linguistic signs by means of other signs of the *same* language. (This obviously presupposes that one can know in the final analysis how to determine rigorously the unity and identity of a language, the decidable form of its limits) There would then be what Jakobson neatly calls translation "proper," *interlingual* translation, which interprets linguistic signs by means of some other language—this appeals to the same presupposition as intralingual translation. Finally there would be intersemiotic translation or transmutation, which interprets linguistic signs by means of systems of nonlinguistic signs. For the two forms of translation which would not be translations "proper," Jakobson proposes a definitional equivalent and another word. The first he translates, so to speak, by another word: intralingual translation or *rewording*. The third likewise: *intersemiotic* translation or *transmutation*. In these two cases, the translation of "translation" is a definitional interpretation. But in the case of translation "proper," translation in the ordinary sense, interlinguistic and post-Babelian, Jakobson does not translate; he repeats the same word: "interlingual translation or translation proper." He supposes that it is not necessary to translate; everyone understands what that means because everyone has experienced it, everyone is expected to know what is a language, the relation of one language to another and especially identity or difference in fact of language. If there is a transparency that Babel would not have impaired, this is surely it, the experience of the multiplicity of tongues and the "proper" sense of the word "translation." In relation to this word, when it is a question of translation "proper," the other uses of the word "translation" would be in a position of intralingual and inadequate translation, like metaphors, in short, like twists or turns of translation in the proper sense. There would thus be a translation in the proper sense and a translation in the figurative sense. And in order to translate the one into the other, within the same tongue or from one tongue to another, in the figurative or in the proper sense, one would engage upon a course that would quickly reveal how this reassuring tripartition can be problematic. Very quickly: at the very moment when pronouncing "Babel" we sense the impossibility of deciding whether this name belongs, properly and simply, to *one* tongue. And it matters that this undecidability is at work in a struggle for the proper name within a scene of genealogical indebtedness. In seeking to "make a name for themselves," to found at the same time a universal tongue and a unique genealogy, the Semites want to bring the world to reason, and this reason can signify simultaneously a colonial violence (since they would thus universalize their idiom) and a peaceful transparency of the human community. Inversely, when God imposes and opposes his name, he ruptures the rational transparency but interrupts also the colonial violence or the linguistic imperialism. He destines them to translation, he subjects them to the law of a translation both necessary and impossible; in a stroke with his translatable-untranslatable name he delivers a universal reason (it will no longer be subject to the rule of a particular nation), but he simultaneously limits its very universality: forbidden transparency, impossible univocity. Translation becomes law, duty and debt, but the debt one can no longer discharge. Such insolvency is found marked in the very name of Babel:

which at once translates and does not translate itself, belongs without belonging to a language and indebts itself to itself for an insolvent debt, to itself as if other. Such would be the Babelian performance.

This singular example, at once archetypical and allegorical, could serve as an introduction to all the so-called theoretical problems of translation. But no theorization, inasmuch as it is produced in a language, will be able to dominate the Babelian performance. This is one of the reasons why I prefer here, instead of treating it in the theoretical mode, to attempt to translate in my own way the translation of another text on translation. The preceding ought to have led me instead to an early text by Walter Benjamin, "On Language as Such and on the Language of Man" (1916), translated by Maurice de Gandillac (*Mythe et Violence*, Paris: Denoël, 1971). Reference to Babel is explicit there and is acccompanied by a discourse on the proper name and on translation. But given the, in my view, overly enigmatic character of that essay, its wealth and its overdeterminations, I have had to postpone that reading and limit myself to "The Task of the Translator" (also translated by Maurice de Gandillac in the same volume). Its difficulty is no doubt no less, but its unity remains more apparent, better centered around its theme. And this text on translation is also the preface to a translation of the *Tableaux parisiens* by Baudelaire, and I refer first to the French translation that Maurice de Gandillac gives us. And yet, translation—is it only a theme for this text, and especially its primary theme?

The title also says, from its first word, the task (*Aufgabe*), the mission to which one is destined (always by the other), the commitment, the duty, the debt, the responsibility. Already at stake is a law, an injunction for which the translator has to be responsible. He *must* also acquit himself, and of something that implies perhaps a fault, a fall, an error and perhaps a crime. The essay has as horizon, it will be seen, a "reconciliation." And all that in a discourse multiplying genealogical motifs and allusions—more or less than metaphorical—to the transmission of a family seed.

The translator is indebted, he appears to himself as translator in a situation of debt; and his task is to *render,* to render that which must have been given. Among the words that correspond to Benjamin's title (*Aufgabe,* duty, mission, task, problem, that which is assigned, given to be done, given to render), there are, from the beginning, *Wiedergabe, Sinnwiedergabe,* restitution, restitution of meaning. How is such a restitution, or even such an acquittance, to be understood? Is it only to be restitution of meaning, and what of meaning in this domain?

For the moment let us retain this vocabulary of gift and debt, and a debt which could well declare itself insolvent, whence a sort of "transference," love and hate, on the part of whoever is in a position to translate, is summoned to translate, with regard to the text to be translated (I do not say with regard to the signatory or the author of the original), to the language and the writing, to the bond and the love which seal the marriage between the author of the "original" and his own language. At the center of the essay, Benjamin says of the restitution that it could very well be impossible: insolvent debt within a genealogical scene. One of the essential themes of the text is the "kinship" of languages in a sense that is no longer tributary of nineteenth-century historical linguistics without being totally foreign to it. Perhaps it is here proposed that we think the very possibility of a historical linguistics.

Benjamin has just quoted Mallarmé, he quotes him in French, after having left in his own sentence a Latin word, which Maurice de Gandillac has reproduced at the bottom of the page to indicate that by "genius" he was not translating from German but from the Latin (*ingenium*). But of course he could not do the same with the third language of this essay, the French of Mallarmé, whose untranslatability Benjamin had measured. Once again: how is a text written in several languages at a time to be translated? Here is the passage on the insolvent (I quote as always the French translation, being content to include here or there the German word that supports my point):

Philosophy and translation are not futile, however, as sentimental artists allege. For there exists a philosophical genius, whose most proper characteristic is the nostalgia for that language which manifests itself in translation.

> Les langues imparfaites en cela que plusieurs, manque la suprême: penser étant écrire sans accessoires ni chuchotement, mais tacite encore l'immortelle parole, la diversité, sur terre, des idiomes empêche personne de proférer les mots qui, sinon, se trouveràient, par une frappe unique, elle-même matériellement la vérité.

If the reality that these words of Mallarmé evoke is applicable, in full rigor, to the philosopher, translation, with the seeds [*Keimen*] that it carries within itself of such a language, is situated midway between literary creation and theory. Its work has lower relief, but it impresses itself just as profoundly on history. If the task of the translator appears in this light, the paths of its accomplishment risk becoming obscure in an all the more impenetrable way. Let us say more: of this task that consists, in the translation, in ripening the seed of a pure language ["den Samen reiner Sprache zur Reife zu bringen"], it seems impossible ever to acquit oneself ["diese Aufgabe . . . scheint niemals lösbar"]; it seems that no solution would permit defining it ["in keiner Lösung bestimmbar"]. Does not one deprive it of any basis if rendering meaning ceases to be the standard?

Benjamin has, first of all, forgone translating the Mallarmé; he has left it shining in his text like the medallion of a proper name; but this proper name is not totally insignificant; it is merely welded to that whose meaning does not allow transport without damage into another language or into another tongue (and *Sprache* is not translated without loss by either word). And in the text of Mallarmé, the effect of being proper and thus untranslatable is tied less to any name or to any truth of adequation than to the unique occurrence of a performative force. Then the question is posed: does not the ground of translation finally recede as soon as the restitution of meaning ("Wiedergabe des Sinnes") ceases to provide the measure? It is the ordinary concept of translation that becomes problematic: it implied this process of restitution, the task (Aufgabe) was finally to render (wiedergeben) what was first *given,* and what was given was, one thought, the meaning. Now, things become obscure when one tries to accord this value of restitution with that of maturation. On what ground, in what ground, will the maturation take place if the restitution of the meaning given is for it no longer the rule?

The allusion to the maturation of a seed could resemble a vitalist or geneticist metaphor; it would come, then, in support of the genealogical and parental code which seems to dominate this text. In fact it seems necessary here to invert this order and recognize what I have elsewhere proposed to call the "metaphoric catastrophe": far from knowing first what "life" or "family" mean whenever we use these familiar values to talk about language and translation; it is rather starting from the notion of a language and its "sur-vival" in translation that we could have access to the notion of what life and family mean. This reversal is operated expressly by Benjamin. His preface (for let us not forget: this essay is a preface) circulates without cease among the values of seed, life, and especially "sur-vival." (*Überleben* has an essential relation with *Übersetzen.*) Now, very near the beginning, Benjamin seems to propose a simile or a metaphor—it opens with "just as . . ."—and right away everything moves in and about *Übersetzen, Übertragen, Überleben:*

> Just as the manifestations of life are intimately connected with the living, without signifying anything for it, a translation proceeds from the original. Indeed not so much from its life as from its survival [Überleben]. For a translation comes after the original and, for the important works that never find their predestined translator at the time of their birth, it characterizes the stage of their survival [*Fortleben,* this time, sur-vival as continuation of life rather than as life post mortem]. Now, it is in this simple reality, without any metaphor ["in völlig unmetaphorischer Sachlichkeit"], that it is necessary to conceive the ideas of life and survival [Fortleben] for works of art.

And according to a scheme that appears Hegelian, in a very circumscribed passage, Benjamin calls us to think life, starting from spirit or history and not from "organic corporeality" alone. There is life at the moment when "sur-vival" (spirit, history, works) exceeds biological life and death: "It is rather in recognizing for everything of which there is history and which is not merely the setting for history that one does justice to this concept of life. For it is starting from history, not from nature . . . , that the domain of life must finally be circumscribed. So is born for the philosopher the task [Aufgabe] of comprehending all natural life starting from this life, of much vaster extension, that is the life of history."

From the very title—and for the moment I stay with it— Benjamin situates the *problem*, in the sense of that which is precisely *before oneself* as a task, as the problem of the translator and not that of translation (nor, be it said in passing, and the question is not negligible, that of the translatoress). Benjamin does not say the task or the problem of translation. He names the subject of translation, as an indebted subject, obligated by a duty, already in the position of heir, entered as survivor in a genealogy, as survivor or agent of sur-vival. The sur-vival of works, not authors. Perhaps the sur-vival of authors' names and of signatures, but not of authors.

Such sur-vival gives more of life, more than a surviving. The work does not simply live longer, it lives more and better, beyond the means of its author. Would the translator then be an indebted receiver, subject to the gift and to the given of an original? By no means. For several reasons, including the following: the bond or obligation of the debt does not pass between a donor and a donee but between two texts (two "productions" or two "creations"). This is understood from the opening of the preface, and if one wanted to isolate theses, here are a few, as brutally as in any sampling:

1/ The task of the translator does not announce itself or follow from a *reception*. The theory of translation does not depend for the essential on any theory of reception, even though it can inversely contribute to the elaboration and explanation of such a theory.

2. Translation does not have as essential mission any *communication*. No more than the original, and Benjamin maintains, secure from all danger of dispute, the strict duality between the original and the version, the translated and the translating, even though he shifts their relation. And he is interested in the translation of poetic or sacred texts, which would here yield the essence of translation. The entire essay extends between the poetic and the sacred, returning from the first to the second, the one that indicates the ideal of all translation, the purely transferable: the intralinear version of the sacred text, the model or ideal (*Urbild*) of any translation at all possible. Now, this is the second thesis: for a poetic text or a sacred text, communication is not the essential. This putting into question does not directly concern the communicative structure of language but rather the hypothesis of a communicable content that could be strictly distinguished from the linguistic act of communication. In 1916, the critique of semiotism and of the "bourgeois conception" of language was already directed against that distribution: means, object, addressee. "There is no content of language." What language first communicates is its "communicability" ("On Language as Such," trans. M. de Gandillac, 85). Will it be said that an opening is thus made toward the performative dimension of utterances? In any case this warns us against precipitation: isolating the contents and theses in "The Task of the Translator" and translating it otherwise than as the signature of a kind of proper name destined to ensure its sur-vival as a work.

3. If there is indeed between the translated text and the translating text a relation of "original" to version, it could not be *representative* or *reproductive*. Translation is neither an image nor a copy.

These three precautions now taken (neither reception, nor communication, nor representation), how are constituted the debt and the genealogy of the translator? Or first, how those of that which is *to-be-translated,* of the to-be-translated?

Let us follow the thread of life or sur-vival wherever it communicates with the movement of kinship. When Benjamin chal-

lenges the viewpoint of reception, it is not to deny it all pertinence, and he will undoubtedly have done much to prepare for a
theory of reception in literature. But he wants first to return to
the authority of what he still calls "the original," not insofar as it
produces its receiver or its translators, but insofar as it requires,
mandates, demands or commands them in establishing the law.
And it is the structure of this demand that here appears most
unusual. Through what does it pass? In a literary—more strictly
speaking in this case, "poetic"—text it does not pass through the
said, the uttered, the communicated, the content or the theme.
And when, in this context, Benjamin still says "communication"
or "enunciation" (*Mitteilung, Aussage*), it is not about the act but
about the content that he visibly speaks: "But what does a literary work [*Dichtung*] 'say'? What does it communicate? Very
little to those who understand it. What it has that is essential is
not communication, not enunciation."

The demand seems thus to pass, indeed to be formulated,
through the *form*. "Translation is a form," and the law of this
form has its first place in the original. This law first establishes
itself, let us repeat, as a demand in the strong sense, a requirement that delegates, mandates, prescribes, assigns. And as for
this law as demand, two questions can arise; they are different in
essence. First question: in the sum total of its readers, can the
work always find the translator who is, as it were, capable? Second question and, says Benjamin, "more properly" (as if this
question made the preceding more appropriate, whereas, we
shall see, it does something quite different): "by its essence does
it [the work] bear translation and if so—in line with the signification of this form—, does it require translation?"

The answers to these two questions could not be of the same
nature or the same mode. *Problematic* in the first case, not
necessary (the translator capable of the work may appear or not
appear, but even if he does not appear, that changes nothing in
the demand or in the structure of the injunction that comes from
the work), the answer is properly *apodictic* in the second case:
necessary, a priori, demonstrable, absolute because it comes

from the internal law of the original. The original requires translation even if no translator is there, fit to respond to this injunction, which is at the same time demand and desire in the very structure of the original. This structure is the relation of life to sur-vival. This requirement of the other as translator, Benjamin compares it to some unforgettable instant of life: it is lived as unforgettable, it *is* unforgettable even if in fact forgetting finally wins out. It will have been unforgettable—there is its essential significance, its apodictic essence; forgetting happens to this unforgettableness only by accident. The requirement of the unforgettable—which is here constitutive—is not in the least impaired by the finitude of memory. Likewise the requirement of translation in no way suffers from not being satisfied, at least it does not suffer in so far as it is the very structure of the work. In this sense the *surviving* dimension is an a priori—and death would not change it at all. No more than it would change the requirement (*Forderung*) that runs through the original work and to which only "a thought of God" can respond or correspond (*entsprechen*). Translation, the desire for translation, is not thinkable without this *correspondence* with a thought of God. In the text of 1916, which already accorded the task of the translator, his Aufgabe, with the response made to the gift of tongues and the gift of names ("Gabe der Sprache," "Gebung des Namens"), Benjamin named God at this point, that of a correspondence authorizing, making possible or guaranteeing the correspondence between the languages engaged in translation. In this narrow context, there was also the matter of the relations between language of things and language of men, between the silent and the speaking, the anonymous and the nameable, but the axiom held, no doubt, for all translation: "the objectivity of this translation is guaranteed in God" (trans. M. de Gandillac, 91). The debt, in the beginning, is fashioned in the hollow of this "thought of God."

Strange debt, which does not bind anyone to anyone. If the structure of the work is "sur-vival," the debt does not engage in relation to a hypothetical subject-author of the original text—

dead or mortal, the dead man, or "dummy," of the text—but to something else that represents the formal law in the immanence of the original text. Then the debt does not involve restitution of a copy or a good image, a faithful representation of the original: the latter, the survivor, is itself in the process of transformation. The original gives itself in modifying itself; this gift is not an object given; it lives and lives on in mutation: "For in its survival, which would not merit the name if it were not mutation and renewal of something living, the original is modified. Even for words that are solidified there is still a postmaturation."

Postmaturation (*Nachreife*) of a living organism or a seed: this is not simply a metaphor, either, for the reasons already indicated. In its very essence, the history of this language is determined as "growth," "holy growth of languages."

4. If the debt of the translator commits him neither with regard to the author (dead insofar as his text has a structure of survival even if he is living) nor with regard to a model which must be reproduced or represented, to what or to whom is he committed? How is this to be named, this what or who? What is the proper name if not that of the author finite, dead or mortal of the text? And who is the translator who is thus committed, who perhaps finds himself *committed* by the other before having committed himself? Since the translator finds himself, as to the survival of the text, in the same situation as its finite and mortal producer (its "author"), it is not he, not he himself as a finite and mortal being, who is committed. Then who? It is he, of course, but in the name of whom or what? The question of proper names is essential here. Where the act of the living mortal seems to count less than the sur-vival of the text in the *translation*— translated and translating—it is quite necessary that the signature of the proper noun be distinguished and not be so easily effaced from the contract or from the debt. Let us not forget that Babel names a struggle for the sur-vival of the name, the tongue or the lips.

From its height Babel at every instant supervises and surprises my reading: I translate, I translate the translation by

Maurice de Gandillac of a text by Benjamin who, prefacing a translation, takes it as a pretext to say to what and in what way every translator is committed—and notes in passing, an essential part of his demonstration, that there could be no translation of translation. This will have to be remembered.

Recalling this strange situation, I do not wish only or essentially to reduce my role to that of a passer or passerby. Nothing is more serious than a translation. I rather wished to mark the fact that every translator is in a position to speak *about* translation, in a place which is more than any not second or secondary. For if the structure of the original is marked by the requirement to be translated, it is that in laying down the law the original begins by indebting itself *as well* with regard to the translator. The original is the first debtor, the first petitioner; it begins by lacking and by pleading for translation. This demand is not only on the side of the constructors of the tower who want to make a name for themselves and to found a universal tongue translating itself by itself; it also constrains the deconstructor of the tower: in giving his name, God also appealed to translation, not only between the tongues that had suddenly become multiple and confused, but first *of his name*, of the name he had proclaimed, given, and which should be translated as confusion to be understood, hence to let it be understood that it is difficult to translate and so to understand. At the moment when he imposes and opposes his law to that of the tribe, he is also a petitioner for translation. He is also indebted. He has not finished pleading for the translation of his name even though he forbids it. For Babel is untranslatable. God weeps over his name. His text is the most sacred, the most poetic, the most originary, since he creates a name and gives it to himself, but he is left no less destitute in his force and even in his wealth; he pleads for a translator. As in *La folie du jour* by Maurice Blanchot, the law does not command without demanding to be read, deciphered, translated. It demands transference (Übertragung and Übersetzung and Überleben). The *double bind* is in the law. Even in God, and it is necessary to follow rigorously the consequence: *in his name.*

Insolvent on both sides, the double indebtedness passes between names. It surpasses a priori the bearers of the names, if by that is understood the mortal bodies which disappear behind the sur-vival of the name. Now, a proper noun does and does not belong, we said, to the language, not even, let us make it precise now, to the corpus of the text to be translated, of the to-be-translated.

The debt does not involve living subjects but names at the edge of the language or, more rigorously, the trait which contracts the relation of the aforementioned living subject to his name, insofar as the latter keeps to the edge of the language. And this trait would be that of the to-be-translated from one language to the other, from this edge to the other of the proper name. This language contract among several languages is absolutely singular. First of all, it is not what is generally called a language contract: that which guarantees the institution of *one* language, the unity of its system, and the social contract which binds a community in this regard. On the other hand it is generally supposed that in order to be valid or to institute anything at all, a contract must take place in a single language or appeal (for example, in the case of diplomatic or commercial treaties) to a transferability already given and without remainder: there the multiplicity of tongues must be absolutely dominated. Here, on the contrary, a contract between two foreign languages as such engages to render possible a translation which *subsequently* will authorize every sort of contract in the originary sense. The signature of this singular contract needs no written document or record: it nevertheless takes place as trace or as trait, and this place takes place even if its space comes under no empirical or mathematical objectivity.

The topos of this contract is exceptional, unique, and practically impossible to think under the ordinary category of contract: in a classical code it would have been called transcendental, since in truth it renders possible every contract in general, starting with what is called the language contract within the limits of a single idiom. Another name, perhaps, for the origin of tongues. Not the origin of language but of languages—before language, languages.

The translation contract, in this transcendental sense, would be the contract itself, the absolute contract, the contract form of the contract, that which allows a contract to be what it is.

Will one say that the kinship among languages presupposes this contract or that the kinship provides a first occasion for the contract? One recognizes here a classic circle. It has always begun to turn whenever one asks oneself about the origin of languages or society. Benjamin, who often talks about the kinship among languages, never does so as a comparatist or as a historian of languages. He is interested less in families of languages than in a more essential and more enigmatic connection, an affinity which is not sure to precede the trait or the contract of the to-be-translated. Perhaps even this kinship, this affinity (*Verwandschaft*), is like an alliance, by the contract of translation, to the extent that the sur-vivals which it associates are not natural lives, blood ties, or empirical symbioses.

> This development, like that of a life original and elevated, is determined by a finality original and elevated. Life and finality—their correlation apparently evident, yet almost beyond the grasp of knowledge, only reveals itself when the goal, in view of which all singular finalities of life act, is not sought in the proper domain of that life but rather at a level more elevated. All finalized vital phenomena, like their very finality, are, after all, finalized not toward life but toward the expression of its essence, toward the representation [*Darstellung*] of its signification. Thus translation has finally as goal to express the most intimate relation among languages.

A translation would not seek to say this or that, to transport this or that content, to communicate such a charge of meaning, but to re-mark the affinity among the languages, to exhibit its own possibility. And that, which holds for the literary text or the sacred text, perhaps defines the very essence of the literary and the sacred, at their common root. I said "re-mark" the affinity among the languages to name the strangeness of an "expression"

("to express the most intimate relation among the languages"),
which is neither a simple "presentation" nor simply anything
else. In a mode that is solely anticipatory, annunciatory, almost
prophetic, translation renders *present* an affinity that is never
present in this presentation. One thinks of the way in which
Kant at times defines the relation to the sublime: a presentation
inadequate to that which is nevertheless presented. Here Benjamin's discourse proceeds in twists and turns:

> It is impossible that it [the translation] be able to reveal this
> hidden relation itself, that it be able to restitute [*herstellen*] it;
> but translation can represent [darstellen] that relation in actualiz-
> ing it in its seed or in its intensity. And this representation of a
> signified ["Darstellung eines Bedeuteten"] by the endeavor, by
> the seed of its restitution, is an entirely original mode of repre-
> sentation, which has hardly any equivalent in the domain of non-
> linguistic life. For the latter has, in analogies and signs, types of
> reference [*Hindeutung*] other than the intensive, that is to say
> anticipatory, annunciatory [*vorgreifende, andeutende*] actualiza-
> tion. But the relation we are thinking of, this very intimate rela-
> tion among the languages, is that of an original convergence. It
> consists in this: the languages are not foreign to one another, but,
> a priori and abstracted from all historical relations, are related to
> one another in what they mean.

The entire enigma of that kinship is concentrated here. What
is meant by "what they mean"? And what about this presentation
in which nothing is presented in the ordinary mode of presence?
    At stake here are the name, the symbol, the truth, the letter.
    One of the basic foundations of the essay, as well as of the 1916
text, is a theory of the name. Language is determined starting
from the word and the privilege of naming. This is, in passing, a
very strong if not very conclusive assertion: "the originary element of the translator" is the word and not the sentence, the
syntactic articulation. As food for thought, Benjamin offers a
curious "image": the sentence (*Satz*) would be "the wall in front
of the language of the original," whereas the word, the word for
word, literality (*Wörtlichkeit*), would be its "arcade." Whereas

the wall braces while concealing (it is *in front of* the original), the arcade supports while letting light pass and the original show (we are not far from the Parisian passages). This privilege of the word obviously supports that of the name and with it what is proper to the proper name, the stakes and the very possibility of the translation contract. It opens onto the *economic* problem of translation, whether it be a matter of economy as the law of the proper or of economy as a quantitative relation (is it translating to transpose a proper name into several words, into a phrase or into a description, and so forth?).

There is some to-be-translated. From both sides it assigns and makes contracts. It commits not so much authors as proper names at the edge of the language, it essentially commits neither to communicate nor to represent, nor to keep an already signed commitment, but rather to draw up the contract and to give birth to the pact, in other words to the *symbolon,* in a sense that Benjamin does not designate by this term but suggests, no doubt with the metaphor of the amphora, let us say, since from the start we have suspected the ordinary sense of metaphor with the ammetaphor.

If the translator neither restitutes nor copies an original, it is because the original lives on and transforms itself. The translation will truly be a moment in the growth of the original, which will complete itself *in* enlarging itself. Now, it has indeed to be, and it is in this that the "seminal" logic must have imposed itself on Benjamin, that growth not give rise to just any form in just any direction. Growth must accomplish, fill, complete (*Ergänzung* is here the most frequent term). And if the original calls for a complement, it is because at the origin it was not there without fault, full, complete, total, identical to itself. From the origin of the original to be translated there is fall and exile. The translator must redeem (erlösen), absolve, resolve, in trying to absolve himself of his own debt, which is at bottom the same—and bottomless. "To redeem in his own tongue that pure language exiled in the foreign tongue, to liberate by transposing this pure language captive in the work, such is the task of the translator."

Translation is a poetic transposition (*Umdichtung*). We will have to examine the essence of the "pure language" that it liberates. But let us note for the moment that this liberation itself presupposes a freedom of the translator, which is itself none other than relation to that "pure language"; and the liberation that it operates, eventually in transgressing the limits of the translating language, in transforming it in turn, must extend, enlarge, and make language grow. As this growth comes also to complete, as it is symbolon, it does not reproduce: it adjoins in adding. Hence this double simile (*Vergleich*), all these turns and metaphoric supplements: (1) "Just as the tangent touches the circle only in a fleeting manner and at a single point, and just as it is this contact, not the point, that assigns to the tangent the law according to which it pursues to infinity its course in a straight line, so the translation touches the original in a fleeting manner and only at an infinitely small point of meaning, to follow henceforth its proper course, according to the law of fidelity in the liberty of language movement." Each time that he talks about the contact (*Berührung*) between the bodies of the two texts in the process of translation, Benjamin calls it "fleeting" (*flüchtig*). On at least three occasions, this "fleeting" character is emphasized, and always in order to situate the contact with meaning, the infinitely small point of meaning which the languages barely brush ("The harmony between the languages is so profound here [in the translations of Sophocles by Hölderlin] that the meaning is only touched by the wind of language in the manner of an Eolian lyre"). What can an infinitely small point of meaning be? What is the measure to evaluate it? The metaphor itself is at once the question and the answer. And here is the other metaphor, the metamphora, which no longer concerns extension in a straight and infinite line but enlargement by adjoining along the broken lines of a fragment. (2) "For, just as the fragments of the amphora, if one is to be able to reconstitute the whole, must be contiguous in the smallest details, but not identical to each other, so instead of rendering itself similar to the meaning of the original, the translation should rather, in a movement of love and in full detail, pass into its own language the mode of intention of the original: thus, just as the debris become recognizable as fragments of the same amphora, original and translations become recognizable as fragments of a larger language."

Let us accompany this movement of love, the gesture of this loving one (*liebend*) that is at work in the translation. It does not reproduce, does not restitute, does not represent; as to the essential, it does not *render* the meaning of the original except at that point of contact or caress, the infinitely small of meaning. It extends the body of languages, it puts languages into symbolic expansion, and symbolic here means that, however little restitution there be to accomplish, the larger, the new vaster aggregate, has still to *reconstitute* something. It is perhaps not a whole, but it is an aggregate in which openness should not contradict unity. Like the urn which lends its poetic topos to so many meditations on word and thing, from Hölderlin to Rilke and Heidegger, the amphora is one with itself though opening itself to the outside—and this openness opens the unity, renders it possible, and forbids it totality. Its openness allows receiving and giving. If the growth of language must also reconstitute without representing, if that is the symbol, can translation lay claim to the truth? Truth—will that still be the name of that which still lays down the law for a translation?

Here we touch—at a point no doubt infinitely small—the limit of translation. The pure untranslatable and the pure transferable here pass one into the other—and it is the truth, "itself materially."

The word "truth" appears more than once in "The Task of the Translator." We must not rush to lay hold of it. It is not a matter of truth for a translation in so far as it might conform or be faithful to its model, the original. Nor any more a matter, either for the original or even for the translation, of some adequation of the language to meaning or to reality, nor indeed of the representation to something. Then what is it that goes under the name of truth? And will it be that new?

Let us start again from the "symbolic." Let us remember the metaphor, or the ammetaphor: a translation espouses the original when the two adjoined fragments, as different as they can be, complete each other so as to form a larger tongue in the course of a sur-vival that changes them both. For the native tongue of the translator, as we have noted, is altered as well. Such at least is my interpretation—my translation, my "task of the translator." It is what I have called the translation contract: hymen or marriage contract with the promise to produce a child whose seed will give rise to history and growth. A marriage contract in the form of a seminar. Benjamin says as much, in the translation the original becomes larger; it grows rather than reproduces itself—and I will add: like a child, its own, no doubt, but with the power to speak on its own which makes of a child something other than a product subjected to the law of reproduction. This promise signals a kingdom which is at once "promised and forbidden where the languages will be reconciled and fulfilled." This is the most Babelian note in an analysis of sacred writing as the model and the limit of all writing, in any case of all Dichtung in its being-to-be-translated. The sacred and the being-to-be-translated do not lend themselves to thought one without the other. They produce each other at the edge of the same limit.

This kingdom is never reached, touched, trodden by translation. There is something untouchable, and in this sense the reconciliation is only promised. But a promise is not nothing, it is not simply marked by what it lacks to be fulfilled. As a promise, translation is already an event, and the decisive signature of a contract. Whether or not it be honored does not prevent the commitment from taking place and from bequeathing its record. A translation that manages, that manages to promise reconciliation, to talk about it, to desire it or make it desirable—such a translation is a rare and notable event.

Here two questions before going closer to the truth. Of what does the untouchable consist, if there is such a thing? And why does such a metaphor or ammetaphor of Benjamin make me think of the hymen, more visibly of the wedding gown?

1. The always intact, the intangible, the untouchable (*unberührbar*) is what fascinates and orients the work of the translator. He wants to touch the untouchable, that which remains of

the text when one has extracted from it the communicable meaning (point of contact which is, remember, infinitely small), when one has transmitted that which can be transmitted, indeed taught: what I do here, after and thanks to Maurice de Gandillac, knowing that an untouchable remnant of the Benjaminian text will also remain intact at the end of the operation. Intact and virgin in spite of the labor of translation, however efficient or pertinent that may be. Pertinency has no bearing here. If one can risk a proposition in appearance so absurd, the text will be even more virgin after the passage of the translator, and the hymen, sign of virginity, more jealous of itself after the other hymen, the contract signed and the marriage consummated. Symbolic completeness will not have taken place to its very end and yet the promise of marriage will have come about—and this is the task of the translator, in what makes it very pointed as well as irreplaceable.

But again? Of what does the untouchable consist? Let us study again the metaphors or the ammetaphors, the Übertragungen which are translations and metaphors of translation, translations (Übersetzungen) of translation or metaphors of metaphor. Let us study all of these Benjaminian passages. The first figure which comes in here is that of the core and the shell, the fruit and the skin (*Kern, Frucht/Schale*). It describes in the final analysis the distinction that Benjamin would never want to renounce or even bother to question. One recognizes a core (the original as such) by the fact that it can bear further translating and restranslating. A translation, *as such*, cannot. Only a core, because it resists the translation it attracts, can offer itself to further translating operations without letting itself be exhausted. For the relation of the content to the language, one would also say of the substance to the form, of the signified to the signifier—it hardly matters here (in this context Benjamin opposes tenor, *Gehalt*, and tongue or language, *Sprache*)—differs from the original text to the translation. In the first, the unity is just as dense, tight, adherent as between the fruit and its skin, its shell or its peel. Not that they are inseparable—one should be able to distinguish them by

rights—but they belong to an organic whole, and it is not insignificant that the metaphor here be vegetal and natural, naturalis-
tic:

> This kingdom it [the original in translation] never fully attains,
> but it is there that is found what makes translating more than
> communicating. More precisely one can define this essential core
> as that which, in the translation, is not translatable again. For, as
> much as one may extract of the communicable in order to trans-
> late it, there always remains this untouchable towards which is
> oriented the work of the true translator. It is not transmissible, as
> is the creative word of the original ["übertragbar wie das Dichter-
> wort des Originals"], for the relation of this tenor to the language
> is entirely different in the original and in the translation. In the
> original, tenor and language form a determinate unity, like that of
> the fruit and the skin.

Let us dissect a bit more the rhetoric of this sequence. It is not
certain that the essential "core" and the "fruit" designate the
same thing. The essential core, that which in the translation is
not translatable again, is not the tenor, but this adherence between the tenor and the language, between the fruit and the
skin. This may seem strange or incoherent (how can a core be
situated between the fruit and the skin?). It is necessary no
doubt to think that the core is first the hard and central unity that
holds the fruit to the skin, the fruit to itself as well; and above all
that, at the heart of the fruit, the core is "untouchable," beyond
reach and invisible. The core would be the first metaphor of
what makes for the unity of the two terms in the second metaphor. But there is a third, and this time one without a natural
provenance. It concerns the relation of the tenor to the language
in the translation and no longer in the original. This relation is
different, and I do not think I give in to artifice by insisting on
this difference in saying that it is precisely that of artifice to
nature. What in fact is it that Benjamin notes, as if in passing, for
rhetorical or pedagogical convenience? That "the language of the
translation envelops its tenor like a royal cape with large folds.
For it is the signifier of a language superior to itself and so

remains, in relation to its own tenor, inadequate, forced, foreign." That is quite beautiful, a beautiful translation: white ermine, crowning, scepter, and majestic bearing. The king has indeed a body (and it is not here the original text but that which constitutes the tenor of the translated text), but this body is only promised, announced and dissimulated by the translation. The clothes fit but do not cling strictly enough to the royal person. This is not a weakness; the best translation resembles this royal cape. It remains separate from the body to which it is nevertheless conjoined, wedding it, not wedded to it. One can of course embroider on this cape, on the necessity of this Übertragung, of this metaphoric translation of translation. For example, one can oppose this metaphor to that of the shell and the core just as one would oppose technology to nature. An article of clothing is not natural; it is a fabric and even—another metaphor of metaphor—a text, and this text of artifice appears precisely on the side of the symbolic contract. Now, if the original text is demand for translation, then the fruit, unless it be the core, insists upon becoming the king or the emperor who will wear new clothes: under its large folds, *in weiten Falten*, one will imagine him naked. No doubt the cape and the folds protect the king against the cold or natural aggressions; but first, above all, it is, like his scepter, the eminent visibility of the law. It is the index of power and of the power to lay down the law. But one infers that what counts is what comes to pass under the cape, to wit, the body of the king, do not immediately say the phallus, around which a translation busies its tongue, makes pleats, molds forms, sews hems, quilts, and embroiders. But always amply floating at some distance from the tenor.

2. More or less strictly, the cape weds the body of the king, but as for what comes to pass under the cape, it is difficult to separate the king from the royal couple. This is the one, this couple of spouses (the body of the king and his gown, the tenor and the tongue, the king and the queen) that lays down the law and guarantees every contract from this first contract. That is why I thought of a wedding gown. Benjamin, we know, does not

push matters in the direction that I give to my translation, reading him always already in translation. More or less faithfully I have taken some liberty with the tenor of the original, as much as with its tongue, and again with the original that is also for me, now, the translation by Maurice de Gandillac. I have added another cape, floating even more, but is that not the final destination of all translation? At least if a translation is destined to arrive.

Despite the distinction between the two metaphors, the shell and the cape (the royal cape, for he said "royal" where others could have thought a cape sufficed), despite the opposition of nature and art, there is in both cases a *unity* of tenor and tongue, natural unity in the one case, symbolic unity in the other. Simply in the translation the unity signals a (metaphorically) more "natural" unity; it promises a tongue or language more originary and almost sublime, sublime to the distended extent that the promise itself—to wit, the translation—there remains inadequate (*unangemessen*), violent and forced (*gewaltig*), and foreign (*fremd*). This "fracture" renders useless, even "forbids," every Übertragung, every "transmission," exactly as the French translation says: the word also plays, like a transmission, with transferential or metaphorical displacement. And the word *Übertragung* imposes itself again a few lines down: if the translation "transplants" the original onto another terrain of language "ironically" more definitive, it is to the extent that it could no longer be displaced by any other "transfer" (Übertragung) but only "raised" (*erheben*) anew on the spot "in other parts." There is no translation of translation; that is the axiom without which there would not be "The Task of the Translator." If one were to violate it, and one must not, one would touch the untouchable of the untouchable, to wit, that which guarantees to the original that it remains indeed the original.

This is not unrelated to truth. Truth is apparently beyond every Übertragung and every possible Übersetzung. It is not the representational correspondence between the original and the translation, nor even the primary adequation between the origi-

nal and some object or signification exterior to it. Truth would be
rather the *pure language* in which the meaning and the letter no
longer dissociate. If such a place, the taking place of such an
event, remained undiscoverable, one could no longer, even by
right, distinguish between an original and a translation. In main-
taining this distinction at all cost, as the original given of every
translation contract (in the quasi-transcendental sense we discussed above), Benjamin repeats the foundation of the law. In so
doing he exhibits the possibility of copyright for works and author, the very possibility by which actual law claims to be sup-
ported. This law collapses at the slightest challenge to a strict
boundary between the original and the version, indeed to the
identity or to the integrity of the original. What Benjamin says
about this relation between original and translation is also found
translated in a language rather wooden but faithfully reproduced
as to its meaning at the opening of all legal treatises concerning
the actual law of translations. And then whether it be a matter of
the general principles of the difference original/translation (the
latter being "derived" from the former) or a matter of the translations of translation. The translation of translation is said to be
"derived" from the original and not from the first translation.
Here are some excerpts from the French law; but there does not
seem to be from this point of view any opposition between it and
the rest of Western law (nevertheless, a study of comparative law
should also concern the translation of legal texts). As we shall
see, these propositions appeal to the polarity expression/ex-
pressed, signifier/signified, form/substance. Benjamin also began by saying: translation is a form, and the symbolizer/sym-
bolized split organizes his whole essay. Now, in what way is this
system of oppositions indispensable to this law? Because only it
allows, starting from the distinction between original and translation, acknowledgment of some originality in the translation.
This originality is determined, and this is one of the many classic
philosophemes at the foundation of this law, as originality of
expression. Expression is opposed to content, of course, and the
translation, which is not supposed to touch the content, must be

original only in its language as *expression;* but expression is also opposed to what French jurists call the *composition* of the original. In general one places composition on the side of form, but here the form of expression in which one can acknowledge some originality to the translator, and for this reason the rights of author-translator, is only the form of linguistic expression, the choice of words in the language, and so forth, but nothing else of the form. I quote Claude Colombet, *Propriété littéraire et artistique* (Paris: Dalloz, 1976), from which I excerpt only a few lines, in accordance with the law of March 11, 1957, recalled at the opening of the book and "authorizing . . . only analyses and short quotations for the purpose of example or illustration," because "every representation or reproduction, integral or partial, made without the consent of the author or of his beneficiaries or executors, is illegal," constituting "therefore an infraction punishable under articles 425 and following of the Penal Code."

54.—Translations are works which are original only by expression; [very paradoxical restriction: the cornerstone of copyright, it is indeed that only the form can become property, and not the ideas, the themes, the contents, which are common and universal property. (Compare all of chapter 1 in this book, *L'absence de protection des idées par le droit d'auteur.*) If a first consequence is good, since it is this form that defines the originality of the translation, another consequence could be ruinous, for it would lead to abandoning that which distinguishes the original from the translation if, excluding expression, it amounts to a distinction of substance. Unless the value of composition, however lax it may be, were still to indicate the fact that between the original and the translation the relation is neither of expression nor of content but of something else beyond these oppositions. In following the difficulty of the jurists—sometimes comic in its casuistic subtlety—so as to draw the consequences from axioms of the type "Copyright does not protect ideas; but these can be, sometimes indirectly, protected by means other than the law of March 11, 1957" (ibid., 21), one measures better the historicity and conceptual fragility of this set of axioms] article 4 of the law cites them among the protected works; in fact it has always been admitted that a translator demonstrates originality in the choice of expressions to render best in one language the meaning of the text in another language. As M. Savatier says, "The genius of each language gives the translated work its own physiognomy; and the translator is not a simple workman. He himself participates in a derived creation for which he bears his own responsibility"; it is that in fact translation is not the result of an automatic process; by the choices he makes among several words, several expressions, the translator fashions a work of the mind; but, of course, he could never modify the composition of the work translated, for he is bound to respect that work.

In his language, Desbois says the same thing, with some additional details:

> *Derived works which are original in expression.* 29. The work under consideration, to be *relatively original* [emphasized by Desbois], need not bear the imprint of a personality at once in composition and expression, like adaptations. It is enough that the author, while following step by step the development of a preexistent work, have performed a personal act in the expression: article 4 attests to this, since, in a nonexhaustive enumeration of derived works, it puts *translations* in the place of honor. "Traduttore, traditore," the Italians are wont to say, in a bit of wit, which, like every coin, has two sides: if there are bad translators, who multiply misreadings, others are cited for the perfection of their task. The risk of a mistake or an imperfection has as counterpart the perspective of an authentic version, which implies a perfect knowledge of the two languages, an abundance of judicious choices, and thus a creative effort. Consulting a dictionary suffices only for mediocre candidates to the baccalaureate: the conscientious and competent translator "gives of himself" and *creates* just like the painter who makes a copy of a model.—The verification of this conclusion is furnished by the comparison of several translations of one and the same text: each may differ from the others without any one containing a misreading; the variety in modes of expression for a single thought demonstrates, with the possibility of choice, that the task of the translator gives room for manifestations of personality. [*Le droit d'auteur en France* (Paris: Dalloz, 1978)]

One will note in passing that the *task of the translator,* confined to the duel of languages (never more than two languages), gives rise only to a "creative effort" (effort and tendency rather than achievement, artisan labor rather than artistic performance), and when the translator "creates," it is like a painter who copies his model (a ludicrous comparison for many reasons; is there any use in explaining?). The recurrence of the word "task" is remarkable enough in any case, for all the significations that it weaves into a network, and there is always the same evaluative interpretation: duty, debt, tax, levy, toll, inheritance and estate tax, nobiliary obligation, but labor midway to creation, infinite task, essential incompletion, as if the presumed creator of the original were not—he too—indebted, taxed, obligated by another text, and a priori translating.

Between the transcendental law (as Benjamin repeats it) and the actual law as it is formulated so laboriously and at times so crudely in treatises on copyright for author or for works, the analogy can be followed quite far, for example in that which concerns the notion of derivation and the translations of translations: these are always derived from the original and not from previous translations. Here is a note by Desbois:

> The translator will not even cease to fashion personal work when he goes to draw advice and inspiration from a preceding translation. We will not refuse the status of author for a work that is derived, *in relation to anterior translations*, to someone who would have been content to choose, among several versions already published, the one that seemed to him the most adequate to the original: going from one to the other, taking a passage from this one, another from that one, he would create a new work, by the very fact of the combination, which renders his work different from antecedent productions. He has exercised creativity, since his translation reflects a new form and results from comparisons, from choices. The translator would still deserve a hearing in our opinion, even if his reflection had led him to the same result as a predecessor, whose work, by supposition, he would not have known: his unintentional replica, far from amounting to plagiarism, would bear the mark of his personality, would present a "subjective novelty," which would call for protection. The two versions, accomplished separately and each without knowledge of the other, gave rise, separately and individually, to manifesta-

tions of personality. *The second will be a work derived vis-à-vis the work that has been translated, not vis-à-vis the first.* [ibid., 41; my emphasis in the last sentence]

Of this right to the truth, what is the relation? Translation promises a kingdom to the reconciliation of languages. This promise, a properly symbolic event adjoining, coupling, marrying two languages like two parts of a greater whole, appeals to a language of the truth ("Sprache der Wahrheit"). Not to a language that is true, adequate to some exterior content, but to a true tongue, to a language whose truth would be referred only to itself. It would be a matter of truth as authenticity, truth of act or event which would belong to the original rather than to the translation, even if the original is already in a position of demand or debt. And if there were such authenticity and such force of event in what is ordinarily called a translation, it is that it would produce itself in some fashion like an original work. There would thus be an original and inaugural way of indebting oneself; that would be the place and date of what is called an original, a work.

To translate well the intentional meaning of what Benjamin means to say when he speaks of the "language of the truth," perhaps it is necessary to understand what he regularly says about the "intentional meaning" or the "intentional aim" ("Intention der Meinung," "Art des Meinens"). As Maurice de Gandillac reminds us, these are categories borrowed from the scholastics by Brentano and Husserl. They play a role that is important if not always very clear in "The Task of the Translator."

What is it that seems intended by the concept of intention (Meinen)? Let us return to the point where in the translation there seems to be announced a kinship among languages, beyond all resemblence between an original and its reproduction and independently of any historical filiation. Moreover, kinship does not necessarily imply resemblence. With that said, in dismissing the historical or natural origin, Benjamin does not exclude, in a wholly different sense, consideration of the origin in general, any more than a Rousseau or a Husserl did in analogous contexts and with analogous movements. Benjamin specifies quite literally: for the most rigorous access to this kinship or to this affinity of languages, "the concept of origin [*Abstammungs-begriff*] remains indispensable." Where, then, is this original affinity to be sought? We see it announced in the plying, re-plying, co-deploying of intentions. Through each language something is intended which is the same and yet which none of the languages can attain separately. They can claim, and promise themselves to attain it, only by coemploying or codeploying their intentional modes, "the whole of their complementary intentional modes." This codeployment toward the whole is a re-plying because what it intends to attain is "the pure language" ("die reine Sprache"), or the pure tongue. What is intended, then, by this co-operation of languages and intentional *modes* is not transcendent to the language; it is not a reality which they would besiege from all sides, like a tower that they would try to surround. No, what they are aiming at intentionally, individually and jointly, in translation is the language itself as a Babelian event, a language that is not the universal language in the Leib-nizian sense, a language which is not the natural language that each remains on its own either; it is the being-language of the language, tongue or language *as such*, that unity without any self-identity, which makes for the fact that there are languages and that they are languages.

These languages relate to one another in translation according to an unheard-of mode. They complete each other, says Ben-jamin; but no other completeness in the world can represent this one, or that symbolic complementarity. This singularity (not rep-resentable by anything in the world) comes no doubt from the intentional mode or from what Benjamin tries to translate in a scholastico-phenomenological language. Within the same inten-tional aim it is necessary to distinguish rigorously between the thing intended, the intended (Gemeinten), and the mode of intention ("die Art des Meinens"). As soon as he sights the origi-nal contract of languages and the hope for the "pure tongue," the task of the translator excludes the intended or leaves it between brackets.

The mode of intention alone assigns the task of translation. Every "thing," in its presumed self-identity (for example, bread *itself*) is intended by way of different modes in each language and in each text of each language. It is among these modes that the translation should seek, produce or reproduce, a complementarity or a "harmony." And since to complete or complement does not amount to the summation of any worldly totality, the value of harmony suits this adjustment, and what can here be called the accord of tongues. This accord lets the pure language, and the being-language of the language, resonate, announcing it rather than presenting it. As long as this accord does not take place, the pure language remains hidden, concealed (*verborgen*), immured in the nocturnal intimacy of the "core." Only a translation can make it emerge.

Emerge and above all develop, make grow. Always according to the same motif (in appearance organicist or vitalist), one could then say that each language is as if atrophied in its isolation, meager, arrested in its growth, sickly. Owing to translation, in other words to this linguistic supplementarity by which one language gives to another what it lacks, and gives it harmoniously, this crossing of languages assures the growth of languages, even that "holy growth of language" "unto the messianic end of history." All of that is announced in the translation process, through "the eternal sur-vival of languages" ("am ewigen Fortleben der Sprachen") or "the infinite rebirth [Aufleben] of languages." This perpetual reviviscence, this constant regeneration (Fort- and Auf-leben) by translation is less a revelation, revelation itself, than an annunciation, an alliance and a promise.

This religious code is essential here. The sacred text marks the limit, the pure even if inaccessible model, of pure transferability, the ideal starting from which one could think, evaluate, measure the essential, that is to say poetic, translation. Translation, as holy growth of languages, announces the messianic end, surely, but the sign of that end and of that growth is "present" (gegenwärtig) only in the "knowledge of that distance," in the Entfernung, *the remoteness* that relates us to it. One can know this remoteness, have knowledge or a presentiment of it, but we cannot overcome it. Yet it puts us in contact with that "language of the truth" which is the "true language" ("so ist diese Sprache der Wahrheit—die wahre Sprache"). This contact takes place in the mode of "presentiment," in the "intensive" mode that renders present what is absent, that allows remoteness to approach as remoteness, *fort:da*. Let us say that the translation is the experience, that which is translated or experienced as well: experience is translation.

The to-be-translated of the sacred text, its pure transferability, that is what would give *at the limit* the ideal measure for all translation. The sacred text assigns the task to the translator, and it is sacred *inasmuch as* it announces itself as transferable, simply transferable, to-be-translated, which does not always mean immediately translatable, in the common sense that was dismissed from the start. Perhaps it is necessary to distinguish here between the transferable and the translatable. Transferability pure and simple is that of the sacred text in which meaning and literality are no longer discernible as they form the body of a unique, irreplaceable, and untransferable event, "materially the truth." Never are the call for translation, the debt, the task, the assignation, more imperious. Never is there anything more transferable, yet by reason of this indistinction of meaning and literality (Wörtlichkeit), the pure transferable can announce itself, give itself, present itself, let itself be translated as untranslatable. From this limit, at once interior and exterior, the translator comes to receive all the signs of remoteness (Entfernung) which guide him on his infinite course, at the edge of the abyss, of madness and of silence: the last works of Hölderlin as translations of Sophocles, the collapse of meaning "from abyss to abyss," and this danger is not that of accident, it is transferability, it is the law of translation, the to-be-translated as law, the order given, the order received—and madness waits on both sides. And as the task is impossible at the approaches to the sacred text which assigns it to you, the infinite guilt absolves you immediately.

That is what is named from here on Babel: the law imposed by the name of God who in one stroke commands and forbids you to translate by showing *and* hiding from you the limit. But it is not only the Babelien situation, not only a scene or a structure. It is also the status and the event of the Babelian text, of the text of Genesis (a unique text in this regard) as sacred text. It comes under the law that it recounts and translates in an exemplary way. It lays down the law it speaks about, and from abyss to abyss it deconstructs the tower, and every turn, twists and turns of every sort, in a rhythm.

What comes to pass in a sacred text is the occurrence of a *pas de sens.* And this event is also the one starting from which it is possible to think the poetic or literary text which tries to redeem the lost sacred and there translates itself as in its model. *Pas de sens*—that does not signify poverty of meaning but no meaning that would be itself, meaning, beyond any "literality." And right there is the sacred. The sacred surrenders itself to translation, which devotes itself to the sacred. The sacred would be nothing without translation, and translation would not take place without the sacred; the one and the other are inseparable. In the sacred text "the meaning has ceased to be the divide for the flow of language and for the flow of revelation." It is the absolute text because in its event it communicates nothing, it says nothing that would make sense beyond the event itself. That event melds completely with the act of language, for example with prophecy. It is literally the literality of its tongue, "pure language." And since no meaning bears detaching, transferring, transporting, or translating into another tongue as such (as meaning), it commands right away the translation that it seems to refuse. It is transferable and untranslatable. There is only letter, and it is the truth of pure language, the truth as pure language.

This law would not be an exterior constraint; it grants a liberty to literality. In the same event, the letter ceases to oppress insofar as it is no longer the exterior body or the corset of meaning. The letter also translates itself of itself, and it is in this self-relation of the sacred body that the task of the translator finds itself engaged. This situation, though being one of pure limit, does not exclude—quite the contrary—gradations, virtuality, interval and in-between, the infinite labor to rejoin that which is nevertheless past, already given, even here, between the lines, already signed.

How would you translate a signature? And how would you refrain, whether it be Yahweh, Babel, Benjamin when he signs right next to his last word? But literally, and between the lines, it is also the signature of Maurice de Gandillac that to end I quote in posing my question: can one quote a signature? "For, to some degree, all the great writings, but to the highest point sacred Scripture, contain between the lines their virtual translation. The interlinear version of the sacred text is the model or ideal of all translation."

Translator's Note

Translation is an art of compromise, if only because the problems of translation have no one solution and none that is fully satisfactory. The best translation is merely better than the worst to some extent, more or less. Compromise also precludes consistency. It would have been possible, and it once seemed plausible, to maintain regular equivalents at least for those terms that figure prominently in the argument. But the result was not worth the sacrifice. There was consolation for so much effort to so little effect in that whatever we did, we were bound to exhibit the true principles of translation announced in our text. And so this translation is exemplary to that extent. To the extent that we were guided in translation, the principles were also those found in the text. Accordingly, a silhouette of the original appears for effect in many words and phrases of the translation.

Publication of the French text is also significant in telling of our situation. Among the many differences in this translation, a few appear already in the original.

The quotations from Walter Benjamin are translated from the French, not the German. The biblical passages are also translated from their French versions, since Derrida works from translations in both cases.

Here are some of the problems for which I found solutions least satisfactory:

"Des Tours de Babel."   The title can be read in various ways. *Des* means "some"; but it also means "of the," "from the," or "about the." *Tours* could be towers, twists, tricks, turns, or tropes, as in a "turn" of phrase. Taken together, *des* and *tours* have the same sound as *détour*, the word for detour. To mark that economy in language the title has not been changed.

langue/langage.   It is difficult to mark this difference in English where "language" covers both. Whenever possible, "tongue" has been used for *langue,* and "language" only in those cases that are clearly specific rather than generic. *Langage* is then translated as "language" in the singular and without modifier, though not always. The German *Sprache* introduces further complications.

survie. The word means "survival" as well as "afterlife"; its use in the text also brings out the subliminal sense of more life and more than life. The hyphenation of "sur-vival" is an admitted cheat.

performance. The French has not the primarily dramatic connotation of the English but rather the sense of prowess and success; its use here also relates to the "performative" of speech acts.

pas-de-sens. With this expression Derrida combines the *pas* of negation with the *pas* of step in a most curious figure. My English suggested a skip.

De ce droit à la vérité quel est le rapport?   This sentence could be translated by any and all of the following: What is the relation between this law and the truth? What is the gain from this law to the truth? What is the relation between this right to the truth and all the rest?

Appendix

Des Tours de Babel

JACQUES DERRIDA

Babel: un nom propre d'abord, soit. Mais quand nous disons Babel aujourd'hui, savons-nous ce que nous nommons? Savons-nous qui? Si nous considérons la survie d'un texte légué, le récit ou le mythe de la tour de Babel, il ne forme pas une figure parmi d'autres. Disant au moins l'inadéquation d'une langue à l'autre, d'un lieu de l'encyclopédie à l'autre, du langage à lui-même et au sens, etc., il dit aussi la nécessité de la figuration, du mythe, des tropes, des tours, de la traduction inadéquate pour suppléer à ce que la multiplicité nous interdit. En ce sens il serait le mythe de l'origine du mythe, la métaphore de la métaphore, le récit du récit, la traduction de la traduction, etc. Il ne serait pas la seule structure à se creuser ainsi mais il le ferait à sa manière (elle même *à peu près* intraduisible, comme un nom propre) et il faudrait en sauver l'idiome.

La "tour de Babel" ne figure pas seulement la multiplicité irréductible des langues, elle exhibe un inachèvement, l'impossibilité de compléter, de totaliser, de saturer, d'achever quelque chose qui est de l'ordre de l'édification, de la construction architecturale, du système et de l'architectonique. Ce que la multiplicité des idiomes vient limiter, ce n'est pas seulement une

traduction "vraie," une entr'expression transparente et adéquate, c'est aussi un ordre structural, une cohérence du con-
structum. Il y a là (traduisons) comme une limite interne à la
formalisation, une incomplétude de la constructure. Il serait facile et jusqu'à un certain point justifié d'y voir la traduction d'un
système en déconstruction.

On ne devrait jamais passer sous silence la question de la
langue dans laquelle se pose la question de la langue et se traduit
un discours sur la traduction.

D'abord: dans quelle langue la tour de Babel fut-elle con-
struite et déconstruite? Dans une langue à l'intérieur de laquelle
le nom propre de Babel pouvait aussi, par confusion, être traduit
par "confusion." Le nom propre Babel, en tant que nom propre,
devrait rester intraduisible mais, par une sorte de confusion
associative qu'une seule langue rendait possible, on put croire le
traduire, dans cette langue même, par un nom commun signifiant ce que *nous* traduisons par confusion. Voltaire s'en étonnait
ainsi dans son *Dictionnaire philosophique*, à l'article Babel:

> Je ne sais pas pourquoi il est dit dans la *Genèse* que Babel signifie
> confusion, car *Ba* signifie père dans les langues orientales, et *Bel*
> signifie Dieu; Babel signifie la ville de Dieu, la ville sainte. Les
> anciens donnaient ce nom à toutes leurs capitales. Mais il est
> incontestable que Babel veut dire confusion, soit parce que les
> architectes furent confondus après avoir élevé leur ouvrage jus-
> qu'à quatre-vingt et un mille pieds juifs, soit parce que les lan-
> gues se confondirent; et c'est évidemment depuis ce temps-là que
> les Allemands n'entendent plus les Chinois; car il est clair, selon
> le savant Bochart, que le chinois est originairement la même
> langue que le haut-allemand.

L'ironie tranquille de Voltaire veut dire que Babel veut dire: ce
n'est pas seulement un nom propre, la référence d'un signifiant
pur à un existant singulier—et à ce titre intraduisible—, mais un
nom commun rapporté à la généralité d'un sens. Ce nom commun veut dire, et non seulement la confusion, encore que "confusion" ait au moins deux sens, Voltaire y est attentif, la confusion des langues mais aussi l'état de confusion dans lequel se

trouvent les architectes devant la structure interrompue, si bien qu'une certaine confusion a déjà commencé à affecter les deux sens du mot "confusion." La signification de "confusion" est confuse, au moins double. Mais Voltaire suggère autre chose encore: Babel ne veut pas seulement dire confusion au double sense de ce mot, mais aussi le nom du père, plus précisément et plus communément, le nom de Dieu comme nom de père. La ville porterait le nom de Dieu le père, et du père de la ville qui s'appelle confusion. Dieu, le Dieu aurait marqué de son patronyme un espace communautaire, cette ville où l'on ne peut plus s'entendre. Et on ne peut plus s'entendre quand il n'y a que du nom propre, et on ne peut plus s'entendre quand il n'y a plus de nom propre. En donnant son nom, un nom de son choix, en donnant tous les noms, le père serait à l'origine du language et ce pouvoir appartiendrait de droit à Dieu le père. Et le nom de Dieu le père serait le nom de cette origine des langues. Mais c'est aussi ce Dieu qui, dans le mouvement de sa colère (comme le Dieu de Böhme ou de Hegel, celui qui sort de lui, se détermine dans sa finitude et produit ainsi l'histoire) annule le don des langues, ou du moins le brouille, sème la confusion parmi ses fils et empoisonne le présent (*Gift-gift*). C'est aussi l'origine des langues, de la multiplicité des idiomes, autrement dit de ce qu'on appelle couramment des langues maternelles. Car toute cette histoire déploie des filiations, des générations et des généalogies: sémitiques. Avant la déconstruction de Babel, la grande famille sémitique était en train d'établir son empire, elle le voulait universel, et sa langue, qu'elle tente aussi d'imposer à l'univers. Le moment de ce projet précède immédiatement la déconstruction de la tour. Je cite deux traductions françaises. Le premier traducteur se tient assez loin de ce qu'on voudrait appeler la "littéralité," autrement dit de la figure hébreue pour dire "langue," là où le second, plus soucieux de littéralité (métaphorique ou plutôt métonymique), dit "lèvre" puisqu'en hébreu on désigne par "lèvre" ce que nous appelons, d'une autre métonymie, "langue." Il faudra dire multiplicité des lèvres et non des langues pour nommer la confusion babelienne. Le pre-

mier traducteur, donc, Louis Segond, auteur de la Bible Segond
parue en 1910, écrit ceci:

> Ce sont là les fils de Sem, selon leurs familles, selon leurs lan-
> gues, selon leurs pays, selon leurs nations. Telles sont les familles
> des fils de Noé, selon leurs générations, selon leurs nations. Et
> c'est d'eux que sont sorties les nations qui se sont répandues sur
> la terre après le déluge. Toute la terre avait une seule langue et
> les mêmes mots. Comme ils étaient partis de l'origine, ils
> trouvèrent une plaine du pays de Schinear, et ils y habitèrent. Ils
> se dirent l'un à l'autre: Allons! faisons des briques, et cuisons-les
> au feu. Et la brique leur servit de pierre, et le bitume leur servit
> de ciment. Ils dirent encore: Allons! bâtissons-nous une ville et
> une tour dont le sommet touche au ciel, et faisons-nous un nom,
> afin que nous ne soyons pas dispersés sur la face de toute la terre.

Je ne sais comment interpréter cette allusion à la substitution ou
à la transmutation des matériaux, la brique devenant pierre et le
bitume servant de mortier. Cela déjà ressemble à une traduction, à une traduction de la traduction. Mais laissons et substi-
tuons une seconde traduction à la première. C'est celle de
Chouraqui. Elle est récente et se veut plus littérale, presque
verbum pro verbo comme Cicero disait qu'il ne fallait surtout pas
faire, dans un de ces premiers conseils au traducteur qu'on peut
lire dans son *Libellus de optima genera oratorum*. Voici:

> Voici les fils de Shem
> pour leurs clans, pour leurs langues,
> dans leurs terres, pour leurs peuples.
> Voilà les clans des fils de Noah pour leur geste,
> dans leurs peuples:
> de ceux-là se scindent les peuples sur terre, après le déluge.
>
> Et c'est toute la terre: une seule lèvre, d'uniques paroles.
> Et c'est à leur départ d'Orient: ils trouvent un cañon,
> en terre de Shine'ar.
> Ils s'y établissent.
> Ils disent, chacun à son semblable:
> «Allons, briquetons des briques,
> Flambons-les à la flambée.»

La brique devient pour eux pierre, le bitume, mortier.
Ils disent:
«Allons, bâtissons-nous une ville et une tour.
Sa tête: aux cieux.
Faisons-nous un nom,
que nous ne soyons dispersés sur la face de toute la terre.»

Que leur arrive-t-il? Autrement dit, de quoi Dieu les punit-il en donnant son nom, ou plutôt, car il ne le donne à rien ni à personne, en clamant son nom, le nom propre de "confusion" qui sera sa marque et son sceau? Les punit-il d'avoir voulu construire à hauteur de cieux? d'avoir voulu accéder au plus haut, jusqu'au Très-Haut? Peut-être, sans doute aussi, mais incontestablement d'avoir voulu ainsi *se faire un nom,* se donner à eux-mêmes le nom, se construire eux-mêmes leur propre nom, s'y rassembler ("que nous ne soyons plus dispersés") comme dans l'unité d'un lieu qui est à la fois une langue et une tour, l'une comme l'autre. Il les punit d'avoir ainsi voulu s'assurer, d'eux-mêmes, une généalogie unique et universelle. Car le texte de la Genèse enchaîne immédiatement, comme s'il s'agissait du même dessein: élever une tour, construire une ville, se faire un nom dans une langue universelle qui soit aussi un idiome, et rassembler une filiation:

Ils disent:
«Allons, bâtissons-nous une ville et une tour.
Sa tête: aux cieux.
Faisons-nous un nom,
que nous ne soyons dispersés sur la face de toute la terre.»

YHWH descend pour voir la ville et la tour
qu'ont bâties les fils de l'homme.
YHWH dit:
«Oui! Un seul peuple, une seule lèvre pour tous:
voilà ce qu'ils commencent à faire! . . .
Allons! Descendons! Confondons là leurs lèvres,
l'homme n'entendra plus la lèvre de son prochain.»

Puis il dissémine les Sem, et la dissémination est ici déconstruction:

YHWH les disperse de là sur la face de toute la terre.
Ils cessent de bâtir la ville.
Sur quoi il clame son nom: Bavel, Confusion,
car là, YHWH confond la lèvre de toute la terre,
et de là YHWH les disperse sur la face de toute la terre.

Ne peut-on alors parler d'une jalousie de Dieu? Par ressenti-
ment contre ce nom et cette lèvre uniques des hommes, il impose son nom, son nom de père; et de cette imposition violente il
entame la déconstruction de la tour comme de la langue universelle, il disperse la filiation généalogique. Il rompt la lignée. Il
impose et interdit *à la fois* la traduction. Il l'impose et l'interdit,
y contraint, mais comme à l'échec, des enfants qui désormais
porteront son nom, le nom qu'*il* donne à la ville. C'est depuis un
nom propre de Dieu, venu de Dieu, descendu de Dieu ou du
père (et il est bien dit que YHWH, nom inprononçable, *descend*
vers la tour), et marqué par lui que les langues se dispersent, se
confondent ou se multiplient, selon une descendance qui dans sa
dispersion même reste scellée du seul nom qui aura été le plus
fort, du seul idiome qui l'aura emporté. Or cet idiome porte en
lui-même la marque de la confusion, il veut dire improprement
l'impropre, à savoir Bavel, confusion. La traduction devient alors
nécessaire et impossible comme l'effet d'une lutte pour l'appropriation du nom, nécessaire et interdite dans l'intervalle entre
deux noms absolument propres. Et le nom propre de Dieu,
donné par Dieu, se divise assez dans la langue, déjà, pour signifier aussi, confusément, "confusion." Et la guerre qu'il dé-
clare, elle a d'abord fait rage au-dedans de son nom: divisé,
bifide, ambivalent, polysémique: Dieu déconstruit. "And he
war," lit-on dans *Finnegans Wake*, et nous pourrions suivre
toute cette histoire du côté de Shem et de Shaun. Le "he war"
ne noue pas seulement, en ce lieu, un nombre incalculable de
fils phoniques et sémantiques, dans le contexte immédiat et dans
tout ce livre babelien, il dit la déclaration de guerre (en anglais)
de celui qui dit Je suis celui qui suis, et qui ainsi fut (*war*), il se
rend intraduisible en sa performance même, *au moins dans ce
fait* qu'il s'énonce en plus d'une langue à la fois, au moins l'an-

glais et l'allemand. Si même une traduction infinie en épuisait le fonds sémantique, elle traduirait encore en *une* langue et perdrait la multiplicité du "he war." Laissons pour une autre fois une lecture moins vite interrompue de ce "he war" et notons une des limites des théories de la traduction: elles traitent trop souvent des passages d'une langue à l'autre et ne considèrent pas assez la possibilité pour des langues d'être impliquées *à plus de deux* dans un texte. Comment traduire un texte écrit en plusieurs langues à la fois? Comment "rendre" l'effet de pluralité? Et si l'on traduit par plusieurs langues à la fois, appellera-t-on cela traduire?

Babel, nous le recevons aujourd'hui comme un nom propre. Certes, mais nom propre de quoi, et de qui? Parfois d'un texte narratif racontant une histoire (mythique, symbolique, allégorique, peu importe pour l'instant), d'une histoire dans laquelle le nom propre, qui alors n'est plus le titre du récit, nomme une tour ou une ville, mais une tour ou une ville qui reçoivent leur nom d'un événement au cours duquel YHWH "clame son nom." Or ce nom propre qui nomme déjà au moins trois fois et trois choses différentes, il a aussi, c'est toute l'histoire, comme nom propre la fonction d'un nom commun. Cette histoire raconte, entre autres choses, l'origine de la confusion des langues, la multiplicité irréductible des idiomes, la tâche nécessaire et impossible de la traduction, sa nécessité *comme* impossibilité. Or on accorde en général peu d'attention à ce fait: c'est en traduction que le plus souvent nous lisons ce récit. Et dans cette traduction, le nom propre garde une destinée singulière puisqu'il n'est pas traduit dans son apparition de nom propre. Or un nom propre en tant que tel reste toujours intraduisible, fait à partir duquel on peut considérer qu'il n'appartient pas rigoureusement, au même titre que les autres mots, à la langue, au système de la langue, qu'elle soit traduite ou traduisante. Et pourtant "Babel," événement dans une seule langue, celle dans laquelle il apparaît pour former un "texte," a aussi un sens commun, une généralité conceptuelle. Que ce soit par un jeu de mot ou une association confuse importe peu: "Babel" pouvait être entendu dans une langue avec le sens de "confusion." Et dès lors, de même que Babel est à la fois nom propre et nom commun, confusion devient aussi nom propre et nom commun, l'un comme l'homonyme de l'autre, le synonyme aussi, mais non l'équivalent car il ne saurait être question de les confondre dans leur valeur. C'est pour le traducteur sans solution satisfaisante. Le recours à l'apposition et à la majuscule ("Sur quoi il clame son nom: Bavel, Confusion") ne traduit pas d'une langue dans une autre. Il commente, explique, paraphrase mais ne traduit pas. Tout au plus reproduit-il approximativement, et en divisant l'équivoque en deux mots là où la confusion se rassemblait en puissance, dans toute sa puissance, dans la traduction interne, si on peut dire, qui travaille le nom en la langue dite originale. Car dans la langue même du récit originaire, il y a une traduction, une sorte de translation qui donne immédiatement (par quelque confusion) l'équivalent sémantique du nom propre qui, par lui-même, en tant que pur nom propre, n'en aurait pas. A vrai dire, cette traduction intralinguistique s'opère immédiatement, ce n'est même pas, au sens strict, une opération. Néanmoins celui qui parle la langue de la Genèse pouvait être attentif à l'effet de nom propre en effaçant l'équivalent conceptuel (comme pierre dans Pierre, et ce sont deux valeurs ou deux fonctions absolument hétérogènes); on serait alors tenté de dire *premièrement* qu'un nom propre, au sens propre, n'appartient pas proprement à la langue; il n'y appartient pas, *bien et parce que* son appel la rend possible (que serait une langue sans possibilité d'appeler d'un nom propre?); par conséquent il ne peut s'inscrire proprement dans une langue qu'en s'y laissant traduire, autrement dit *interpréter* dans son équivalent sémantique: dès ce moment il ne peut plus être reçu comme nom propre. Le nom "pierre" appartient à la langue française, et sa traduction dans une langue étrangère doit en principe transporter son sens. Ce n'est plus le cas pour "Pierre" dont l'appartenance à la langue française n'est pas assurée et en tout cas pas du même type. Peter en ce sens n'est pas une *traduction* de Pierre, pas plus que Londres n'est une traduction de London, etc. Et *deuxièmement*, le sujet dont la langue dite maternelle serait la langue de la Genèse peut bien entendre Babel comme "confusion," il opère alors une traduction *confuse* du nom propre dans son équivalent commun sans avoir besoin d'un autre mot. C'est comme s'il y avait là deux mots, deux homonymes dont l'un a valeur de nom propre et l'autre de nom commun: entre les deux une traduction qu'on peut très diversement évaluer. Appartient-elle à ce genre que Jakobson appelle traduction intralinguale ou reformulation (*rewording*)? Je ne le crois pas: le "rewording" concerne des rapports de transformation entre noms communs et phrases ordinaires. L'essai "On translation" (1959) distingue trois formes de traductions. La traduction *intralinguale* interprète des signes linguistiques au moyen d'autres signes de la *même* langue. Cela suppose évidemment qu'on sache en dernière instance comment déterminer rigoureusement l'unité et l'identité d'une langue, la forme décidable de ses limites. Il y aurait ensuite ce que Jakobson appelle joliment la traduction "proprement dite," la traduction *interlinguale* qui interprète des signes linguistiques au moyen d'une autre langue, ce qui en appelle à la même présupposition que la traduction intralinguale. Il y aurait enfin la traduction intersémiotique ou *transmutation* qui interprète des signes linguistiques au moyen de systèmes de signes non-linguistiques. Pour les deux formes de traduction qui ne seraient pas des traductions "proprement dites" Jakobson propose un équivalent définitionnel et un autre mot. La première, il la traduit si on peut dire par un autre mot: traduction *intralinguale* ou *reformulation, rewording*. La troisième également: traduction *intersémiotique* ou *transmutation*. Dans ces deux cas, la traduction de "traduction" est une interprétation définitionnelle. Mais dans le cas de la traduction "proprement dite," de la traduction au sens courant, interlinguistique et post-babelien, Jakobson ne traduit pas, il reprend le même mot: "la traduction interlinguale ou traduction proprement dite." Il suppose qu'il n'est pas nécessaire de traduire, tout le monde comprend ce que cela veut dire parce que tout le monde en a l'expérience, tout le monde est censé savoir ce qu'est une langue, le rapport d'une langue à l'autre et surtout l'identité ou la différence en fait de langue. S'il y a une transparence que Babel n'aurait pas entamée, c'est bien cela, l'expérience de la multiplicité des langues et le sens "proprement dit" du mot "traduction." Par rapport à ce mot, quand il s'agit de traduction "proprement dite," les autres usages du mot "traduction" seraient en situation de traduction intralinguale et inadéquate, comme des métaphores, en somme, des tours ou tournures de la traduction au sens propre. Il y aurait donc une traduction au sens propre et une traduction au sens figuré. Et pour traduire l'une dans l'autre, à l'intérieur de la même langue ou d'une langue à l'autre, au sens figuré ou au sens propre, on s'engagerait dans des voies qui révéleraient vite ce que cette tripartition rassurante peut avoir de problématique. Très vite: à l'instant même où prononçant Babel nous éprouvons l'impossibilité de décider si ce nom appartient, proprement et simplement, à *une* langue. Et il importe que cette indécidabilité travaille une lutte pour le nom propre à l'intérieur d'une scène d'endettement généalogique. En cherchant à "se faire un nom," à fonder à la fois une langue universelle et une généalogie unique, les Sémites veulent mettre à la raison le monde, et cette raison peut signifier simultanément une violence coloniale (puisqu'ils universaliseraient ainsi leur idiome) et une transparence pacifique de la communauté humaine. Inversement, quand Dieu leur impose et oppose son nom, il rompt la transparence rationnelle mais interrompt aussi la violence coloniale ou l'impérialisme linguistique. Ils les destine à la traduction, il les assujettit à la loi d'une traduction nécessaire et impossible; du coup, de son nom propre traduisible-intraduisible il délivre une raison universelle (celle-ci ne sera plus soumise à l'empire d'une nation particulière) mais il en limite simultanément l'universalité même: transparence interdite, univocité impossible. La traduction devient la loi, le devoir et la dette mais de la dette on ne peut plus s'acquitter. Telle insolvabilité se trouve marquée à même le nom de Babel: qui à la fois se traduit et ne se traduit pas, appartient sans appartenir à une langue et s'endette auprès de lui-même d'une dette insolvable, auprès de lui-même comme autre. Telle serait la performance babelienne.

Cet exemple singulier, à la fois archétypique et allégorique, pourrait introduire à tous les problèmes dits théoriques de la traduction. Mais aucune théorisation, dès lors qu'elle se produit dans une langue, ne pourra dominer la performance babelienne. C'est une des raisons pour lesquelles je préfère ici, au lieu d'en traiter sur le mode théorique, tenter de traduire à ma manière la traduction d'un autre texte sur la traduction. Ce qui précède aurait dû me conduire plutôt vers un autre texte de Walter Benjamin, "Sur le langage en général et sur le langage humain" (1916) (traduit par Maurice de Gandillac dans *Mythe et Violence*, Denoël, 1971). La référence à Babel y est explicite et s'y accompagne d'un discours sur le nom propre et sur la traduction. Mais devant le caractère à mes yeux trop énigmatique de cet essai, sa richesse et ses surdéterminations, j'ai dû ajourner cette lecture et m'en tenir à "La tâche du traducteur" (également traduit par M. de Gandillac dans le même volume). Sa difficulté n'est sans doute pas moindre, mais son unité reste plus apparente, mieux centrée autour de son thème. Et ce texte sur la traduction est aussi la préface à une traduction des *Tableaux parisiens* de Baudelaire, et je le lis d'abord dans la traduction française que nous en donne Maurice de Gandillac. Et pourtant, la traduction, est-ce seulement un thème pour ce texte, et surtout son premier thème?

Le titre dit aussi, dès son premier mot, la tâche (*Aufgabe*), la mission à laquelle on est (toujours par l'autre) destiné, l'engagement, le devoir, la dette, la responsabilité. Il y va déjà d'une loi, d'une injonction dont le traducteur doit répondre. Il *doit* s'acquitter aussi, et de quelque chose qui implique peut-être une faille, une chute, une faute et peut-être un crime. L'essai a pour horizon, on le verra, une "réconciliation." Et tout cela dans un discours multipliant les motifs généalogiques et les allusions— plus ou moins que métaphoriques—à la transmission d'une semence familiale. Le traducteur est endetté, il s'apparaît comme traducteur dans la situation de la dette; et sa tâche c'est de *rendre,* de rendre ce qui doit avoir été donné. Parmi les mots qui répondent au titre de Benjamin (*Aufgabe*, le devoir, la mission, la tâche, le problème, ce qui est assigné, donné à faire, donné à rendre), c'est, dès le début, *Wiedergabe, Sinn-wiedergabe,* la restitution, la restitution du sens. Comment entendre une telle restitution voire un tel acquittement? Sera-ce seulement restitution du sens, et quoi du sens en ce domaine?

Retenons pour l'instant ce lexique du don et de la dette, et d'une dette qui pourrait bien s'annoncer comme insolvable, d'où une sorte de "transfert," amour et haine, de qui est en situation de traduire, sommé de traduire, à l'égard du texte à traduire (je ne dis pas du signataire ou de l'auteur de l'original), de la langue et de l'écriture, du lien et de l'amour qui signe la noce entre l'auteur de l'"original" et sa propre langue. Au centre de l'essai, Benjamin dit de la restitution qu'elle pourrait bien être impossible: dette insolvable à l'intérieur d'une scène généalogique. Un des thèmes essentiels du texte est la "parenté" des langues en un sens qui n'est plus tributaire de la linguistique historique du XIXème siècle, sans lui être tout à fait étranger. Peut-être nous est-il ici proposé de penser la possibilité même d'une linguistique historique.

Benjamin vient de citer Mallarmé, il le cite en français, après avoir laissé dans sa propre phrase un mot latin, que Maurice de Gandillac a reproduit en bas de page pour bien marquer que par "génie" il ne traduisait pas de l'allemand mais du latin (*ingenium*). Mais bien entendu il ne pouvait en faire autant avec la troisième langue de cet essai, le français de Mallarmé dont Benjamin avait mesuré l'intraduisibilité. Une fois encore: comment traduire un texte écrit dans plusieurs langues à la fois? Voici ce passage sur l'insolvable (je cite comme toujours la traduction française, me contentant d'inclure ici ou là le mot allemand qui soutient mon propos):

> Philosophie et traduction ne sont pas cependant des futilités, comme le prétendent les artistes sentimentaux. Car il existe un génie philosophique, dont le caractère le plus propre est la nostalgie de ce langage qui s'annonce dans la traduction:
>
>> Les langues imparfaites en cela que plusieurs, manque la suprême: penser étant écrire sans accessoires ni chuchotement, mais tacite encore l'immortelle parole, la diversité, sur

terre, des idiomes empêche personne de proférer les mots qui, sinon, se trouveraient, par une frappe unique, elle-même matériellement la vérite.

Si la réalité qu'évoquent ces mots de Mallarmé, est applicable, en toute rigueur, au philosophe, la traduction, avec les germes [*Keimen*] qu'elle porte en elle d'un tel langage, se situe à mi-chemin de la création littéraire et de la théorie. Son oeuvre a moins de relief mais s'imprime tout aussi profondément dans l'histoire. Si la tâche du traducteur apparaît sous cette lumière, les chemins de son accomplissement risquent de s'obscurcir de façon d'autant plus impénétrable. Disons plus: de cette tâche qui consiste, dans la traduction, à faire mûrir la semence d'un pur langage ["den Samen reiner Sprache zur Reife zu bringen"], il semble impossible de jamais s'acquitter ["diese Aufgabe . . . scheint niemals lösbar"], il semble qu'aucune solution ne permette de la définir ["in keiner Lösung bestimmbar"]. Ne la prive-t-on pas de toute base si rendre le sens cesse d'être l'étalon?

Benjamin vient d'abord de renoncer à traduire Mallarmé, il l'a laissé briller comme la médaille d'un nom propre dans son texte; mais ce nom propre n'est pas totalement insignifiant, il se soude seulement à ce dont le sens ne se laisse pas transporter sans dommage dans un autre langage ou dans une autre langue (et *Sprache* ne se traduit pas sans perte par l'un ou l'autre mot). Et dans le texte de Mallarmé, l'effet de propriété intraduisible se lie moins à du nom ou à de la vérité d'adéquation qu'à l'unique événement d'une force performative. Alors se pose la question: le sol de la traduction n'en vient-il pas à se retirer dès l'instant où la restitution du sens ("Wiedergabe des Sinnes") cesse de donner la mesure? C'est le concept courant de la traduction qui devient problématique: il impliquait ce procès de restitution, la tâche (Aufgabe) revenait à rendre (wiedergeben) ce qui était d'abord *donné*, et ce qui était donné, c'était, pensait-on, le sens. Or les choses s'obscurcissent quand on essaie d'accorder cette valeur de restitution avec celle de maturation. Sur quel sol, dans quel sol aura lieu la maturation si la restitution du sens donné n'en est plus la règle?

L'allusion à la maturation d'une semence pourrait ressembler

à une métaphore vitaliste ou génétiste; elle viendrait alors
soutenir le code généalogiste et parental qui semble dominer ce
texte. En fait il paraît ici nécessaire d'inverser cet ordre et de
reconnaître ce que j'ai ailleurs proposé d'appeler la "catastrophe
métaphorique": loin que nous sachions d'abord ce que veut dire
"vie" ou "famille" au moment où nous nous servons de ces valeurs familières pour parler de langage et de traduction, c'est au
contraire à partir d'une pensée de la langue et de sa "survie" en
traduction que nous accéderions à la pensée de ce que vie et
famille veulent dire. Ce retournement est expressément opéré
par Benjamin. Sa préface (car ne l'oublions pas, cet essai est une
préface) circule sans cesse entre les valeurs de semence, de vie
et surtout de "survie" (*Überleben* a un rapport essentiel avec
Übersetzen). Or très près du début, Benjamin semble proposer
une cmparaison ou une métaphore—elle s'ouvre par un "de
même que"—et d'emblée tout se déplace entre *Übersetzen,
Übertragen, Überleben:*

> De même que les manifestations de la vie, sans rien signifier pour
> le vivant, sont avec lui dans la plus intime corrélation, ainsi la
> traduction procède de l'original. Certes moins de sa vie que de sa
> "survie" [Überleben]. Car la traduction vient après l'original et,
> pour les oeuvres importantes qui ne trouvent jamais leur traduc-
> teur prédestiné au temps de leur naissance, elle caractérise le
> stade de leur survie [*Fortleben*, cette fois, la survie comme con-
> tinuation de la vie plutôt que comme vie post mortem]. Or c'est
> dans leur simple réalité, sans aucune métaphore ["in völlig un-
> metaphorischer Sachlichkeit"] qu'il faut concevoir pour les
> oeuvres d'art les idées de vie et de survie [Fortleben].

Et selon un schéma d'apparence hegelien, dans un passage
très circonscrit, Benjamin nous appelle à penser la vie depuis
l'esprit ou l'histoire et non pas depuis la seule "corporalité
organique." Il y a vie au moment où la "survie" (l'esprit, l'histoire, les oeuvres) excède la vie et la mort biologique: "C'est en
reconnaissant bien plutôt la vie à tout ce dont il y a histoire et qui
n'en est pas seulement le théâtre qu'on rend justice à ce concept
de vie. Car c'est à partir de l'histoire, non de la nature . . . qu'il

faut finalement circonscrire le domaine de la vie. Ainsi naît pour le philosophe la tâche [Aufgabe] de comprendre toute vie naturelle à partir de cette vie, de plus vaste extension, qui est celle de l'histoire."

Dès son titre—et pour l'instant je m'y tiens—Benjamin situe le *problème*, au sens de ce qui précisément est *devant soi* comme une tâche, comme celui du traducteur et non de la traduction (ni d'ailleurs, soit dit au passage et la question n'est pas négligeable, de la traductrice). Benjamin ne dit pas la tâche ou le problème de la traduction. Il nomme le sujet de la traduction, comme sujet endetté, obligé par un devoir, déjà en situation d'héritier, inscrit comme survivant dans une généalogie, comme survivant ou agent de survie. La survie des oeuvres, non pas des auteurs. Peut-être la survie des noms d'auteurs et des signatures, mais non des auteurs.

Telle survie donne un plus de vie, plus qu'une survivance. L'oeuvre ne vit pas seulement plus longtemps, elle vit plus et mieux, au-dessus des moyens de son auteur. Le traducteur serait-il alors un récepteur endetté, soumis au don et à la donnée d'un original? Nullement. Pour plusieurs raisons dont celle-ci: le lien ou l'obligation de la dette ne passe pas entre un donateur et un donataire mais entre deux textes (deux "productions" ou deux "créations"). Cela s'entend dès l'ouverture de la préface et si l'on voulait isoler des thèses, en voici quelques-unes avec la brutalité du prélèvement:

1. La tâche du traducteur ne s'annonce pas depuis une *réception*. La théorie de la traduction ne relève pas pour l'essentiel de quelque théorie de la réception, même si elle peut inversement contribuer à la rendre possible et à en rendre compte.

2. La traduction n'a pas pour destination essentielle de *communiquer*. Pas plus que l'original, et Benjamin maintient à l'abri de toute contestation possible ou menaçante, la dualité rigoureuse entre l'original et la version, le traduit et le traduisant, même s'il en déplace le rapport. Et il s'intéresse à la traduction de textes poétiques ou sacrés qui livrerait ici l'essence de la traduction. Tout l'essai se déploie entre le poétique et le sacré,

pour remonter du premier au second, lequel indique l'idéal de toute traduction, le traductible pur: la version intralinéaire du texte sacré, le modèle ou l'idéal (*Urbild*) de toute traduction possible en général. Or, c'est la deuxième thèse, pour un texte poétique ou pour un texte sacré, la communication n'est pas l'essentiel. Cette mise en question ne concerne pas directement la structure communicante du langage, mais plutôt l'hypothèse d'un contenu communicable qui se distinguerait rigoureusement de l'acte linguistique de la communication. En 1916, la critique du sémiotisme et de la "conception bourgeoise" du langage visait déjà cette distribution: moyen, objet, destinataire. "Il n'y a pas de contenu du langage." Ce que communique d'abord le langage, c'est sa "communicabilité" ("Sur le langage" tr. M. de Gandillac, p. 85). Dira-t-on qu'une ouverture est ainsi faite vers la dimension performative des énoncés? En tout cas cela nous met en garde devant une précipitation: isoler des contenus et des thèses dans "La tâche du traducteur," et le traduire autrement que comme la signature d'une sorte de nom propre destinée à assurer sa survie comme oeuvre.

3. S'il y a bien entre texte traduit et texte traduisant un rapport d'"original" à version, il ne saurait être *représentatif* ou *reproductif*. La traduction n'est ni une image ni une copie.

Ces trois précautions prises (ni réception, ni communication, ni représentation), comment se constituent la dette et la généalogie du traducteur? ou d'abord de ce qui est *à-traduire,* de l'à-traduire?

Suivons le fil de vie ou de survie, partout où il communique avec le mouvement de la parenté. Quand Benjamin récuse le point de vue de la réception, ce n'est pas pour lui dénier toute pertinence, et il aura sans doute beaucoup fait pour préparer à une théorie de la réception en littérature. Mais il veut d'abord revenir à l'instance de ce qu'il appelle encore l'"original," non pas en tant qu'elle produit ses récepteurs ou ses traducteurs, mais en tant qu'elle les requiert, mande, demande ou commande en posant la loi. Et c'est la structure de cette demande qui paraît ici la plus singulière. Par où passe-t-elle? Dans un texte littéraire—disons plus rigoureusement dans ce cas "poéti-que"—elle ne passe pas par le dit, l'énoncé, le communiqué, le contenu ou le thème. Et quand, dans ce contexte, Benjamin dit encore "communication" ou "énonciation" (*Mitteilung, Aus-sage*), ce n'est pas de l'acte mais du contenu que visiblement il parle: "Mais que "dit" une oeuvre littéraire (*Dichtung*)? Que communique-t-elle? Très peu à qui la comprend. Ce qu'elle a d'essentiel n'est pas communication, n'est pas énonciation."

La demande semble donc passer, voire être formulée par la *forme*. "La traduction est une forme" et la loi de cette forme a son premier lieu dans l'original. Cette loi se pose d'abord, ré-pétons-le comme une demande au sens fort, une exigence qui délègue, mande, prescrit, assigne. Et quant à cette loi comme demande, deux questions peuvent surgir; elles sont d'essence différente. Première question: parmi la totalité de ses lecteurs, l'oeuvre peut-elle chaque fois trouver le traducteur qui en soit en quelque sorte capable? Deuxième question et, dit Benjamin, "plus proprement" (comme si cette question rendait la précé-dente plus appropriée alors que, nous allons le voir, il lui fait un sort tout autre): "par son essence [l'oeuvre] supporte-t-elle et s'il en est ainsi—conformément à la signification de cette forme—, exige-t-elle d'être traduite?"

A ces deux questions la réponse ne saurait être de même nature ou de même mode. *Problématique* dans le premier cas, non nécessaire (le traducteur capable de l'oeuvre peut apparaître ou ne pas apparaître, mais même s'il n'apparaît pas, cela ne change rien à la demande et à la structure de l'injonction venue de l'oeuvre), la réponse est proprement *apodictique* dans le se-cond cas: nécessaire, apriori, démontrable, absolue car elle vient de la loi intérieure de l'original. Celui-ci exige la traduction même si aucun traducteur n'est là, en mesure de répondre à cette injonction qui est en même temps demande et désir dans la structure même de l'original. Cette structure est le rapport de la vie à la survie. Cette exigence de l'autre comme traducteur, Benjamin la compare à tel instant inoubliable de la vie: il est vécu comme inoubliable, il *est* inoubliable même si en fait l'oubli

finit par l'emporter. Il aura été inoubliable, c'est là sa signification essentielle, son essence apodictique, l'oubli n'arrive à cet
inoubliable que par accident. L'exigence de l'inoubliable—qui
est ici constitutive—n'est pas le moins du monde entamée par la
finitude de la mémoire. De même l'exigence de la traduction ne
souffre en rien de n'être pas satisfaite, du moins ne souffre-t-elle
pas en tant que structure même de l'oeuvre. En ce sens la
dimension *survivante* est un apriori—et la mort n'y changerait
rien. Pas plus qu'à l'exigence (*Forderung*) qui traverse l'oeuvre
originale et à laquelle seule peut répondre ou correspondre (*entsprechen*) "une pensée de Dieu." La traduction, le désir de
traduction n'est pas pensable sans cette *correspondance* avec
une pensée de Dieu. Dans le texte de 1916 qui accordait déjà la
tâche du traducteur, son Aufgabe, à la réponse faite au don des
langues et au don du nom ("Gabe der Sprache," "Gebung des
Namens"), Benjamin nommait Dieu en ce lieu, celui d'une correspondance autorisant, rendant possible ou garantissant la correspondance entre les langages engagés en traduction. Dans ce
contexte étroit, il s'agissait aussi bien des rapports entre langage
des choses et langage des hommes, entre le muet et le parlant,
l'anonyme et le nommable, mais l'axiome valait sans doute pour
toute traduction: "l'objectivité de cette traduction est garantie
en Dieu" (tr. M. de Gandillac, p. 91). La dette, au commence-
ment, se forme dans le creux de cette "pensée de Dieu."

Etrange dette, qui ne lie personne à personne. Si la structure
de l'oeuvre est "survie," la dette n'engage pas auprès d'un sujet-
auteur présumé du texte original—mort ou mortel, le mort du
texte—mais à autre chose que représente la loi formelle dans
l'immanence du texte original. Ensuite la dette n'engage pas à
restituer une copie ou une bonne image, une représentation
fidèle de l'original: celui-ci, le survivant, est lui-même en procès
de transformation. L'original se donne en se modifiant, ce don
n'est pas d'un objet donné, il vit et survit en mutation: "Car dans
sa survie, qui ne mériterait pas ce nom, si elle n'était mutation et
renouveau du vivant, l'original se modifie. Même pour des mots
solidifiés il y a encore une post-maturation."

Post-maturation (*Nachreife*) d'un organisme vivant ou d'une semence: ce n'est pas non plus, simplement, une métaphore, pour les raisons déjà entrevues. Dans son essence même, l'histoire de la langue est déterminée comme "croissance," "sainte croissance des langues."

4. Si la dette du traducteur ne l'engage ni à l'égard de l'auteur (mort même s'il est vivant dès lors que son texte a structure de survie), ni à l'égard d'un modèle qu'il faudrait reproduire ou représenter, envers quoi, envers qui engage-t-elle? Comment nommer cela, ce quoi ou ce qui? Quel est le nom propre si ce n'est celui de l'auteur fini, mort ou mortel du texte? Et qui est le traducteur qui s'engage ainsi, qui se trouve peut-être *engagé* par l'autre avant de s'être engagé lui-même? Comme le traducteur se trouve, quant à la survie du texte, dans la même situation que son producteur fini et mortel (son "auteur"), ce n'est pas lui, pas lui-même en tant que fini et mortel qui s'engage. Alors qui? C'est certes lui mais au nom de qui et de quoi? La question des noms propres est ici essentielle. Là où l'acte du vivant mortel paraît moins compter que la survie du texte *en traduction*—traduit et traduisant—, il faut bien que la signature du nom propre s'en distingue et ne s'efface pas si facilement du contrat ou de la dette. N'oublions pas que Babel nomme une lutte pour la survie du nom, de la langue ou des lèvres.

De sa hauteur Babel à chaque instant surveille et surprend ma lecture: je traduis, la traduction par Maurice de Gandillac d'un texte de Benjamin qui, préfaçant une traduction, en prend prétexte pour dire à quoi et en quoi tout traducteur est engagé et note au passage, pièce essentielle de sa démonstration, qu'il ne saurait y avoir de traduction de la traduction. Il faudra s'en souvenir.

Rappelant cette étrange situation, je ne veux pas seulement, pas essentiellement réduire mon rôle à celui d'un passeur ou d'un passant. Rien n'est plus grave qu'une traduction. Je voulais plutôt marquer que tout traducteur est en position de parler *de* la traduction, à une place qui n'est rien moins que seconde ou secondaire. Car si la structure de l'original est marquée par l'exigence d'être traduit, c'est qu'en faisant la loi l'original commence par s'endetter *aussi* à l'égard du traducteur. L'original est le premier débiteur, le premier demandeur, il commence par manquer et par pleurer après la traduction. Cette demande n'est pas seulement du côté des constructeurs de la tour qui veulent se faire un nom et fonder une langue universelle se traduisant d'elle-même; elle contraint aussi le déconstructeur de la tour: en donnant son nom, Dieu en a aussi appelé à la traduction, non seulement entre les langues devenues tout à coup multiples et confuses, mais d'abord *de son nom,* du nom qu'il a clamé, donné, et qui doit se traduire par confusion pour être entendu, donc pour laisser entendre qu'il est difficile de le traduire et ainsi de l'entendre. Au moment où il impose et oppose sa loi à celle de la tribu, il est aussi demandeur de traduction. Il est aussi endetté. Il n'a pas fini de pleurer après la traduction de son nom alors même qu'il l'interdit. Car Babel est intraduisible. Dieu pleure sur son nom. Son texte est le plus sacré, le plus poétique, le plus originaire puisqu'il crée un nom et se le donne, il n'en reste pas moins indigent en sa force et en sa richesse même, il pleure après un traducteur. Comme dans *La folie du jour* de Maurice Blanchot, la loi ne commande pas sans demander d'être lue, déchiffrée, traduite. Elle demande le transfert (Übertragung et Übersetzung et Überleben). Le *double bind* est en elle. En Dieu même, et il faut en suivre rigoureusement la conséquence: *en son nom.*

Insolvable de part et d'autre, le double endettement passe entre des noms. Il déborde a priori les porteurs des noms si l'on entend par là les corps mortels qui disparaissent derrière la survie du nom. Or un nom propre appartient et n'appartient pas, disions-nous, à la langue, ni même, précisons-le maintenant, au corpus du texte à traduire, de l'à-traduire.

La dette n'engage pas des sujets vivants mais des noms au bord de la langue ou, plus rigoureusement, le trait contractant le rapport dudit sujet vivant à son nom, en tant que celui-ci se tient au bord de la langue. Et ce trait serait celui de l'à-traduire d'une langue à l'autre, de ce bord à l'autre du nom propre. Ce contrat de langue entre plusieurs langues est absolument singulier. D'abord il n'est pas ce qu'on appelle en général contrat de langue: ce qui garantit l'institution d'*une* langue, l'unité de son système et le contrat social qui lie une communauté à cet égard. D'autre part on suppose en général que pour être valable ou instituer quoi que ce soit, tout contrat doit avoir lieu dans une seule langue ou en appeler (par exemple dans le cas de traités diplomatiques ou commerciaux) à une traductibilité déjà donnée et sans reste: la multiplicité des langues doit y être absolument dominée. Ici au contraire un contrat entre deux langues étrangères en tant que telles engage à rendre possible une traduction qui *ensuite* autorisera toute sorte de contrats au sens courant. La signature de ce contrat singulier n'a pas besoin d'une écriture documentée ou archivée: elle n'en a pas moins lieu comme trace ou comme trait, et ce lieu a lieu même si son espace ne relève d'aucune objectivité empirique ou mathématique.

Le topos de ce contrat est exceptionnel, unique, pratiquement impossible à penser sous la catégorie courante de contrat: dans un code classique on l'aurait dit transcendantal puisqu'en vérité il rend possible tout contrat en général, à commencer par ce qu'on appelle le contrat de langue dans les limites d'un seul idiome. Autre nom, peut-être, pour l'origine des langues. Non pas l'origine du langage mais des langues—avant le langage, *les* langues.

Le contrat de traduction, en ce sens transcendantal, serait le contrat lui-même, le contrat absolu, la forme-contrat du contrat, ce qui permet à un contrat d'être ce qu'il est.

La parenté entre les langues, dira-t-on qu'elle suppose ce contrat ou qu'elle lui donne son premier lieu? On reconnaît là un cercle classique. Il a toujours commencé à tourner quand on s'interroge sur l'origine des langues ou de la société. Benjamin, qui parle souvent de parenté entre les langues, ne le fait jamais en comparatiste ou en historien des langues. Il s'intéresse moins à des familles de langues qu'à un apparentement plus essentiel et plus énigmatique, à une affinité dont il n'est pas sûr qu'elle précède le trait ou le contrat de l'à-traduire. Peut-être même cette parenté, cette affinité (*Verwandschaft*), est-elle comme une alliance, par le contrat de traduction, dans la mesure où les survies qu'elle associe ne sont pas des vies naturelles, des liens de sang ou des symbioses empiriques.

> Ce développement, comme celui d'une vie originale et de niveau élevé, est déterminé par une finalité originale et de niveau élevé. Vie et finalité—leur corrélation apparemment évidente, et qui pourtant échappe presque à la connaissance, ne se révèle que lorsque le but en vue duquel agissent toutes les finalités singulières de la vie n'est point cherché dans le domaine propre de cette vie, mais bien à un niveau plus élevé. Tous les phénomènes vitaux finalisés, comme leur finalité même, sont en fin de compte finalisés non vers la vie, mais vers l'expression de son essence, vers la représentation [*Darstellung*] de sa signification. Ainsi la traduction a finalement pour but d'exprimer le rapport le plus intime entre des langues.

La traduction ne chercherait pas à dire ceci ou cela, à transporter tel ou tel contenu, à communiquer telle charge de sens mais à re-marquer l'affinité entre les langues, à exhiber sa propre possibilité. Et cela, qui vaut pour le texte littéraire ou le texte sacré, définit peut-être l'essence même du littéraire et du sacré, à leur racine commune. J'ai dit "re-marquer" l'affinité entre les langues pour nommer l'insolite d'une "expression" ("exprimer le rapport le plus intime entre les langues") qui n'est ni une simple "présentation" ni simplement autre chose. La traduction rend *présente* sur un mode seulement anticipateur, annonciateur, quasiment prophétique, une affinité qui n'est jamais présente dans cette présentation. On pense à la manière dont Kant définit parfois le rapport au sublime: une présentation inadéquate à ce qui pourtant s'y présente. Ici le discours de Benjamin s'avance à travers des chicanes:

> Il est impossible qu'elle [la traduction] puisse révéler ce rapport caché lui-même, qu'elle puisse le restituer [*herstellen*]; mais elle peut le représenter [darstellen] en l'actualisant dans son germe

ou dans son intensité. Et cette représentation d'un signifié ["Darstellung eines Bedeuteten"] par l'essai, par le germe de sa restitution, est un mode de représentation tout à fait original, qui n'a guère d'équivalent dans le domaine de la vie non-langagière. Car cette dernière connaît, dans des analogies et des signes, d'autres types de référence [*Hindeutung*] que l'actualisation intensive, c'est-à-dire anticipatrice, annonciatrice [*vorgreifende, andeutende*]. Mais le rapport auquel nous pensons, ce rapport très intime entre les langues, est celui d'une convergence originale. Elle consiste en ceci, que les langues ne sont pas étrangères l'une à l'autre, mais, *a priori* et abstraction faite de toutes relations historiques, sont apparentées l'une à l'autre en ce qu'elles veulent dire.

Toute l'énigme de cette parenté se concentre ici. Que veut dire "ce qu'elles veulent dire"? Et qu'en est-il de cette présentation dans laquelle rien ne se présente sur le mode courant de la présence?

Il y va du nom, du symbole, de la vérité, de la lettre.

Une des assises profondes de l'essai, comme du texte de 1916, c'est une théorie du nom. Le langage y est déterminé à partir du mot et du privilège de la nomination. C'est, au passage, une affirmation très ferme sinon très démonstrative: "l'élément originaire du traducteur" est le mot et non la proposition, l'articulation syntaxique. Pour le donner à penser, Benjamin propose une curieuse "image": la proposition (*Satz*) serait "le mur devant la langue de l'original," alors que le mot, le mot à mot, la littéralité (*Wörtlichkeit*) en serait l'"arcade." Alors que le mur étaie en cachant (il est *devant* l'original), l'arcade soutient en laissant passer le jour et en donnant à voir l'original (nous ne sommes pas loin des passages parisiens). Ce privilège du mot soutient évidemment celui du nom et avec lui la propriété du nom propre, enjeu et possibilité du contrat de traduction. Il ouvre sur le problème *économique* de la traduction, qu'il s'agisse de l'économie comme loi du propre ou de l'économie comme rapport quantitatif (est-ce traduire que transposer un nom propre en plusieurs mots, en une phrase ou en une description, etc?).

Il y a de l'à-traduire. Des deux côtés il assigne et contracte. Il

engage moins des auteurs que des noms propres au bord de la
langue, il n'engage essentiellement ni à communiquer ni à représenter, ni à tenir un engagement déjà signé, plutôt à établir
le contrat et à donner naissance au pacte, autrement dit au *symbolon*, en un sens que Benjamin ne désigne pas sous ce nom
mais suggère sans doute par la métaphore de l'amphore, disons,
puisque dès le début nous avons suspecté le sens courant de la
métaphore, par l'ammétaphore.

Si le traducteur ne restitue ni ne copie un original, c'est que
celui-ci survit et se transforme. La traduction sera en vérité un
moment de sa propre croissance, il s'y complètera *en* s'agrandis-
sant. Or il faut bien que la croissance, et c'est en cela que la
logique "séminale" a dû s'imposer à Benjamin, ne donne pas lieu
à n'importe quelle forme dans n'importe quelle direction. La
croissance doit accomplir, remplir, compléter (*Ergänzung* est ici
le mot le plus fréquent). Et si l'original appelle un complément,
c'est qu'à l'origine il n'était pas là sans faute, plein, complet,
total, identique à soi. Dès l'origine de l'original à traduire il y a
chute et exil. Le traducteur doit racheter (erlösen), absoudre,
résoudre en tâchant de s'absoudre lui-même de sa propre dette,
qui est au fond la même—et sans fond. "Racheter dans sa propre
langue ce pur langage exilé dans la langue étrangère, libérer en
le transposant ce pur langage captif dans l'oeuvre, telle est la
tâche du traducteur." La traduction est transposition poétique
(*Umdichtung*). Ce qu'elle libère, le "pur langage," nous aurons à
en interroger l'essence. Mais notons pour l'instant que cette
libération suppose elle-même une liberté du traducteur qui n'est
elle-même que rapport à ce "pur langage"; et la libération
qu'elle opère, éventuellement en transgressant les limites de la
langue traduisante en la transformant à son tour, doit étendre,
agrandir, faire croître le langage. Comme cette croissance vient
aussi compléter, comme elle est symbolon, elle ne reproduit
pas, elle ajointe en ajoutant. D'où cette double comparaison
(*Vergleich*), tous ces tours et suppléments métaphoriques: (1)
"De même que la tangeante ne touche le cercle que de façon
fugitive et en un seul point et que c'est ce contact, non le point,

qui lui assigne la loi selon laquelle elle poursuit à l'infini sa marche en ligne droite, ainsi la traduction touche à l'original de façon fugitive et seulement en un point infiniment petit du sens, pour suivre ensuite sa marche la plus propre, selon la loi de fidélité dans la liberté du mouvement langagier." Chaque fois qu'il parle du contact (*Berührung*) entre le corps des deux textes au cours de la traduction, Benjamin le dit "fugitif" (*flüchtig*). Au moins à trois reprises, ce caractère "fugitif" est souligné, et toujours pour situer le contact avec le sens, le point infiniment petit du sens que les langues effleurent à peine ("L'harmonie entre les langues y est si profonde [il s'agit des traductions de Sophocle par Hölderlin] que le sens n'est touché par le vent du langage qu'à la manière d'une harpe éolienne"). Que peut être un point infiniment petit du sens? A quelle mesure l'évaluer? La métaphore même est à la fois la question et la réponse. Et voici l'autre métaphore, la métamphore, qui ne concerne plus l'extension en ligne droite et infinie mais l'agrandissement par ajointement selon les lignes brisées du fragment. (2) "Car, de même que les débris d'une amphore, pour qu'on puisse reconstituer le tout, doivent être contigus dans les plus petits détails, mais non identiques les uns aux autres, ainsi au lieu de se rendre semblable au sens de l'original, la traduction doit bien plutôt, dans un mouvement d'amour et jusque dans le détail, faire passer dans sa propre langue le mode de visée de l'original: ainsi, de même que les débris deviennet reconnaissables comme fragments d'une même amphore, original et traductions deviennent reconnaissables comme fragments d'un langage plus grand."

Accompagnons ce mouvement d'amour, le geste de cet aimant (*liebend*) qui oeuvre dans la traduction. Il ne reproduit pas, ne restitue pas, ne représente pas, pour l'essentiel il ne *rend* pas le sens de l'original sauf en ce point de contact ou de caresse, l'infiniment petit du sens. Il étend le corps des langues, il met la langue en expansion symbolique; et symbolique ici veut dire que, si peu de restitution qu'il y ait à accomplir, le plus grand, le nouvel ensemble plus vaste doit encore *reconstituer* quelque chose. Ce n'est peut-être pas un tout, mais c'est un ensemble dont l'ouverture ne doit pas contredire l'unité. Comme la cruche qui donne son topos poétique à tant de méditations sur la chose et la langue, de Hölderlin à Rilke et à Heidegger, l'amphore est une avec elle-même tout en s'ouvrant au-dehors—et cette ouverture ouvre l'unité, elle la rend possible et lui interdit la totalité. Elle lui permet de recevoir et de donner. Si la croissance du langage doit aussi reconstituer sans représenter, si c'est là le symbole, la traduction peut-elle prétendre à la vérité? Vérité, sera-ce encore le nom de ce qui fait encore la loi pour une traduction?

Nous touchons ici—en un point sans doute infiniment petit— à la limite de la traduction. L'intraduisible pur et le traductible pur y passent l'un dans l'autre—et c'est la vérité, "elle-même matériellement."

Le mot de "vérité" apparaît plus d'une fois dans "La tâche du traducteur." Il ne faut pas se hâter de s'en saisir. Il ne s'agit ni de la vérité d'une traduction en tant qu'elle serait conforme ou fidèle à son modèle, l'original. Ni davantage, du côté de l'original ou même de la traduction, de quelque adéquation de la langue au sens ou à la réalité, voire de la représentation à quelque chose. Alors de quoi s'agit-il sous le nom de vérité? Et sera-ce nouveau à ce point?

Repartons du "symbolique." Rappelons la métaphore ou l'ammétaphore: une traduction épouse l'original quand les deux fragments ajointés, aussi différents que possible, se complètent pour former une langue plus grande, au cours d'une survie qui les change tous les deux. Car la langue maternelle du traducteur, nous l'avons noté, s'y altère également. Telle est du moins mon interprétation—ma traduction, ma "tâche du traducteur." C'est ce que j'ai appelé le contrat de traduction: hymen ou contrat de mariage avec promesse de produire un enfant dont la semence donnera lieu à histoire et croissance. Contrat de mariage comme séminaire. Benjamin le dit, dans la traduction l'original grandit, il croît plutôt qu'il ne se reproduit—et j'ajouterai comme un enfant, le sien sans doute mais avec la force de parler tout seul qui fait d'un enfant autre chose qu'un produit assujetti à la loi de la reproduction. Cette promesse fait signe vers un royaume à la fois "promis et interdit où les langues se réconcilieront et s'accompliront." C'est la note la plus babélienne d'une analyse de l'écriture sacrée comme modèle et limite de toute écriture, en tout cas de toute Dichtung dans son être-à-traduire. Le sacré et l'être-à-traduire ne se laissent pas penser l'un sans l'autre. Ils se produisent l'un l'autre au bord de la même limite.

Ce royaume n'est jamais atteint, touché, foulé par la traduction. Il y a de l'intouchable et en ce sens la réconciliation est seulement promise. Mais une promesse n'est pas rien, elle n'est pas seulement marquée par ce qui lui manque pour s'accomplir. En tant que promesse, la traduction est déjà un événement, et la signature décisive d'un contrat. Qu'il soit ou non honoré n'empêche pas l'engagement d'avoir lieu et de léguer son archive. Une traduction qui arrive, qui arrive à promettre la reconciliation, à en parler, à la désirer ou faire désirer, une telle traduction est un événement rare et considérable.

Ici deux questions avant d'aller plus près de la vérité. En quoi consiste l'intouchable, s'il y en a? Et pourquoi telle métaphore ou ammétaphore de Benjamin me fait penser à l'hymen, plus visiblement à la robe de mariage?

1. Le toujours intact, l'intangible, l'intouchable (*unberührbar*), c'est ce qui fascine et oriente le travail du traducteur. Il veut toucher à l'intouchable, à ce qui reste du texte quand on en a extrait le sens communicable (point de contact, on s'en souvient, infiniment petit), quand on a transmis ce qui se peut transmettre, voire enseigner: ce que je fais ici, après et grâce à Maurice de Gandillac, sachant qu'un reste intouchable du texte benjaminien restera, lui aussi, intact au terme de l'opération. Intact et vierge malgré le labeur de la traduction, et si efficiente, si pertinente qu'elle soit. Ici la pertinence ne touche pas. Si on peut risquer une proposition en apparence aussi absurde, le texte sera encore plus vierge après le passage du traducteur, et l'hymen, signe de virginité, plus jaloux de lui-même après l'autre hymen, le contrat passé et la consommation du mariage. La complétude symbolique n'aura pas eu lieu jusqu'à son terme et

pourtant la promesse de mariage sera advenue—et c'est la tâche du traducteur, en ce qu'elle a de très aigu comme d'irremplaçable.

Mais encore? En quoi consiste l'intouchable? Etudions encore les métaphores ou les ammétaphores, les Übertragungen qui sont des traductions et des métaphores de la traduction, des traductions (Übersetzungen) de traduction ou des métaphores de métaphore. Etudions tous ces passages benjaminiens. La première figure qui vient ici, c'est celle du noyau et de l'écorce et du fruit et de l'enveloppe (*Kern, Frucht/Schale*). Elle décrit en dernière instance la distinction à laquelle Benjamin ne voudra jamais renoncer ni même consacrer quelques questions. On reconnaît un noyau (l'original en tant que tel) à ceci qu'il peut se laisser de nouveau traduire et retraduire. Une traduction, elle, ne le peut pas *en tant que telle*. Seul un noyau, parce qu'il résiste à la traduction qu'il aimante, peut s'offrir à une nouvelle opération traductrice sans se laisser épuiser. Car le rapport du contenu à la langue, on dirait aussi du fond à la forme, du signifié au signifiant, peu importe ici (dans ce contexte Benjamin oppose teneur, *Gehalt*, et langue on langage, *Sprache*), diffère du texte original à la traduction. Dans le premier, l'unité en est aussi serrée, stricte, adhérente qu'entre le fruit et sa peau, son écorce ou sa pelure. Non qu'ils soient inséparables, on doit pouvoir les distinguer en droit, mais ils appartiennent à un tout organique et il n'est pas insignifiant que la métaphore soit ici végétale et naturelle, naturaliste:

> Ce royaume il [l'original en traduction] ne l'atteint jamais complètement, mais c'est là que se trouve ce qui fait que traduire est plus que communiquer. Plus précisément on peut définir ce noyau essentiel comme ce qui, dans la traduction, n'est pas à nouveau traduisible. Car, autant qu'on en puisse extraire du communicable pour le traduire, il reste toujours cet intouchable vers quoi s'oriente le travail du vrai traducteur. Il n'est pas transmissible comme l'est la parole créatrice de l'original ["übertragbar wie das Dichterwort des Originals"], car le rapport de la teneur au langage est tout à fait différent dans l'original et dans la traduc-

tion. Dans l'original, teneur et langage forment une unité déterminée, comme celle du fruit et de l'enveloppe.

Décortiquons un peu plus la rhétorique de cette séquence. Il n'est pas sûr que le "noyau" essentiel et le "fruit" désignent la même chose. La noyau essentiel, ce qui n'est pas, dans la traduction, à nouveau traduisible, ce n'est pas la teneur mais cette adhérence entre la teneur et la langue, entre le fruit et l'enveloppe. Cela peut paraître étrange ou incohérent (comment un noyau pourrait-il se situer entre le fruit et l'enveloppe?) Il faut sans doute penser que le noyau est d'abord l'unité dure et centrale qui fait tenir le fruit à l'enveloppe, le fruit à lui-même aussi; et surtout que, au coeur du fruit le noyau est "intouchable," hors d'atteinte et invisible. Le noyau serait la première métaphore de ce qui fait l'unité des deux termes dans la seconde métaphore. Mais il y en a une troisième, et cette fois elle n'a pas de provenance naturelle. Elle concerne le rapport de la teneur à la langue dans la traduction, et non plus dans l'original. Ce rapport est différent et je ne crois pas céder à l'artifice en insistant sur cette différence pour dire qu'elle est précisément celle de l'artifice à la nature. Qu'est-ce que Benjamin note en effet, comme au passage, par commodité rhétorique ou pédagogique? Que "le langage de la traduction enveloppe sa teneur comme un manteau royal aux larges plis. Car il est le signifiant d'un langage supérieur à lui-même et reste ainsi, par rapport à sa propre teneur, inadéquat, forcé, étranger." C'est très beau, une belle traduction: hermine blanche, couronnement, sceptre et démarche majestueuse. Le roi a bien un corps (et ce n'est pas ici le texte original mais ce qui constitue la teneur du texte traduit) mais ce corps est seulement promis, annoncé et dissimulé par la traduction. L'habit sied mais ne serre pas assez strictement la personne royale. Ce n'est pas une faiblesse, la meilleure traduction ressemble à ce manteau royal. Elle reste séparée du corps auquel cependant elle se conjoint, l'épousant sans l'épouser. On peut certes broder sur ce manteau, sur la nécessité de cette Übertragung, de cette traduction métaphorique de la traduction. Par exemple on peut opposer cette métaphore à celle de l'écorce et du noyau comme on opposerait la technique à la nature. Un vêtement n'est pas naturel, c'est un tissu et même, autre métaphore de la métaphore, un texte, et ce texte d'artifice apparaît justement du côté du contrat symbolique. Or si le texte original est demande de traduction, le fruit, à moins que ce ne soit le noyau, exige ici de devenir le roi, ou l'empereur qui portera les habits neufs: sous ses larges plis, *in weiten Falten*, on le devinera nu. Le manteau et les plis protègent sans doute le roi contre le froid ou les aggressions naturelles; mais d'abord, surtout, c'est, comme son sceptre, la visibilité insigne de la loi. C'est l'indice du pouvoir et du pouvoir de faire la loi. Mais on en infère que ce qui compte, c'est ce qui se passe sous le manteau, à savoir le corps du roi, ne dites pas tout de suite le phallus, autour duquel une traduction affaire sa langue, fait des plis, moule des formes, coud des ourlets, pique et brode. Mais toujours amplement flottante à quelque distance de la teneur.

2. Plus ou moins strictement, le manteau épouse le corps du roi, mais pour ce qui se passe sous le manteau, il est difficile de séparer le roi du couple royal. C'est lui, ce couple d'époux (le corps du roi et sa robe, la teneur et la langue, le roi et la reine) qui fait la loi et garantit tout contrat depuis ce premier contrat. C'est pourquoi j'ai pensé à une robe de mariage. Benjamin, on le sait, ne pousse pas les choses dans le sens où je les traduis moi-même, le lisant toujours déjà en traduction. Plus ou moins fidèlement j'ai pris quelque liberté avec la teneur de l'original, autant qu'avec sa langue, et encore avec l'original qu'est aussi pour moi, maintenant, la traduction de Maurice de Gandillac. J'ai ajouté un manteau à l'autre, ça flotte encore plus, mais n'est-ce pas la destination de toute traduction? Si du moins une traduction se destinait à arriver.

Malgré la distinction entre les deux métaphores, l'écorce et le manteau (le manteau royal, car il a dit "royal" là où d'autres auraient pu penser qu'un manteau suffisait), malgré l'opposition de la nature et de l'art, dans les deux cas il y a *unité* de la teneur et de la langue, unité naturelle dans un cas, unité symbolique dans l'autre. Simplement dans la traduction l'unité fait signe vers une unité (métaphoriquement) plus "naturelle," elle promet une langue ou un langage plus originaires et comme sublimes, sublimes dans la mesure démesurée où la promesse elle-même, à savoir la traduction, y reste inadéquate (*unangemessen*), violente et forcée (*gewaltig*) et étrangère (*fremd*). Cette "brisure" rend inutile, "interdit" même toute Übertragung, toute "transmission" dit justement la traduction française: le mot joue aussi, comme la transmission, avec le déplacement transférentiel ou métaphorique. Et le mot "Übertragung" s'impose encore quelques lignes plus loin: si la traduction "transplante" l'original sur un autre terrain de langue "ironiquement" plus définitif, c'est dans la mesure où l'on ne pourrait plus le déplacer de là par aucun autre "transfert" (Übertragung) mais seulement l'"ériger" (*erheben*) à nouveau sur place "en d'autres parties." Il n'y a pas de traduction de la traduction, voilà l'axiome sans lequel il n'y aurait pas "La tâche du traducteur." Si on y touchait on toucherait, et il ne le faut pas, à l'intouchable de l'intouchable, à savoir ce qui garantit à l'original qu'il reste bien l'original.

Cela n'est pas sans rapport avec la vérité. Elle est apparemment au delà de toute Übertragung et de toute Übersetzung possible. Elle n'est pas la correspondance représentative entre l'original et la traduction, ni même adéquation première entre l'original et la traduction et quelque objet ou signification hors de lui. La vérité serait plutôt le *langage pur* en lequel le sens et la lettre ne se dissocient plus. Si un tel lieu, l'avoir-lieu de tel événement restait introuvable, on ne pourrait plus, fût-ce en droit, distinguer entre un original et une traduction. En maintenant à tout prix cette distinction, comme la donnée originaire de tout contrat de traduction (au sens quasi-transcendantal dont nous parlions plus haut), Benjamin répète le fondement du droit. Ce faisant il exhibe la possibilité d'un droit des oeuvres et d'un droit d'auteur, celle-là même sur laquelle prétend s'appuyer le droit positif. Celui-ci s'effondre dès la moindre contestation d'une frontière rigoureuse entre l'original et la version, voire de l'identité à soi ou de l'intégrité de l'original. Ce que dit

Benjamin de ce rapport entre original et traduction, on le retrou-
ve, traduit dans une langue de bois mais fidèlement reproduit en
son sens au seuil de tous les traités juridiques concernant le droit
positif des traductions. Et cela qu'il s'agisse des principes génér-
aux de la différence original/traduction (celle-ci étant "dérivée"
de celui-là) ou qu'il s'agisse des traductions de traduction. La
traduction de traduction est dite "dérivée" de l'original et non de
la première traduction. Voici quelques extraits du Droit français;
mais il ne semble pas y avoir de ce point de vue opposition entre
celui-ci et d'autres droits occidentaux (il reste qu'une enquête de
droit comparé devrait aussi concerner la traduction des textes de
droit). On va le voir, ces propositions en appellent à la polarité
expression/exprimé, signifiant/signifié, forme/fond. Benjamin
commençait aussi par dire: la traduction est une forme; et le
clivage symbolisant/symbolisé organise tout son essai. Or en
quoi ce système d'opposition est-il indispensable à ce droit?
C'est que seul il permet, à partir de la distinction entre l'original
et la traduction, de reconnaître quelque originalité à la traduction. Cette originalité est déterminée et c'est un des nombreux
philosophèmes classiques au fondement de ce droit, comme
originalité de *l'expression.* Expression s'oppose à contenu certes,
et la traduction, censée ne pas toucher au contenu, doit n'être
originale que par la langue *comme expression;* mais expression
s'oppose aussi à ce que les juristes français appellent la *composi-*
tion de l'original. En général on situe la composition du côté de
la forme, mais ici la forme d'expression dans laquelle on peut
reconnaître de l'originalité au traducteur et à ce titre un droit
d'auteur-traducteur, c'est seulement la forme d'expression linguistique, le choix des mots dans la langue, etc., mais rien d'autre de la forme. Je cite Claude Colombet, *Propriété littéraire et*
artistique, Paris: Dalloz, 1976, dont j'extrais seulement quelques
lignes, conformément à la loi du 11 mars 1957, rappelée à
l'ouverture du livre et "n'autorisant . . . que les analyses et les
courtes citations dans un but d'exemple et d'illustration," car
"toute représentation ou reproduction intégrale, ou partielle,
faite sans le consentement de l'auteur ou de ses ayants droit ou

ayants cause, est illicite," constituant "donc une contrefaçon sanctionnée par les articles 425 et suivants du Code Pénal.":

54.—Les traductions sont des oeuvres qui sont originales seulement par l'expression; [restriction très paradoxale: la pierre angulaire du droit d'auteur, c'est en effet que seule la forme peut devenir propriété, et non les idées, les thèmes, les contenus, qui sont propriété commune et universelle. (Cf. tout le chapitre 1 de ce livre *L'absence de protection des idées par le droit d'auteur.*) Si une première conséquence est bonne, puisque c'est cette forme qui définit l'originalité de la traduction, une autre conséquence en pourrait être ruineuse car elle devrait conduire à abandonner ce qui distingue l'original de la traduction si, à l'exclusion de l'expression, il revient à une distinction de fond. A moins que la valeur de composition, si peu rigoureuse qu'elle soit, ne reste l'indice du fait qu'entre l'original et la traduction le rapport n'est ni d'expression ni de contenu mais d'autre chose au-delà de ces oppositions. A suivre l'embarras des juristes—parfois comique dans sa subtilité casuistique—pour tirer les conséquences des axiomes du type "Le droit d'auteur ne protège pas les idées; mais celles-ci peuvent être, parfois indirectement, protégées par d'autres moyens que par la loi du 11 mars 1957," ibid., p. 21, on mesure mieux l'historicité et la fragilité conceptuelle de cette axiomatique] l'article 4 de la loi les cite parmi les oeuvres protégées; en effet il a toujours été admis que le traducteur fait preuve d'originalité dans le choix des expressions pour rendre au mieux en une langue le sens du texte en une autre langue. Comme le dit M. Savatier "Le génie de chaque langue donne à l'oeuvre traduite une physionomie propre; et le traducteur n'est pas un simple ouvrier. Il participe lui-même à une création dérivée dont il porte la responsabilité propre"; c'est qu'en effet la traduction n'est pas le résultat d'un processus automatique; par les choix qu'il opère entre plusieurs mots, plusieurs expressions, le traducteur fait une oeuvre de l'esprit; mais, bien entendu, il ne saurait modifier la composition de l'oeuvre traduite, car il est tenu au respect de cette oeuvre.

Dans sa langue, Desbois dit la même chose, avec quelques précisions suplémentaires:

Les oeuvres dérivées qui sont originales par l'expression. 29. Point n'est besoin que l'oeuvre considérée, pour être *relativement originale* [souligné par Desbois], porte l'empreinte d'une personnalité à la fois par la composition et l'expression comme les adaptations. Il suffit que l'auteur, tout en suivant pas à pas le développement d'une oeuvre préexistante, ait fait acte personnel dans l'expression: l'article 4 en fait foi, puisque, dans une énumération non-exhaustive des oeuvres dérivées il situe à la place d'honneur les *traductions*. "Traduttore, traditore," disent volontiers les Italiens, en une boutade, qui, comme toute médaille, a un avers et un revers: s'il est de mauvais traducteurs, qui multiplient les contre-sens, d'autres sont cités grâce à la perfection de leur tâche. Le risque d'une erreur ou d'une imperfection a pour contrepartie la perspective d'une version authentique, qui implique une parfaite connaissance des deux langues, une foison de choix judicieux, et partant un effort créateur. La consultation d'un dictionnaire ne suffit qu'aux candidats médiocres au baccalauréat: le traducteur consciencieux et compétent "met du sien" et crée tout comme le peintre qui fait la copie d'un modèle.—La vérification de cette conclusion est fournie par la comparaison de plusieurs traductions d'un seul et même texte: chacune pourra différer des autres, sans qu'aucune contienne un contre-sens; la variété des modes d'expression d'une même pensée démontre, par la possibilité d'un choix, que la *tâche* du traducteur donne prise à des manifestations de personnalité. [*Le droit d'auteur en France*, Paris: Dalloz, 1978]

On relèvera au passage que la *tâche du traducteur,* confinée dans le duel des langues (jamais plus de deux langues), ne donne lieu qu'à "effort créateur" (effort et tendance plutôt qu'achèvement, labeur artisanal plutôt que performance d'artiste), et quand le traducteur "crée," c'est comme un peintre qui copie son modèle (comparaison saugrenue à plus d'un titre, est-il utile de l'expliquer?). Le retour du mot "tâche" est assez remarquable en tout cas, par toutes les significations qu'il tisse en réseau, et c'est toujours la même interprétation évaluatrice: devoir, dette, taxe, redevance, impôt, charge d'héritage et succession, noble obligation mais labeur à mi-chemin de la création, tâche infinie, inachèvement essentiel, comme si le présumé créateur de l'original n'était pas lui aussi, endetté, taxé, obligé par un autre texte, a priori traducteur.

Entre le droit transcendantal (tel que Benjamin le répète) et le droit positif tel qu'il se formule si laborieusement et parfois si grossièrement dans les traités du droit d'auteur ou du droit des oeuvres, l'analogie peut être suivie très loin, par exemple en ce qui concerne la notion de dérivation et les traductions de traductions: celles-ci sont toujours dérivées de l'original et non de traductions antérieures. Voici une note de Desbois:

> Le traducteur ne cessera pas même de faire oeuvre personnelle, lorsqu'il ira puiser conseil et inspiration dans une précédente traduction. Nous ne refuserons pas la qualité d'auteur d'une oeuvre dérivée, *par rapport à des traductions antérieures*, à celui qui se serait contenté de choisir, entre plusieurs versions déjà publiées, celle qui lui paraît la plus adéquate à l'original: allant de l'une à l'autre, prenant un passage à celle-ci, un autre à celle-là, il créerait une oeuvre nouvelle, par le fait même de la combinaison, qui rend son ouvrage différent des productions antécédentes. Il a fait acte de création, puisque sa traduction reflète une forme nouvelle, résulte de comparaisons, de choix. Le traducteur serait encore, selon nous, digne d'audience, malgré qu'il eût été conduit par ses réflexions au même résultat qu'un devancier, dont il aurait par hypothèse ignoré le travail: sa réplique involontaire, loin de constituer un plagiat, porterait la marque de sa personnalité, présenterait une "nouveauté subjective," qui appellerait protection. Les deux versions, accomplies à l'insu, séparément l'une de l'autre, ont donné lieu séparément et isolément, à des manifestations de personnalité. *La seconde sera une oeuvre dérivée vis-à-vis de l'oeuvre qui a été traduite, non vis-à-vis de la première.* [Ibid., p. 41; j'ai souligné cette dernière phrase]

De ce droit à la vérité, quel est le rapport?

La traduction promet un royaume à la réconcilation des langues. Cette promesse, événement proprement symbolique ajointant, accouplant, mariant deux langues comme les deux parties d'un tout plus grand, en appelle à une langue de la vérité ("Sprache der Wahrheit"). Non pas à une langue vraie, adéquate à quelque contenu extérieur, mais à une vraie langue, à une langue dont la vérité ne serait référée qu'à elle-même. Il s'agirait de la vérité comme authenticité, vérité d'acte ou d'événement qui appartiendrait à l'original plutôt qu'à la traduction, même si l'original est déjà en situation de demande ou de dette. Et s'il y avait une telle authenticité et une telle force d'événement dans ce qu'on appelle couramment une traduction, c'est qu'elle se produirait de quelque façon comme oeuvre originale. Il y aurait donc une manière originale et inaugurale de s'endetter, ce serait le lieu et la date de ce qu'on appelle un original, une oeuvre.

Pour bien traduire le sens intentionnel de ce que veut dire Benjamin quand il parle de "langue de la vérité," peut-être faut-il entendre ce qu'il dit régulièrement du "sens intentionnel" ou de la "visée intentionnelle" ("Intention der Meinung," "Art des Meinens"). Comme le rappelle Maurice de Gandillac, ce sont là des catégories empruntées à la scolastique par Brentano et Husserl. Elles jouent un rôle important, sinon toujours très clair dans "La tâche du traducteur."

Qu'est-ce qui paraît visé sous ce concept de visée (Meinen)? Reprenons au point où dans la traduction semble s'annoncer une parenté des langues, au-delà de toute ressemblance entre un original et sa reproduction, et indépendamment de toute filiation historique. D'ailleurs la parenté n'implique pas nécessairement la ressemblance. Cela dit, en écartant l'origine historique ou naturelle, Benjamin n'exclut pas, en un tout autre sens, la considération de l'origine en général, pas plus que ne le font dans des contextes et par des mouvements analogues un Rousseau ou un Husserl. Benjamin le précise même littéralement: pour l'accès le plus rigoureux à cette parenté ou à cette affinité des langues "le concept d'origine [*Abstammungsbegriff*] reste indispensable." Où chercher alors cette affinité originaire? Nous la voyons s'annoncer dans un ploiement, un reploiement et un co-déploiement des visées. A travers chaque langue quelque chose est visé qui est le même et que pourtant aucune des langues ne peut atteindre séparément. Elles ne peuvent prétendre l'atteindre, et se le promettre, qu'en co-employant ou co-déployant leurs visées intentionnelles, "le tout de leurs visées intentionnelles complémentaires." Ce co-déploiement vers le tout est un reploiement car ce qu'il vise à atteindre, c'est "le langage pur" ("die reine Sprache"), ou la pure langue. Ce qui est alors visé par cette co-opération des langues et des visées intentionnelles n'est pas transcendant à la langue, ce n'est pas un réel qu'elles investiraient de tous côtés comme une tour dont elles tenteraient de faire le tour. Non, ce qu'elles visent intentionnellement chacune et ensemble dans la traduction, c'est la langue même comme événement babelien, une langue qui n'est pas la langue universelle au sens leibnizien, une langue qui n'est pas davantage la langue naturelle que chacune reste de son côté, c'est l'être-langue de la langue, la langue ou le langage *en tant que tels*, cette unité sans aucune identité à soi qui fait qu'il y a des langues, et que ce sont des langues.

Ces langues se rapportent l'une à l'autre dans la traduction selon un mode inouï. Elles se complètent, dit Benjamin; mais aucune autre complétude au monde ne peut représenter celle-ci, ni cette complémentarité symbolique. Cette singularité (non représentable par rien qui soit dans le monde) tient sans doute à la visée intentionnelle ou à ce que Benjamin essaie de traduire dans le langage scolastico-phénoménologique. A l'intérieur de la même visée intentionnelle il faut rigoureusement distinguer entre la chose visée, le visé (Gemeinten), et le mode de la visée ("die Art des Meinens"). La tâche du traducteur, dès qu'il prend en vue le contrat originaire des langues et l'espérance de la "langue pure," exclut ou laisse entre parenthèses le "visé."

Le mode de visée seul assigne la tâche de traduction. Chaque "chose," dans son identité présumée à soi (par exemple le pain *lui-même*) est visée selon des modes différents dans chaque langue et dans chaque texte de chaque langue. C'est entre ces modes que la traduction doit chercher, produire ou reproduire une complémentarité ou une "harmonie." Et dès lors que compléter ou complémenter ne revient à la sommation d'aucune totalité mondaine, la valeur d'harmonie convient à cet ajustement, à ce qu'on peut appeler ici l'accord des langues. Cet accord laisse résonner, l'annonçant plutôt qu'il ne le présente, le pur langage, et l'être-langue de la langue. Tant que cet accord n'a pas lieu, le pur langage reste caché, célé (*verborgen*), muré dans l'intimité nocturne du "noyau." Seule une traduction peut l'en faire sortir.

Sortir et surtout développer, faire croître. Toujours selon le même motif (d'apparence organiciste ou vitaliste), on dirait alors que chaque langue est comme atrophiée dans sa solitude, maigre, arrêtée dans sa croissance, infirme. Grâce à la traduction, autrement dit à cette supplémentarité linguistique par laquelle une langue donne à l'autre ce qui lui manque, et le lui donne harmonieusement, ce croisement des langues assure la croissance des langues, et même cette "sainte croissance des langues" "jusqu'au terme messianique de l'histoire." Tout cela s'annonce dans le processus traducteur, à travers "l'éternelle survie des langues" ("am ewigen Fortleben der Sprachen") ou "la renaissance [Aufleben] infinie des langues." Cette perpétuelle reviviscence, cette régénérescence constante (Fort- et Auf-leben) par la traduction, c'est moins une révélation, la révélation elle-même, qu'une annonciation, une alliance et une promesse.

Ce code religieux est ici essentiel. Le texte sacré marque la limite, le modèle pur, même s'il est inaccessible, de la traductibilité pure, l'idéal à partir duquel on pourra penser, évaluer, mesurer la traduction essentielle, c'est à dire poétique. La traduction, comme sainte croissance des langues, annonce le terme messianique, certes, mais le signe de ce terme et de *cette croissance* n'y est "présent" (gegenwärtig) que dans le "savoir de cette distance," dans l'Entfernung, *l'éloignement* qui nous y rapporte. Cet éloignement, on peut le savoir, en avoir le savoir ou le pressentiment, on ne peut le vaincre. Mais il nous met en rapport avec cette "langue de la vérité" qui est le "véritable langage" ("so ist diese Sprache der Wahrheit—die wahre Sprache"). Cette mise en rapport a lieu sur le mode du "pressentiment," sur le mode "intensif" qui se rend présent ce qui est absent, laisse venir l'éloignement comme éloignement, *fort:da.* Disons que la traduction est l'expérience, ce qui se traduit ou s'éprouve aussi: l'expérience est traduction.

L'à-traduire du texte sacré, sa pure traductibilité, voilà ce qui donnerait *à la limite* la mesure idéale de toute traduction. Le texte sacré assigne sa tâche au traducteur, et il est sacré *en tant qu'il* s'annonce comme traductible, simplement traductible, à-traduire; ce qui ne veut pas toujours dire immédiatement traduisible, au sens commun qui fut écarté dès le début. Peut-être faut-il distinguer ici entre le traductible et le traduisible. La traductibilité pure et simple est celle du texte sacré dans lequel le sens et la littéralité ne se discernent plus pour former le corps d'un événement unique, irremplaçable, intransférable "matériellement la vérité." Jamais l'appel à la traduction, la dette, la tâche, l'assignation ne sont plus impérieuses. Jamais il n'y a plus traductible, mais en raison de cette indistinction du sens et de la littéralité (Wörtlichkeit), le traductible pur peut s'annoncer, se donner, se présenter, se laisser traduire comme intraduisible. Depuis cette limite, à la fois intérieure et extérieure, le traducteur en vient à recevoir tous les signes de l'éloignement (Entfernung) qui le guide en sa démarche infinie, au bord de l'abîme, de la folie et du silence: les dernières oeuvres de Hölderlin comme traductions de Sophocle, l'effondrement du sens "d'abîme en abîme," et ce danger n'est pas celui de l'accident, c'est la traductibilité, c'est la loi de la traduction, l'à-traduire comme loi, l'ordre donné, l'ordre reçu—et la folie attend des deux côtés. Et comme la tâche est impossible aux abords du texte sacré qui vous l'assigne, la culpabilité infinie vous absout aussitôt.

C'est ce qui se nomme ici désormais Babel: la loi imposée par le nom de Dieu qui du même coup vous prescrit et vous interdit de traduire en vous montrant et en vous dérobant la limite. Mais ce n'est pas seulement la situation babelienne, pas seulement une scène ou une structure. C'est aussi le statut et l'événement du texte babelien, du texte de la Genèse (texte à cet égard unique) comme texte sacré. Il relève de la loi qu'il raconte et qu'il traduit exemplairement. Il fait la loi dont il parle, et d'abîme en abîme il déconstruit la tour, et chaque tour, les tours en tous genres, selon un rythme.

Ce qui se passe dans un texte sacré, c'est l'événement d'un *pas de sens*. Et cet événement est aussi celui à partir duquel on peut penser le texte poétique ou littéraire qui tend à racheter le sacré perdu et s'y traduit comme dans son modèle. Pas-de-sens, cela

ne signifie pas la pauvrété mais pas de sens qui soit lui-même,
sens, hors d'une "littéralité." Et c'est là le sacré. Il se livre à la
traduction qui s'adonne à lui. Il ne serait rien sans elle, elle
n'aurait pas lieu sans lui, l'un et l'autre sont inséparables. Dans
le texte sacré "le sens a cessé d'être la ligne de partage pour le
flot du langage et pour le flot de la révélation." C'est le texte
absolu parce qu'en son événement il ne communique rien, il ne
dit rien qui fasse sens hors de cet événement même. Cet événement se confond absolument avec l'acte de langage, par exemple
la prophétie. Il est littéralement la littéralité de sa langue, le
"langage pur." Et comme aucun sens ne s'en laisse détacher,
transférer, transporter, traduire dans une autre langue comme
tel (comme sens), il commande aussitôt la traduction qu'il semble refuser. Il est traductible et intraduisible. Il n'y a que de la
lettre, et c'est la vérité du langage pur, la vérité comme langage
pur.

   Cette loi ne serait pas une contrainte extérieure, elle accorde
une liberté à la littéralité. Dans le même événement, la lettre
cesse d'opprimer dès lors qu'elle n'est plus le corps extérieur ou
le corset de sens. Elle se traduit aussi d'elle-même, et c'est dans
ce rapport à soi du corps sacré que se trouve engagée la tâche du
traducteur. Cette situation, pour être celle d'une pure limite,
n'exclut pas, au contraire, les degrés, la virtualité, l'intervalle et
l'entre-deux, le labeur infini pour rejoindre ce qui pourtant est
passé, déjà donné, ici même, entre les lignes, déjà signé.

   Comment traduiriez-vous une signature? Et comment vous en
abstiendriez-vous, qu'il s'agisse de Iaweh, de Babel, de Benjamin quand il signe tout près de son dernier mot? Mais à la
lettre, et entre les lignes, c'est aussi la signature de Maurice de
Gandillac que pour finir je cite en posant ma question: peut-on
citer une signature? "Car, à un degré quelconque, toutes les
grandes écritures, mais au plus haut point l'Ecriture sainte, con-
tiennent entre les lignes leur traduction virtuelle. La version
intralinéaire du texte sacré est le modèle ou l'idéal de toute
traduction."

Contributors

Alan Bass received his Ph. D. from the Johns Hopkins University and then went on to psychoanalytic training in New York City, where he is now a practicing analyst. He has translated and annotated four books by Jacques Derrida and has lectured and written widely on deconstruction and psychoanalysis.

Cynthia Chase, assistant professor of English at Cornell University, has published essays on Freud, Wordsworth, Rousseau, and George Eliot. She is currently working on intertextual relationships in romantic writing.

Jacques Derrida is director of studies at L'Ecole des Hautes Etudes and also directs the Collège International de Philosophie. His work already translated includes *Speech and Phenomena* (1973), *Of Grammatology* (1976), *Writing and Difference* (1978), *Spurs* (1978), *Archeology of the Frivolous* (1980), *Dissemination* (1981), *Positions* (1981), and *Margins of Philosophy* (1982).

Joseph F. Graham teaches French at Tulane University. He has written mostly about theories of language and literature. His new work will appear first in *Onomatopoetics* and later in *Principles for Literary Criticism.*

Barbara Johnson is professor of French at Harvard University. She is the author of *Défigurations du langage poétique* (1979) and *The Critical Difference* (1980), translator of Jacques Derrida's *Dissemination* (1981), and editor of *The Pedagogical Imperative: Teaching as a Literary Genre* (1982).

Philip E. Lewis teaches in the Department of Romance Studies at Cornell University and writes about seventeenth-century French literature and contemporary criticism. He was the editor of *Diacritics* from 1976 to 1981.

Robert J. Matthews is associate professor of philosophy at Rutgers University, with principal research interests in the philosophy of psychology and aesthetics. He has held appointments as visiting professor at Harvard University, Massachusetts Institute of Technology, and the University of Western Ontario.

Richard Rand has edited and translated Jacques Derrida's *Signéponge,* and has published a number of articles and reviews on British romantic poetry.

Index

Page numbers in parentheses refer to the Appendix.

Library of Congress Cataloging in Publication Data
Main entry under title:

Difference in translation.

    Includes index.
    Contents: The measure of translation effects /
Philip E. Lewis—Paragon, parergon / Cynthia Chase—
O'er-brimmed / Richard Rand—[etc.]
    1. Translating and interpreting—Addresses, essays,
lectures. I. Graham, Joseph F.
P306.D45   1985   418'.02   84-15622
ISBN 0-8014-1704-X

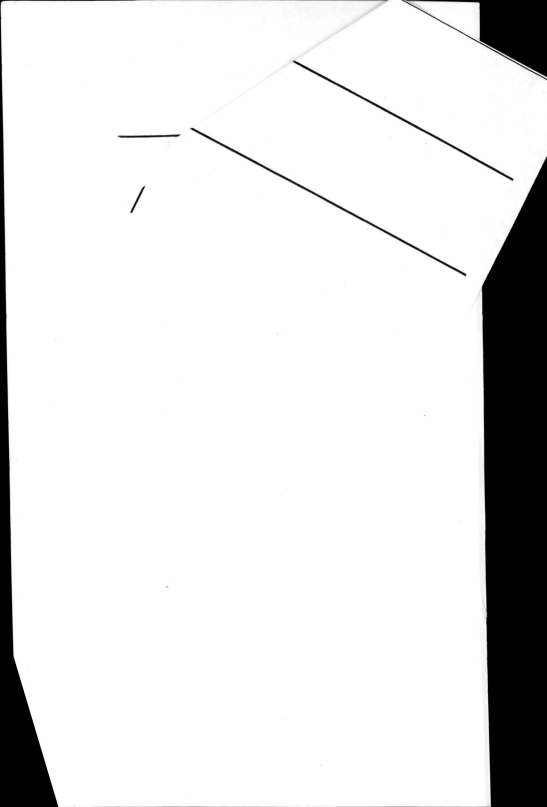